ISLAND BORN

FRANK BURNABY

Baby Island ©1981 by Frank Burnaby, Original Treatment
Island Born © 2006 by Frank Burnaby
All Rights Reserved

All rights reserved. No part of this book may be reproduced or transmitted in any form or by any means, electronic or mechanical, including photocopying, recording, or by any information storage and retrieval system, without the permission in writing from the publisher.

Published by Sandy Back Press July, 2012

ISBN: 978-0-9832669-1-4
E-book ISBN: 978-0-9832669-0-7
First Edition

FrankBurnaby.com

Cover Illustration by John Macdonald
Map "Journey of the Joya" by Briony Penn

Createspace and eBook Conversion·Araby Greene·webbishbooks.com

JOURNEY OF THE JOYA

- START TRIP JULY 19, 1974 — Falmouth H., ENGLAND
- FORCE 10/11 SW GALE — BAY OF BISCAY
- Coruña, SPAIN
- LARGE MISTRAL GALE FOR 3 DAYS
- Cagliari
- SOJOURN IN GREEK ISLES TO AWAIT OPENING OF SUEZ CANAL
- SIROCO, FREAK GIANT WAVE
- Valleta
- Suez Canal
- FLIPPED COIN TO GO WEST OR EAST
- SHIP REPAIRS IN MALTA
- ARRESTED BY EGYPTIAN ARMY OFFICER IN UNDERPANTS
- FOLLOWED BY WHALE SHARK 1 DAY
- RED SEA
- YEMEN
- UNINHABITED DRY VOLCANIC ISLANDS
- HANISH ISLAND
- HEADWINDS & NO WATER FOR A MONTH WITH ONLY DISTILLED SEAWATER TO DRINK
- ERITREAN WAR ON THE WEST SIDE OF THE RED SEA
- ARRESTED BY GUNBOAT FROM ETHIOPIA
- Assab
- HEAD WINDS FROM SOUTH
- TOWED TO ASSAB
- ETHIOPIA
- STRANDED WHILE CIVIL WAR RAGING DURING GALES OF SW MONSOON
- HANISH
- INSET 1: STRAITS OF BAB EL MANDEB

ISLAND BORN

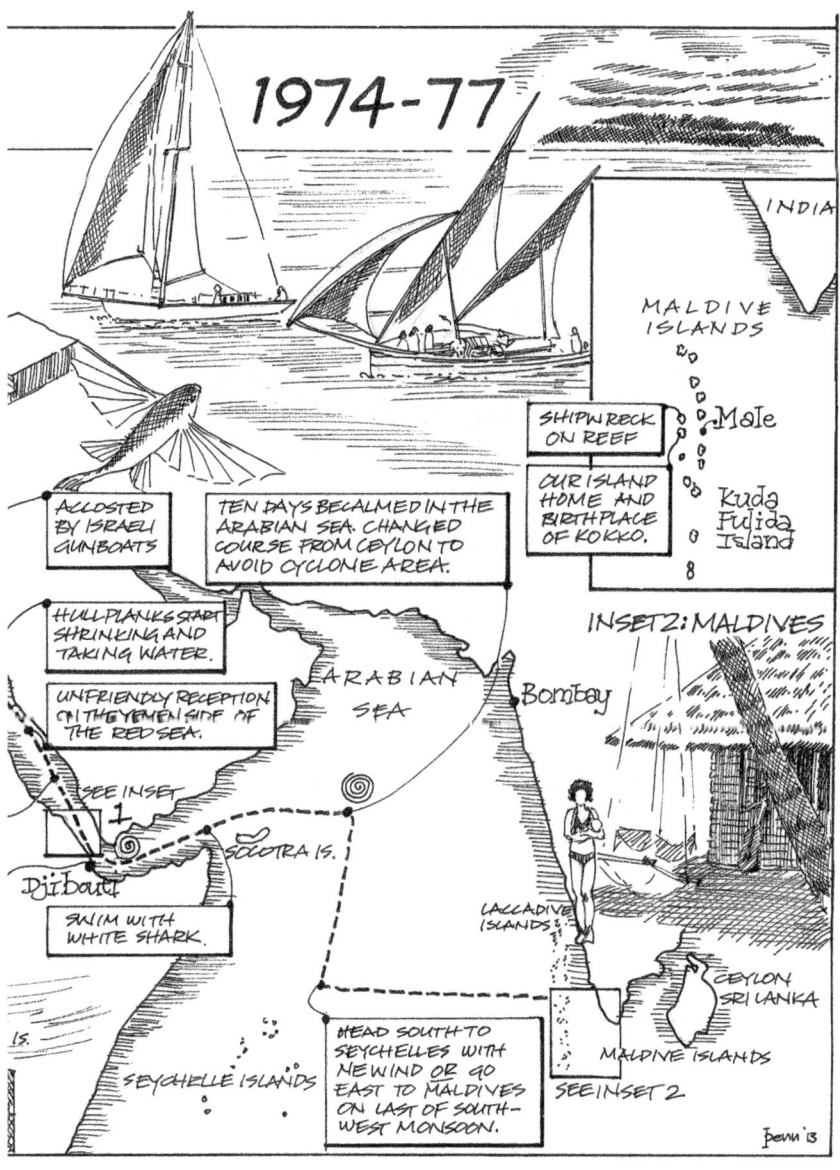

Gayle and Frank
Djibouti Photo Booth
1976

To Gayle for her courage and prevailing spirit in her short life, and for establishing a beachhead in our hearts for the wholeness of women, as well as men; to my son Kokko and his wise soul for guiding us to an island within.

Acknowledgments

With gratitude forever to my wife Annica, for her unwavering intuitive wisdom and support during the years it took to write this book, and to my younger boys Matthew and Willem for whispering outside my door and who taught me how to be a father.

Special thanks to my sister, Sara, for shining like the sun on this manuscript with her invaluable editing and encouragement, and to my brother John for sailing the Indian Ocean with me and being my brother in every way.

Also thanks to Peter Levitt and Shirley Graham for their visionary and steadfast support, as well as others including Ralph and Mallory Pred, Pearl Luke, Denise Bukowski at The Bukowski Agency in Toronto, Betsy Amster at Betsy Amster Literary Enterprises in Los Angeles, and friends and family.

Author's Note

It was difficult to leave out of the narrative the stories of a number of crew members we took on from port to port over the years. Gayle and I were in it for the long haul, and these segments were finally incidental or unrelated to the developing themes in Island Born.

Most notably, I would like to honor my younger brother, John, for his courage and heart to sail across the Indian Ocean with Gayle and me. I will be forever guilty of not having the largesse to know how to write that story in. And then there is my good friend and early sailing partner, Michael Kyne, who contributed great spirit and effort to make this voyage happen.

Contents

Prologue xvii

Part I LAYING A COURSE   1

  1 The Calling 3

  2 My Partner 7

  3 An Inheritance 17

  4 The Ship Joya 21

  5 My Mentor 25

  6 Gayle Arrives 29

  7 Strength 33

  8 As We Are Able 37

  9 Navigation 43

  10 O'Riordan's Hurricane 47

  11 Taking O'Riordan to Sea 51

  12 Bay of Biscay 57

  13 An Old Boot 63

  14 Running the Gauntlet 67

PART II CROSSING BORDERS   73

  15 Sailing out of a Bottle 75

  16 No Fresh Water – Hanish Islands 85

  17 Red Sea Escape 91

  18 On the Brink 97

  19 O'Riordan's Bed 101

  20 Djibouti and Terror du Mondo 105

  21 Gayle's Love 109

22 Coming of Age	117
23 Back to Back	121
24 Fleeing Djibouti	125
25 Fire Poppies in the Arabian Sea	131

PART III PARADISE NET 141

26 Blooms in Waves – The Maldives	143
27 Illegally Ashore	147
28 Upon a Reef	151
29 The Land	157
30 Congratulations	163
31 Dragged from the Sea	169
32 Gambling Joya	173
33 Moonless Dark	181
34 Shore Leave	187
35 Evicted from Land	191
36 Searching Seaward	193
37 Relying upon Wind	197
38 Last Stop	199
39 Island Siblings	205
40 Hospitality	211
41 The Agreement	215
42 Stepping Ashore	221
43 An Elder's Decision	225
44 Joya's Sale	231
45 Parting Maelstrom	235

PART IV ISLAND EXPEDITION 241

46 Unnatural Worries	243

47 Singapore 247

48 Medical Grip 253

49 The Map 257

50 Last Errand 259

51 Back to the Maldives 263

52 Our Island 271

PART V OUR NEW VILLAGE   279

53 The House 281

54 Jungle Camp 289

55 Without Clocks 295

56 Just Two of Us 301

57 Taking Shelter 305

58 Far from Alone 309

59 Appropriating Privacy 315

60 Mosabe's Prediction 319

PART VI FROM THIS MATRIX   325

61 A Baby 327

62 Violet Waters 341

63 Soft Knocking 347

64 Honoring Family 351

65 Storm Riding 355

66 Kokko's Name 359

67 The Chess Crisis 363

68 Reclaiming 367

69 Feridu Medicine Man 373

70 Poison 377

71 Assimilation 381

72 Seeking Allies	387
73 Mosabe's Checkmate	393
74 Baking	401
75 Fitting In	407
76 Swallowed Up	409
77 Seeds	413
78 Sowing	419
79 O'Riordan's Laugh	423
80 Casting Off	425
About the Author	431

Prologue

She was too young to be dying, fasting to death on her mother's couch. She quietly waited with her chapped lips parted in an oval, her eye lids halfway down. No apparent breath behind her teeth. I placed a gardenia beneath her nose, which I brought to remind her of our island. Her eye seemed to gather the light from the white petals, either staring or waiting, I couldn't tell.

She asked what I was doing, and I told her that I had brought her a gardenia.

She tilted her eyes down to see. "Beautiful," she whispered.

I placed the damp flower into her hand, and helped raise it to her nose, waiting to be sure she breathed the fragrance in.

"Thank you" she whispered.

I put my face down to the coolness of her skin, that ached in my skin, that no longer felt heat from our tears, or water droplets from the gardenia in her palm, and I whispered into her ear, "No, thank you, Gayle. Thank you."

She was nearly at the end of her fast, and the cancer would not get her now. Once again, she had taken the helm of her life. She had declined a last desperate surgery, choosing death with her unflinching courage, that fearless embrace which had taken her so far beyond her wildest dream.

Our son, Kokko, had asked his mom to die with his crystal around her neck, and to live inside it for the rest of his life. The call came early in the morning from Gayle's mother. "She's gone," she said calmly.

    We found her lying in the window seat when we arrived. Kokko's crystal lay in the hollow of her throat, aglow in the morning sunlight. He knelt and bent his head by her shoulder, as if listening to her. When he looked up, he smiled, his 14 year old eyes insolent with light, the unbearable light. Then he unfastened the crystal from around his mom's neck, and put it around his own.

Beneath the veneer of civilization... lies not the barbarian and animal, but the human in us who knows the rightness of birth in gentle surroundings, the necessity of a rich nonhuman environment, play at being animals... the cultivation of metaphorical significance of natural phenomena of all kinds... There is a secret person undamaged in every individual, aware of the validity of these, sensitive to their right moments in our lives.

—Paul Shepard[1]

[1]Shepard, Paul. *Nature and Madness*. Athens, GA: Univ. of Georgia Press, 1998, c.1982. p129.

Part I
LAYING A COURSE

1
The Calling

There were no parking places as I cruised the end of Washington Boulevard in Venice Beach. It was my lunch break, and the height of summer. The sandy food-stained sidewalks swarmed with crowds from the city. Parked cars nosed up to the curb like beached whales. It had only been a few months earlier that I had been surging across the Java Sea on an Indonesian *prahu*, sleeping on deck on a grass mat with the cook-fire flickering on patchwork sails. The *prahu* I had planned to purchase from a shipyard in the Celebes had sunk in a tropical storm. Now after two years on the road, I had wound up back where I started. All my friends had graduated from university and begun their careers. That left me at twenty-seven years old with no sensible ambition at all. At least nothing I could justify, that wouldn't have made anyone laugh. So I kept my plans to myself. But I was burning up inside with a calling I must have been born with, that neither my upbringing nor my family's appeals could stop from charging out.

The young woman I was about to meet this blistering afternoon in August 1972, would begin a voyage that would take me to the ends of the earth, and to the very brink of losing myself. I spotted her walking along the curb barefoot, placing one foot in front of the other, balancing with her arms extended, as if she were treading the edge of the world. She was only about sixteen, pretty with long auburn hair, and slender hips in cutoff jeans. She noticed me watching her. A shadow of acknowledgement slid across her face, as it must have mine, an eclipse that blocked out the traffic and crowds around us.

I slammed the brakes, kissing the rear bumper of the car in front of me. The guy glared back, shook his fist at me, and drove on.

The girl laughed heartily and sauntered off through the crowd. I craned my neck, for a sign of her among the bikini shops, bike rentals, and fast-food windows.

Unable to find a parking place, I headed back to the vintage Baltic Trader where I worked as an apprentice shipwright in the marina. Without any funds of my own, she was close as I could get to such a lovely ship. Originally designed for sea voyages in the North Atlantic, she was tied up to the wharf with a sagging yard arm, like a forgotten ancestor. I got hired to help convert her into a floating condo for a local developer, replete with a Jacuzzi tub and a couch in the living room. With each rasp of my saw I realized, then twenty-seven, how circumstances could cut away at one's own future.

The young girl with the eclipsing eyes appeared to be homeless. I caught glimpses of her hanging out with drunks and bums in alleys clutching their bottles in brown bags in the midst of spilled trash and prowling dogs, or sometimes she was shooting pool inside a reeking, street-end bar, laughing with adult men in the smoky light. This particular evening, I spotted her in the alley as I drove to my apartment. I cruised slowly by as she tipped back a bottle with some vagrants, a young man with filthy bare feet playing guitar, and some bums feeling important. She held her head high and her eyes shone, as if they were laughing into mine.

I waved indifferently as I passed.

"Hi, Bye," she sung.

I sat in my car in the dark outside my apartment, as if I weren't going back in. What was she doing on the streets so young? So defiant and at ease in her circumstances, as if a regular life were immaterial? She might be a teenage alcoholic, I thought. Definitely young enough to get me arrested. But there was something unsettling in her eyes. She reminded me of a naked sadhu I met on the banks of the Ganges, in India. He had looked at me just as she had, sitting there smeared in white ash in front of his sacred fire. And I had just stood there unable to speak, while he stared at me with that same fearless twinkling, as if there was something obvious about me.

2
My Partner

A couple of weeks later on my lunch break again down at the pier, I pulled up a chair in the Cheese and the Olive, at one of the resin surfaced cargo hatch covers salvaged off a ship for a table. I looked behind me, and there she was, sitting at a table alone eating a salad. Her presence flustered me, as if I'd already been caught in a contradiction. My plans definitely did not include falling in love. She blushed with her fork frozen between her lips, her auburn hair in ringlets under her chin.

"My name is Frank."

"Gayle," she said, smiling, without averting her eyes, woodsy green eyes, womanly eyes. My staring embarrassed her. Her cheeks swelled with peach freckles over her cheek bones.

I was certainly an outlandish sight, in my straw top hat with a tuft under my lower lip, my sharp Scottish nose slightly crooked from the tennis racket that had broken it in prep school. My hair was rusted by the sun, clumps glued together with white paint. Wood chips and sawdust drizzled to the floor around me. My feet were stuck into dented Dutch clogs with my shirt hanging open in the heat. I was skinny and taut as a ship's halyard.

I bit off the end of a hot pepper with the last mouthful of a Swiss cheese sandwich and pushed back my chair, already cursing myself for not going over to her, I nodded as I left.

"Bye." She said, raising her hand.

I wove as smoothly as possible toward the door, to avoid crashing into tables and chairs on my way out.

A few days later while taking a shower, I heard a commotion at my front door. It was Gayle arguing with my houseguest. He refused to let her in because she was soaking wet, and smelled of alcohol.

"I'm a friend of Frank's," she said, trying to elbow her way in. "Are you going to make a lady stand outside when she's freezing?"

"It's okay, Milton," I shouted out. "Let her in."

Gayle stepped indignantly past him. "Sourpuss."

She turned to me, her summer dress twisted around her body, and her hair plastered to her head with wet sand, "Some guys threw me in the ocean... I was in the neighborhood."

Not wanting her to feel humiliated or uncomfortable, I stepped aside, holding my towel around me and opening my free hand to the bathroom. "The shower's in there, if you want to use it."

"Thank you." She glided past me, waving her hand in an exaggerated flourish of grace and composure.

We met for dinner at the Fish Shanty, a couple of blocks over from my place. It had ship's hawsers looped through wooden pilings leading up to a door with a large brass porthole. Anyone longing for the sea, even the fried smell of the sea, could crawl up into this place like a hermit crab. We sat at a table covered with a red and white checked table cloth and waited for our food to be served in red plastic baskets. Gayle looked older than she was, scrubbed clean without makeup, eyes wild as a Gypsy's. She flicked her cigarette nervously into the ash tray, trying to be polite by not slugging down her rum and coke while I sipped mine.

"What was that sword thing hanging on the wall in your apartment, something you brought back from travelling?"

"Yeah."

"Where'd you get it?

"Borneo. But don't get me started about that."

She looked down modestly. "I was just wondering."

"I just don't want to ruin our first dinner together going on about my travels."

"I can always leave."

"Exactly. I tend to spoil the conversation telling travel stories. My family just changes the subject. My friends ignore me."

"I haven't got any travel stories, so I don't mind."

"You haven't travelled anywhere?"

"Only to Arizona with some friends. We drove there and back in 2 days."

"What about with your family?"

"Nope."

"You've never been on a plane?"

"Nope."

I had never met anyone like her, closed up here on the streets of LA like a pea in a pod. But there was hunger in her eyes. Something she imagined. I don't know what.

"Okay, I was on an Indonesian cattle freighter off the coast of eastern Borneo. Nearly capsizing in a storm. The cattle were all sliding to one side, sliding on their bellies and backs, groaning. The decks were running with urine and cow shit, right into the canvas sided area where I was huddled with about fifty other deck passengers. Almost everyone was barfing into the mix. I couldn't stand it anymore and clamored up into the wheel house where I wedged myself under the stairs. Some officers tried to get me to come out…"

Realizing I was already in deeper than I intended, I hesitated.

"Are you going to tell me about this friggin sword or not?"

I continued about the cranky missionaries in a small tin-roofed Catholic mission who put me up that first night after I arrived. They had insisted my long hair would frighten the natives upriver, and I had allowed them to buzz cut me.

"Frighten *them*!" I said. "I wish you could have seen these jungly looking dudes who picked me up. The local boat I was on had reached the end of navigable part of the river. Up ahead were rapids through an otherwise impassable wilderness. The Dyaks pulled alongside in a long dugout canoe with an outboard motor. They had black hair down below their shoulders and eagle feathers stuck in it like arrows! The backs of their hands were tattooed to the tips of their fingers. They wore nothing but a pair of shorts made out of tree bark, and had swords in bark scabbards lying beside them. Their thighs were massive. I climbed in going *Holy Shit* to myself, and we zoomed off. One of them sat backwards facing me with a transistor radio playing Led Zeppelin. He never took his eyes off me, or relaxed his insane grinning with shiny black teeth stained from chewing beetle nut."

Gayle laughed. "The buzz cut probably saved you. It made you too ugly for those guys to want your head." She took a swig of her drink.

My account hadn't put her off at all, no matter how prone I was to disorienting details. I took a swig of my brown English ale, and stared at the discolored foam. Something inside me wanted to test her. See how far she would go. I went on about the decomposing pig I sat next to for a week, which they cut chunks off of and boiled for dinner. How we slept on hunks of peeled bark in the jungle. And of the leeches swollen up with my blood. Dangling off my thighs when I helped shoulder the rattan pouches full of salt through the jungle up beyond some rapids.

"So did you see any shrunken heads?"

"Did I mention shrunken heads?"

"It's Borneo, right?"

"They don't walk around with shrunken heads. They were imprisoned by the Dutch colonials for head hunting."

"Come on. You knew they hid them somewhere."

"Ok I thought they must have. I had heard you might be able to see them up where I was, near the mountains crossing over to Sarawak, which is the Malaysian part of Borneo."

"And...?"

"And finally I couldn't resist. I kinda gestured from my head to an empty basket in this longhouse where I was staying. But I realized my mistake instantly. There were several families squatting around and all their expressions just sank. They looked really disturbed, frowning at me with their mouths puckered up like they had eaten something sour."

"That's because you're from L.A. Imagine what they would have thought if one of 'em had to ride in a friggin' bus full of weirdoes up Venice Boulevard," she laughed. "You should've just snooped around."

"I'm not snooping around a Dyak house full of limb and head lopping natives. I stood out like a sore thumb."

"I would have never gone up there."

"How could you know that, until you got there?"

"I don't think I could be a primitive person."

"What is primitive?"

"Well let's put it this way, you ain't four feet tall with black teeth."

"And I never grew up feeling connected with my world or had the inner confidence these people seemed to be born with, from the youngest to the oldest. They left me with the women husking rice all day while they went about the jungle on bamboo poles in the trees. They wanted me to join them, but could see I wasn't the man they were. One night they allowed me to accompany them on a hunt, but I gave up after running for miles in a creek. Some eight year old kids took me back. But they kept trying. One night they gave me some foamy white stuff in a wooden cup. It made me delirious for days. I don't know how many. A bare-breasted old woman fed me broth with my head in her lap. The wrinkles in her stomach looked as if she'd birthed the whole village. Metal rings stretched down from her earlobes in long loops of skin below her sagging tits. They swung over my nose, kinda like pendulums keeping time. The men gave me the sword when I left, like I had earned it. But they still wanted some money for it. So yes, I felt each experience took me deeper than where I started."

"That's what I want to do," Gayle said without pause. "See the world. I'm not scared. I dropped out of school and took care of myself since I was thirteen. L.A.'s gotta be worse than a jungle."

We sat there for a moment. Gayle lit a cigarette which looked strange in such a young mouth. She took a drag, and brought her bare leg up with her heel on the edge of her seat, exhaling with her cigarette hand draped over a lovely knee.

"Now that I've told you this much, Gayle, I just want to tell you about my plan."

"Your plan?"

"Yeah, I got a plan. It came to me standing on the shore in Penang. I still had not made any sense of my life, and L.A. felt too close, with only Southeast Asia and the Pacific between me and a flight back. It was dark and starting to rain. My bush hat had worn out. I still had a piece of bone woven into a vine for a headband that I made in Nepal. Cold rain began soaking into my hair and leaking down my face, but I could not move a step in any direction.

Up on the road there was this crazy old Chinese prostitute waiting in my trishaw, waving for me to come in out of the rain. She had been following me everywhere. Her face was pure white with some kind of flour paste she put on it. She always had a flower behind her ear. She was probably pretty once. The Chinese owner of the run down hotel where I stayed would not let her inside. She would just wait out in the street. She was always there. Outside the opium den too, where junkies fed opium to monkeys that came to the window ledge. Penang was only a small two-story town then. I'd let her ride around with me. Fact was we were sort of companions. I wrote my Dad that I was destitute, but he sent me a plane ticket home instead of money. I knew my complete failure to discover how to live my life would become concrete forever if I returned; that it would be the death of me. But I didn't seem to have any more of a future than she did. Still I refused to think I was like her. Crazy with nowhere to go. But she's another story."

"I'll bet."

"Really, I was her friend. But the reason I came to Penang was because a fellow traveler got me excited about Chinese junks. I'd never seen one, other than in pictures. Some boatmen playing cards over crates in a tent told me the junks were coming back. So I stood there on the muddy bank as it grew dark. The swells were smoking in the rain as the first heavy timbered ships emerged, huge battened sails, soiled brown in the mist. Anchors plunged into the muddy water. All of a sudden boat people were shouting and handling hemp hawsers.

I paced back and forth through the slippery goose shit for days, staring at them, unable to think of what to do next. I was mesmerized by every detail. The laundry flapping from the rigging in a breeze, fish spinning on tethers to dry in the sun, and kids sculling their launches ashore. It was a floating village!

Then one morning they were gone. Every boat vanished. That's what really got me. I remember staring out over the dull sparkle of the water that day. It was as if my own heart had sailed off and left an empty space in me. Then I had it. I remembered napping in my mom's lap at the beach in Santa Monica. That hollow sound of pounding waves in the background. The groans of gulls. The smells of drying seaweed and hot sand. You probably felt the same as a California kid... Right? The love of the sea?"

"We didn't belong to a Beach Club."

"Come on. Didn't you go to the beach?"

"Not much. It was hard to get there."

"I grew up surfing, hanging out like seals in the waves. They didn't belong to a beach club either."

"Well I did spend a fair amount of time in the Porpoise Lounge."

"That's not funny Gayle. I'm talking about suddenly opening your eyes, and seeing what you love about who you are. The sea has always taught me how to love my life. That's what I realized on that shore in Penang. The sea is my home!"

Gayle shrugged, seeming less confident. "I get seasick on the ferry to Catalina."

"Everyone gets seasick on the ferry to Catalina. You have to look out to the horizon to keep from getting sick. That's what you do on a boat. It's like looking inside yourself. Because you never get to the horizon. Just to what you dream."

"So that's your plan? To go off on a boat?"

"Yes."

Gayle fell silent and showed no interest in hearing more or speaking further.

After dinner, we drove down a dark stretch of Pacific Avenue on the way back to my apartment. The silence had grown uncomfortable, like the marine fog enveloping our headlights. I glanced over at her shape outlined by the dash lights.

When I turned my eyes back to the road, a ragged man loomed up in our headlights, stiff as a scarecrow and bent over some agony at his middle, hurrying across the road.

I screeched on the brakes, swerving and cursing the terror of almost killing someone. I gripped the steering wheel, grumbling under my breath, heart pounding.

Gayle stared oddly off into the corner of the windshield as if nothing had happened. "Now you've met my father," she said.

I started to brake. "Should we go back?"

"No," she snapped.

I coasted slowly along for a moment to calm myself. "Where does he live?"

"Nowhere... He won't stay in a shelter. He only comes around Mom's at the end of the month for his welfare check."

Gayle made love with me that night, and several of the next, showing up at my door after she cleaned houses for someone named Sammy. She was business-like about sex, as if she had earned a meal she fully intended to enjoy. Then she vanished, sometimes for weeks at a time, saying that "Guys always think they can own you." I set a precedent by not interfering with her decisions, and watched as paper sacks of her things began to accumulate against the bedroom wall: a tarnished silver necklace from India rolled up in a white cotton blouse, new leather sandals, a pair of meticulously folded jeans reserved for going out, and some crumpled photographs including a mug shot of some tough-looking guy. There was also a paper sack full of pink curlers and a mini hairdryer. It seemed I had now been included in the few valuables she would come back for.

In spite of her meager beginnings, Gayle never complained, or even uttered a derogatory remark about her father. "Dad used to hold me on his lap," she said. "He made me lots of nice promises. He never kept any, but I dreamed he would. Mom won't let him inside anymore. He just stands outside shouting."

Mom had to be tough to raise us six kids by herself in the projects." Gayle laughed. "I will always remember the first swear word that came out of my mouth. All five of my brothers said they were going to tell Mom. I got so scared I went up and washed my own mouth out with soap. But when she got home, they told her anyway. And she made me do it all over again. Because Mom was a good Mormon. Ivory soap! Blech!"

When I came over, Phyllis whipped up mashed potatoes and trays of chocolate chip cookies for us. It was obvious there was love in this household. Phyllis listened and smiled easily, selfless and nonjudgmental as the moon. With five boys it was easy to see how much she adored her renegade and only daughter. The wall was covered in photos of her children, nieces, nephews and other family members, most with that pastel blue background that makes a person look packaged. The furniture was cheap and tasteless Penny's Americana. The TV was on all the time. And the air was stale with the windows always closed, probably cause of the noise off the street. The family lived in low income housing projects. Gayle's Christmas presents came from the fire department. Her spirit had grown strong and free being so adored and accepted by her mother, and at the same time unattached to the material things she never had.

I felt like a monster of both deprivation and privilege by comparison to Gayle's tightly knit family. Mine made an art of being together without any revealing interaction. We lived in a large Spanish colonial house in an expensive neighborhood in Los Angeles with a live-in cook and housemaid, and a huge garden and gardener. I attended private schools and summer camps. My parents gave me a car when I was sixteen. And all along I yearned to be free from it all. To be someone real, like Gayle.

The drone of rush hour traffic in the distance around my Los Angeles Hancock Park neighborhood felt like a moat of sorrow and hopelessness growing up. But there was a path I had never considered. Doing it right with someone who also went missing in their circumstances. Gayle had awakened that man in me. If she had been three years old I would have wanted to adopt her. If she had been a hundred and three years old, I would have given her my companionship.

3
An Inheritance

The sun rose in the west that spring day when my father told me Aunt Beth had passed away. She had left me a small inheritance. Actually she was my father's mother, but my parents never told us kids anything about her. She had been hidden from us, a tempestuous beauty, considered a family renegade because she had rejected my sternly Victorian grandfather. She took my father away and raised him in hotels, and then spent the last third of her life secluded in the antique smelling darkness of her house in Beverly Hills, the drapes never drawn back. What I did not know was that dad visited her in that darkness every single day after work. He never mentioned her or anything about his side of the family. Not a word. My mom led me to believe that he just worked late all those years.

My inheritance from Aunt Beth was just enough to purchase a sailboat, plus a few hundred dollars a month to live on. I told Dad that I was leaving again, but this time to sail the world. His condemnation was, of course, what I expected. He had offered me a salesman position to begin my climb to taking over his lumber company. He was proud, had always trotted me through his offices and around the yards, boasting to his employees that I would be "the new boss." But now he was silent, not a word of detraction towards me, like a jailer leaving the key in the lock on purpose.

Mom told me that my ancestors had sailed off to the Australian gold rush of 1851, wheeled over mountainous waves around the Horn, taking position lines off stars with whitewater roaring down the decks. I felt directly descended, setting sail with some mitochondrial DNA under my own mast step that had taken a few generations to get back to sea.

The sailing books I had been reading were all English publications, so I decided to go to England to look for a ship. I figured that the lineage of maritime traditions in such fierce English weather, the generations of seamen, shipwrights, and lives lost, would be in the design of the ship I would find.

When I told Gayle about my inheritance at our usual table for dinner in the Fish Shanty, she looked at me hard, as if my good fortune were now a sea between us.

"Why don't you come with me?" I half whispered, completely at a loss to make this real for her or myself - that we had drawn so inexplicably together to meet the challenge of a lifetime.

Gayle looked back at me wide-eyed, stunned to be confronted with such an immediate step, one that would spontaneously transport her from her marginalized young life in L.A. Then she looked down, thoughtfully working her finger around a knothole in the table. "But you don't know how to sail. Right?"

"We'll find a boat first. Then we'll learn to sail."

Gayle stared out the window at the clutter of shabby storefronts bathed in that golden southwestern light at sunset. Solitary fishermen leaned with their shadows stretching back over their catch buckets along the pier railing.

"Well, I don't mind sailing around the world on a yacht," she said, with her typically wry air of bravado.

Her eyes already had the beauty of a storm in them. Names are often so prophetic. Gayle! Yes, she was born a goddess of tempestuous waters.

"I'll join you soon as I can earn enough for my plane ticket."

I took a long breath. "But I can buy you a ticket."

"Partners have to stand on their own feet to be real partners. You go ahead."

4
The Ship Joya

In London I bought a 750cc barrel-chested Norton Commando motorcycle, expecting to duck in and out of every harbor on the English coastline to find my boat. Its weight fell over on me at the first stoplight and a man jumped out of his car to help me pick it up. I figured plenty of horsepower was what I needed to make a dream come true.

I headed for the South coast. Although it was late July, the drizzle was freezing. I rode with my hands in a pair of socks, pulling under overpasses to shiver in the downpours. In the small village of Lymington, my Norton rumbled like a Sherman tank between the white plaster storefronts. I pulled up High Street to a cottage overlooking the river, home of a yacht broker I had telephoned from London.

He laid newspapers on the couch before allowing me to sit down while he sorted through his listings. He pulled out a photograph of a vintage sailing vessel, and continued thumbing specification sheets of more boats. I knew instantly that the boat in my hands was mine, exactly what I had dreamed. "It's more than you can afford," he said over his magnifiers.

"But I want to see this one," I insisted.

"But you haven't looked at the others."

"This is the only boat I am interested in."

We stood on a grassy hillock in drifts of mist over the small marina in the river. He pointed down at her in her slip. She was breathtaking, a 40-foot cutter, gleaming black with varnished spars. Her sails were red, the traditional tanned color, her main neatly flaked along the top of her boom, and her foresails bundled at the base of her forestays. She was solid Burmese teak, built in 1937 with teak decks, bronze winches and bronze deck hardware. At first sight my future was already rove through every one of her blocks, and smoothed to the curve of every plank.

Her name was Joya, Spanish for jewel, but the broker, Alistair, pronounced her name with a hard "J." She had been lavishly cared for by her owner, who owned the internationally famous boatyard adjacent the marina, Berthon Boat Company in Lymington, Hampshire.

Alistair did not want to submit my offer. "It's too low," he said. "And in any case, she's much too much boat for your experience."

I had not confessed that I had absolutely no sailing experience, or that the cost of the boat was my entire inheritance. It was one of those inexplicable things that happens. The dream just slips into another dreamer, as if fulfilling its own destiny. I told Alistair that I already knew Joya was mine, that I had envisioned this exact boat. I told him to deliver a personal message with my offer: *I will sail her around the world.*

To my yacht broker's astonishment, my offer was accepted the next day.

It was near midnight when I walked to the red iron phone box just up the street from the shipyard to telephone Gayle. She had taken a dayshift as a waitress at a 24-hour restaurant named "Ships" in Westwood, writing me that the other waitresses did not believe she was actually going to sail around the world. That was Gayle to get a job at a place named Ships, before she went off on one.

Gayle answered. "I was hoping you would call this morning."

"I've got the boat!"

A reverberation in the connection echoed my words back to me in a tiny voice, as if some part of me still could not be heard. I had to remember that silence was her way of answering. Gayle and my father were both that way. He carried words in his body like shrapnel. He paced the halls alone at night when his company was too leveraged to allow him to sleep. He did not speak a word when I first wrecked the family car, or even when I surprised my parents returning home unannounced after two years away, not even a single word to me about his mother's death, or when I most recently departed to sail around the world.

"I bought a boat, Gayle. Do you hear me?"

Still no answer. The night over the Atlantic seemed a void, collapsing into itself. Only the sound of Gayle's breath.

"She's beautiful," I said. "Deep and long-keeled. Seaworthy. All her gear bronze and oversize. She's black with red sails like the Bristol Channel Pilot cutter I once showed you."

Still no answer.

"Her name is Joya. That means jewel in Spanish."
I stared at the gauzy reflections of myself upon the black glass of the phone box. It was August, but cold enough to feel like winter. "Have you changed your mind about coming?" I asked.

A long silence. "No," Gayle responded.

"Do you need money for a ticket?"

"No, I have my own money."

"Then what?"

"Do you still want me to come?"

A remarkable ship had just come into my possession, a divine treasure, truly a jewel. An ark for the two of us! Wasn't that the answer for everything, at least for now?

"Of course, I want you to come... I thought we'd already decided..."

"Then I'll call you," she said, "when I know what time to pick me up at the train station in Lymington."

I hung up and leaned back against phone box. We had always been abrupt. That was our way with each other. But I couldn't shake the gnawing sense that this voyage would turn into more than either of us had ever bargained for. I grabbed the receiver back off the hook, thinking she might still be on the line, to tell her how much her coming meant to me, how I knew already that I loved her, how much.... but the line was dead. There was just the movement of trees outside the glass panes, their branches scratching in the wind.

5
My Mentor

Gayle wrote that she had *not yet* saved enough money to join me. *Not yet!* But I had a ship for us! However shy and afraid she might have been, that little teenage waitress was not balking at leaving the country for the first time, or sailing out into a vast ocean wilderness, or at any other obstacle. Her courage to do what was right came through loud and clear. It was all or nothing for Gayle. Always would be.

I began the job of fitting out Joya on my own. First, I would repaint her with copper-based antifouling paint while she was in the shipyard for her marine survey, up on the "hard," as the English refer to a ship on land. Evenings I poured through my reference materials, books such as Hiscock's *Cruising under Sail,* and Adlard Coles's *Heavy Weather Sailing,* Beiser's *The Proper Yacht,* and Jurd's *Yacht Construction.*

The name Mr. O'Riordan began popping up when the townspeople discovered I had no sailing experience. "Yes, he might appreciate having something to do and someone to talk to," Mrs. Bateman said, in her bakery next to her bed and breakfast. "He's quite an eccentric old gentleman." She straightened her arms against the counter. "He shocked the whole town some years back. It was a fisherman that spotted him rowing straight out to sea in his skiff one night. Sea rescue could not find him till late the next afternoon. He was trying to row around the Isle of Wight, he told them. He was seventy-three years old, mind you!"

What had possessed the man? Especially a man Mr. O'Riordan's age. For years afterward I thought about it. Tides and willpower were all he could predict in those gale-swept seas. He had rowed out of the Lymington estuary opposite the Isle of Wight before dawn on the ebb tide, then rowed for all he was worth into the confluence of waters around the Needles light. Hugging the ghostly white cliffs on the seaward side of the Isle of Wight, he must have picked up the flood to round the island's midpoint at St. Catherine's. That was where the coast guard picked him up about 2 p.m., flying with the tide and a following southwesterly wind to boot. The old man in his little boat might have made it home by ten the same night, riding the races of three tides around the island over a distance of fifty or sixty miles!

Alistair Easton, our yacht broker, said that O'Riordan had sailed across the Atlantic and survived a hurricane in a twenty-six foot Vertue, a small yacht designed by the famous English naval architect, Laurent Giles. "A good boat, but O'Riordan and his friend were almost seventy at the time." Alistair laughed. "They became quite famous in the boating world, a book and so on. Most people in town would prefer the old boy just go have a nap every day, lean on a nurse's arm. But not O'Riordan."

"Yes. Yes. Come anytime," Mr. O'Riordan shouted in a raspy voice when I telephoned. "I'm usually always here, except Tuesday afternoons when I go to market, or Thursday mornings when I go down to the river to my boat."

That fall day I first went to see O'Riordan, the roadside path was puddled from a succession of storms. Large elm trees had begun to lose their leaves. Hard gusts swayed the branches stiffly overhead. The cold wind bent the field grasses back and forth like green candle flames in the afternoon sun. I turned in at O'Riordan's number carved on a granite corner stone at the top of High Street. The gravel driveway led up to the gray stone house. It was overgrown with weeds, and the front garden was tangled by raking winds, and overshaded by wilding hedges.

I rapped the iron knocker upon a heavy plank door. Then again. It flung suddenly open upon a stout white-haired man with a lion's jaw. "Come in. Come in. I didn't hear you knocking. I was doing some work in the back of the house. Come in. Come in." As I introduced myself, he stood slightly sideways to me, seeming to split his difficulty hearing and seeing. "Yes, Yes. Come in." O'Riordan was handsome, not tall but powerful. A red wool boatneck sweater sat squarely on his shoulders. It was the same moth-holed sweater he would wear every day.

We settled in a dim library filled with books and navigation instruments. Gazing about me I took note of a number of instruments I had only seen in sailing books including a celestial globe, a gimbaled compass off a ship, and a barocyclonometer with its insect leg of a needle on a graphing disk for tracking cyclones. In the musty dark wooden shelves of books sat some varnished boxes with tarnished brass clasps: a sextant and a case for an old Walker log which is an instrument for logging miles traveled by trailing an impeller on a line behind a yacht. On a round oak table in the center of the room, an oversize magnifying glass, a pair of calipers and parallel rulers lay on top of a stack of nautical charts.

O'Riordan leaned forward from his crinkled leather easy chair and asked me to tell him about my plans "to sail off into the world." I had not gotten very far before he interrupted.

"Yes, yes, that's fine," he said. "I'll teach you what I can. But what makes me wonder is, why would you want to go to all this trouble?"

What kind of question is that? I thought. "The way of life," I answered. "The adventure."

My words sounded trite. How could I explain the thrill a vintage wooden ship held for me, how often I had imagined myself surging over the waves in search of an unspoiled place, not just in the world, but deep within myself? And if such a place existed and I were able to find it, that would be how I wanted to honor my life, no matter how briefly, or how daunting the challenge. Maybe O'Riordan at eighty-nine years old, having lived a whole lifetime, could ask a young man if going to all this trouble would ever come to anything. But I had the energy to begin. I could not accept myself as I had been taught to be. Nature would be my teacher. I would take the chance of a lifetime now, rather than wait.

O'Riordan leaned forward in his chair with both hands on his cane, as if he knew exactly what I was thinking. "Yes, but I can assure you this is no picnic - long voyages on the ocean. You can never come back completely. I've seen the worst of it - what the power of the sea can do to a ship. Ohhhh… and what it can do to a man. You cannot imagine."

There was a silence as Mr. O'Riordan bent forward to relight his pipe.

"You should understand Mr. O'Riordan that I don't plan on coming back. Not in the usual sense."

"Yes, you are young… and maybe foolish," he mused, taking a long draw. "You deserve your chance." He wheezed with a long laugh under his breath, suddenly clenching his jaw tight on his pipe stem. "I'll have to come down and inspect this boat you've bought."

6
Gayle Arrives

Gayle had doubts about entrusting our lives and education to an eighty nine year old half-blind town eccentric. Probably she had never entrusted her safety to anyone. "I better learn how to sail this boat myself, if I ever want to see my family again," she announced on the phone.

I waited for her on the train platform in front of the one room station outside Lymington. My battered old Morris van was the only car in the muddy parking lot. Reflections of storm clouds drifted over the silvered surface of rain-filled potholes, surrounded by vibrant green fields. Besides me, only an elderly man and lady in overcoats waited on the platform. The hills began to rumble from the approaching train, and the gentleman folded his newspaper and slipped it into his coat pocket. The rumble grew louder. I was suddenly shaken by how little Gayle and I knew each other. Four months had elapsed since she had waved goodbye at the airport. She was essentially a stranger to me, gambling with her life, gambling on intuitions, gambling on each other. As Gayle approached I began to feel like a stranger even to myself.

A thin long legged young woman stepped down from the train onto the landing. She wore a short maroon skirt and a small brimmed felt hat that she'd found in a used clothing store. She stumbled as if she were being tackled by the weight of a huge suitcase she lugged off the steps. The zipper had burst and it was cinched around the middle with a rope. She swung it down with a thud before I could reach for it.

She stood staring at me, dark blue under her eyes from lack of sleep, her hair disheveled. She shivered slightly in the autumn chill, squeezing her shoulders together in a full length purple overcoat. We hesitated, and then collided when I tried to kiss her hello.

"First I started going to the wrong city," Gayle said, "Leamington up north somewhere, instead of Lymington. Thank God a bus driver realized my mistake. I lugged my bag up and down steps and overpasses about a hundred times before I got here."

"But you made it. You can calm down now."

"Then there was the perv that lurked around after me."

"Oh, I'm sorry…." I paused, and her eyes met mine. "Would you like to see our boat," I asked, trying not to appear too excited. "It's on the way to our B&B."

"I've been in these clothes for twenty hours. I stink. I'm itchy and cold. I gotta get washed up."

By the time Gayle showered, the B&B owners, the Batemans, had made a little celebration dinner, for the arrival of "my fiancée," an assumption that surprised both of us. A couple of B&B guests also attended. Gayle was very uncomfortable with "English formality" she called it, not to mention their need to have us engaged.

"I'm not sure you would make a good husband," she said, climbing the narrow stairs back up to our room, which had been converted from an attic storage space with baby blue wall paper.

She turned to face me at the bed, and boldly undressed. She stood there naked as if that were her duty. I put my arm around her and turned her toward the bed.

"I already miss home," she said.

I cuddled her to sleep, while she clung to me like a child.

At breakfast in the parlor, she thought the other B&B guests were casting "opinionated" glances at her. Even the English tea cozy made her feel out of place. "It's like dressing your dog," she said.

I was anxious for her to see Joya, and we drove directly to the shipyard after breakfast. I shuttled her into the old boat shed. She stopped, and stared into the cavernous dark. The hulking, dismasted shape of Joya sat in a goliath cradle, hauled up on lard-greased rails that reached back into the murky water.

"It stinks in here," she said, as I steadied the tall ladder up to Joya's deck. Gayle climbed, holding the rungs with her finger tips to avoid the wedges of mud mixed with lard scraped off shoes climbing up. Inside Joya's main saloon she looked at the chaos of boat parts, boxes of boat junk, everything layered in thick dust.

"Isn't she beautiful? All her cabinetry is cherry." I wiped the dust from a cupboard panel. "There's a separate cabin with a sink forward, and our own cabin is aft. Look at these beautiful paneled doors with bronze hardware. They're cherry too. Those are library bookshelves, and here's the galley. Look how the plate racks drain over the sink."

"What a mess," she said.

The rest of the day we lugged boxes around and cleaned up our new home.

Joya's marine survey gave her a top rating; the sale was finalized. We launched her with a silver dollar under her mast step, as is the ancient tradition. Once back in her slip along the river, we moved aboard. White swans glided around our stern in the emerald water, eddying out toward the cold sea.

The moment Mr. O'Riordan met Gayle, his manner changed. His eyebrows raised, watching every move she made. He became uncharacteristically silent around his crackling fireplace evenings, rather than rallying his memories of facing storms or explanations of sailing technique.

"Her grit to tackle an ocean voyage around the world is crucial to your success," he said. "Few women have ever lasted long at sea."

One afternoon I rushed in, late to my lesson, and found Gayle and O'Riordan sitting on the couch. He had taken both her hands in his, his face concentrated, his eyes misty and out of focus. He lifted her hands close to his face to study them, maybe feeling their heat. Gayle had hands that were strong as a man's, but remarkably pliant and graceful.

"It was in her touch," O'Riordan said suddenly of his deceased wife. "Anything she touched came to life. The way the sea touches a boat. She had healing hands." Then he wheezed with laughter, mysteriously bemused, releasing Gayle's hands as if he had stepped ashore.

Healing hands! I was surprised by revelations O'Riordan made about his past, such as his twenty-seven year career as a police chief in India. I think his wife's name was Margaret, but I am not certain he ever said so.

"I marked the bearings of constellations out in the garden," he mused. "If you have a sharp eye you might see the top of a stake or two out there." He pointed from memory out through the leaded library windows, toward some shrubs in an overgrown patch of grass. Sure enough, I saw the tip of a stake.

"They were known to sleep out there together all night, even in the snow," Mrs. Bateman reported.

Gayle and I went to visit every evening. To keep us late he would eventually pull a bottle of whisky out of the cupboard. The hurricane he had survived crossing the Atlantic was what he mostly went on about. Not the horror of the storm, but the beauty of it. Eventually he would always come to it by the end of the evening, sitting in front of his dying fire. Describing those seas in such a trance, as if he were instructing us how to dance over the waves.

7
Strength

To visit us down on the river, O'Riordan walked more than two miles from his house, thumping his white cane down High Street, as villagers turned to watch and gossip about him. The first time I spotted O'Riordan coming down the floats, I was forty feet aloft in the bosun's chair, lock-wiring shackles in the diamond strut rigging that supports the top mast section. The job was made more difficult as the bosun's chair twisted about in the freezing December wind.

"Ahoy, Joya! Ahoy!" he shouted, leaning hard on his cane, gliding on it like a keel in the turbulence.

"You're in for it," Gayle said, as she cranked me down to the deck with the main halyard winch.

O'Riordan climbed aboard clutching the neck of his cane. I hurried ahead to give him a hand down the companionway ladder into our main saloon. Instead he took hold of the ladder rails and clambered down himself, scraping the bulkheads like a giant crab. He sat sturdily at the saloon table, staring ahead waiting for the black Colombian coffee Gayle was brewing. Cirrus cloud wisps of white hairs marched over his nearly bald head. Too blind to make out any details about Joya, he sat contemplating the feel of her through his seat, the way she responded to the undercurrents and undulations making their way up river from the open sea. His ox sized shoulders swayed just enough for his posture to find support in Joya's bones. The ribs of his own ship had been stove in when she fell from the cliff face of a giant wave during the hurricane. "The near fatal rent in her hull may as well have been in my own chest," he told us. "But the sea decided to spare us a little longer." He laughed long and silently under his breath, which made him seem slightly insane. Then he fell abruptly silent, feeling the movement of our ship again, as the cabin filled with the aroma of brewing coffee.

O'Riordan stirred suddenly, thumping his cane on the cabin sole. "This seems to be quite a fine ship you have here."

O'Riordan adopted us without asking our permission. Several times a week he came, no matter how violent the weather. Winter southwesterlies whined through the rigging and frothing ocean surges charged upriver from a body of water called the Solent, lying between the Isle of Wight and the mainland. His hailing cut through it all, "Ahoy, Joya! Ahoy!"

I always rushed out to escort him, as he short-stepped his way along the pitching flotation docks, holding his yellow sou'wester hat on with the hook of his cane, shouting out in the blasts of spray. I kept close to his elbow to prevent him from being pitched into the sea, and sinking like a stone statue with his cane outstretched in his hand. The first time I tried to steady him, he cast me off with his shoulder, very nearly knocking me off the dock as he passed by.

"I have no choice but to come," he said in gruff voice. "You have put something in your coffee that has made me addicted." He was addicted all right, addicted to imaginings only the sea and our ship could inspire.

"Where is Gayle?" he demanded, leaning around the kitchen bulkhead. "She has the magic touch with the coffee."

"She's in our cabin, writing a letter home."

"It's all the shouting. Tell her to come, and I'll promise to remember, that I'm the one who is deaf, and not her."

Gayle wrote her mother: *He has threatened to send the water patrollers after us if we leave without knowing what we are doing, and I think he should.*

He asked questions, and then wheezed with laughter over my zealous efforts to prepare ourselves. "That is as strong a fitting as I've ever seen," he said, his fingertips taking a measure of the massive 3/8" thick stainless steel stem fitting I had just fabricated.

"It was a complicated piece," I said, "with eight angles, and it fits perfectly." O'Riordan just smiled, rocking slightly in his seat. Why would he be amused by such a piece of hard work? Had I made it too strong? Or was he laughing at how futile the strongest piece would prove to be?

8
As We Are Able

That winter we worked seven days a week into the night, until we were stiff with cold and exhaustion. O'Riordan beamed knowingly. He sung out this poem for us from time to time:

For the first five days
We work hard as we're able
On the sixth and seventh
We holystone the decks
And scrape the cable.

I walked across to Berthon boatyard up the river bank from Joya's slip where I could get advice from old salts still working at the trades of their forefathers.

"Old Molly's got a reverse twist to'er," Bert said, his elbows working his marlin spike into the twisted steel in the dim yellow light of the rigging shack. He coughed horribly on the cigarette he clamped between his lips like the rigging wire in his vise.

My own lungs began to pump for the few molecules of air to be found in the odorous reek of tar and oiled hemp, the oxidized steel rigging, dank gunny sacks, and rotting canvas. Rusting scraps mounded undisturbed as shipwrecks under the wooden work benches. Then add a hundred years of stale cigarette smoke into the windowless shed. "The girls gets stubborn at times," he said, twisting the spike back around to open the lay. "Just give'er a little leeway as you bring'er round. She'll settle home by'erself. Like a woman."

The wire strand snapped, tightening itself into the groove as if it were alive. "Like that," he said.

We worked nights till just before the pubs closed. I plunged my head down the hatch to check our ship's clock on the aft cabin bulkhead. "That's it!" I called out. "We've got fifteen minutes! Let's go."

Gayle and I ran full tilt down the dock, as if our lives depended on it, and crossed the gravel lot to our rusted wreck of a Morris van. I scraped a wound in the ice across the windshield. The battery was always dead. Gayle pushed from behind, as I laid my shoulder to the doorjamb. If it only went *pomp pomp pomp* and stopped at the end of the lot, I tried the hand crank at the front of the engine. As a last resort, I whacked its iron head with a wrench. "I really love the simple life," Gayle scoffed. Her first complaints were no more significant than this. Our adventure had begun. Hard work and uncomfortable, but exciting, I thought, as we wheeled through the small town, shivering in fumes of noxious exhaust wafting up through the rusted out floorboards.

Gayle wrote to her mom: *I've been saving money by doing half our laundry by hand, and putting a little bit down each week on this nice corduroy jacket. You should see my purple long coat, it's close to threads now. The lining completely fell out. Mark Bateman, who is the B&B landlady's son, gave me his old school jacket which is pretty warm.*

And in another letter to her mom: *I make our own bread cause I figure we can only spend about $2.50 a day on food, and when a loaf of bread is $.50, you make your own . My wheat bread turns into a rock after it cools, and I have to chisel it into small pieces for the swans. And while I'm complaining, the cheapest crummiest cigarettes you can buy cost $.65, but I know what you would say about that. So now I'm going to the vegetable shop and say "Ghooooooh" as the English do when they hear the price.*

We spent all our money at the ship's chandlery and the pubs. There was a workingman's pub named The Ship's Inn down Quay Road that let us in filthy as we always were. All our clothes were stained and torn, doughy with teak dust, gilded with bronze filings, splattered with paint, and hardened in patches with linseed oil, varnish, and glue. Our pockets were full of resident bits and pieces, notes, and odd scraps that just fell in. At a glance, other seagoing folk could recognize what type of work we were doing, as well as what type of boat we were on.

At the sound of the ship's bell for last call, net pullers, fishermen, boat builders, all began waving beefy forearms with fish scales still stuck on, their gear-grease-stained fingers clutching empty mugs. We crowded in hurrying to order light and bitters backed up with scotches "neat", then leaning back out of reach of the barman as he began picking up.

The landlady at the King's Head on High Street sometimes let us in for meal dressed as we were. She had us sit at a hallway table behind the kitchen, out of sight of her guests dressed appropriately in sport coats and ties out front. We ordered the vegetable curry. While we waited, Gayle examined her hands. They were heavily calloused and stained, her nails broken, her cuticles split. She tried to preserve her femininity by concealing them when we went out. She picked at a hardened glob on the back of her hand, and then looked up at me.

"We've been working without a break for four months. Is this going to be our boat life, Frank?"

Her female nature was bound to surface. I knew I was getting away with having absolute authority over the management of our preparations. So far she had agreed that my male energy was what was needed to get us launched, and on our way. Whenever she interrupted a meal to speak about something, I knew it was not going to be good. Her unspoken thoughts sat in her stomach undigested, and ruined her appetite.

"You keep saying we are going to leave: in another three weeks, another month... How can anyone live in this damp? I'm getting purple pimples. My flesh is rotting."

The Pub lady's husband Mort set our plates down as if he were handling explosives. The inn must have been his wife's idea. I'd heard he had once been a seaman. Arms and shoulders muscular as his did not get that way from lifting a spatula. Now he wore a patch of white apron that looked too small on him.

"Listen to that wind outside!" Gayle whispered, as Mort went back through the swinging door into the kitchen. "Even the seagulls won't leave town." She stared up at the plaster ceiling, ignoring her dinner steaming under her chin. "I'm scared, Frank. The wind has gotta be a lot worse out in the Bay of Biscay. Neither of us knows what we're doing."

"Alistair says he's going to send two of his clients," I said, "instructors from Glenan Sailing School in France, to come down and talk to us. Don't worry. Eat your dinner while it's hot."

"It's not only that. Who do I have to talk to? You're like talking to the typical male-hell-bent-to-do-something. I'm lonely for girlfriends."

I put my fork down. Trouble had been brewing from a few days back. I suspected it when she had been so intent on finding out if money had been wired to her by her brother, for her share of a car he sold in L.A. "What about what's-her-name... Emily? The girl from the laundromat."

"What about her?"

"I just thought that..."

"No one here relates to us 'cause we wear a bunch of dirty rags, drive a heap of junk, and own a yacht."

Then and there I knew Gayle was going to leave, and there was nothing I could do about it. We walked back to Joya in silence. The flotation docks slammed against their pilings in the river waves.

Joya's mast rocked against the granite sheen of the sky. Gayle climbed below, but I remained on deck adjusting our dock lines.

I'd seen small sailing vessels come into port from great distances, a steel one all dented between its ribs with its railings flattened to the deck by a monstrous weight, another dismasted; I'd seen some setting out with equipment mended with tape, lashings, or simply left in disrepair, boats sailed across the sea like broken ironing boards. How did they ever make it? What combination of timing, intuition, spontaneity, grit, or fearlessness gets them there? Some choices you just can't argue with. There's a rightness about them that can't be explained. Gayle was ready to leave, and I wasn't.

Our bodies were so sore that it hurt to make love that night. We laughed about it as the sea leapt and crinkled around the hull like broken glass. She made love as if she would never leave me, but I could not sleep. Pain in my arms from overwork forced me to sit up most of the night. Gayle slept in a ball to ease the pain in her back.

At dawn I lay in my bunk listening to Gayle out in the galley. She plunged her hands through the thin layer of ice in the water bucket, growling as she sloshed the frozen slush into her face. The sun yellowed a patch of sky through the deck skylight. I prayed it would brighten our day. That Gayle would not leave. But by the time I got up, the winter gloom had engulfed us.

"It's just going to be for awhile, Frank. I've got to get out of here. I'm going to France. I'll call you."

I swallowed on that one, a big lump that wouldn't go down. She's trying to make it easier on me. I will never see her again, I thought.

She refused to let me take her to the train station. To help her in any way. She trudged across the marina parking lot in her long purple coat, weaving through the puddles with her coattails flapping defiantly behind her, the same coat she arrived wearing at the Lymington train station only a few months back.

She stopped and turned at the path leading out through the tangle of blackberry bushes to the road. She peered back at me, holding the sweep of her hair out of her face. Her eyes looked dark and bruised. Was it the distance casting such a shadow? How could I not have noticed! Then she was gone.

9
Navigation

O'Riordan clamped his jaw at our navigation lesson, sensing the weight of Gayle's absence. "And where is Gayle? Is she fed up with all our sailing talk?"

"She went to France for a few days."

O'Riordan waited for more, but I could not confess it. How the challenge for me now was to accept that my dream involved another. That being swept up in a dream had become losing control of it. Of course O'Riordan knew all about that. How love demands being free, whatever the consequences.

He nodded, not questioning me further. Then stamping his cane, "All right then! Where is the star globe?"

O'Riordan insisted on teaching me how to project trigonometric theories upon the heavens: Meridian Angles and Altitudes, Amplitudes, Logarithms of Trigonometric Functions, Haversines. He loved how it all worked, but I just got denser by the day. How did I get into this? What hope was there of ever getting out of harbor if I was to be Mr. O'Riordan's astronomy student?

"Are these academics really necessary?" I asked in mathematical distress. "Can't I just learn the mechanics of celestial navigation? I want to cross oceans, not the sky."

O'Riordan set the star globe firmly back on the shelf. "If that is what you want, then I will teach you how to do it. Not how it works. But you could learn that from anyone."

Was O'Riordan fed up too? Was my heart bent to a mast in too much wind? I never thought of myself as desperate, but I was manically disciplined in spite of any cost to myself or anyone else, including Gayle, and capable of taking any risk to get there.

After forty-five minutes of my lesson, O'Riordan began to snore, his head fixed in an upright position, and I went out to make tea. His kitchen reeked of gas seeping from an old porcelain countertop burner. Years of neglect had left the sinks stained a deep yellow. The cleaning lady never bothered to clean what O'Riordan could not see. So the dirtiest parts of the kitchen were a sort of eye chart he had failed. And it was getting worse. Everything had to be put exactly back in its place, where O'Riordan's hands knew to feel for what he needed. I laid the large spoon alongside the sugar can in the cupboard, the stick matches to the left just under the gas burners, and so on.

I returned with tea and O'Riordan heard the china clink when I put the tray down.

"Where was I?" O'Riordan sputtered, stamping his feet. He reached into the empty space over his head, as if he were feeling for the canvas canopy of his old boat languishing down in the harbor.

Gayle's absence brought me face to face with the wild non-negotiable truth of us. She was both my barometer and my storm. Had I paid attention I would have seen it coming. I must have made some kind of deal with God, behind my own back. It was now so obvious, Gayle without the y, embodied what was most unpredictable and violent about the sea. It was also what was most beautiful. What O'Riordan had fallen in love with forever. The storm that had almost killed him.

Joya's cabin smelled of her coffee, her soap and clothes. I breathed her in standing beside her bunk. I anthropomorphized everything. Her missing blue toothbrush in the sink rack had sided with her for a better life, her work socks crumpled on the floor stayed behind to haunt me, all her prettiest clothes, missing on empty shelves, had snubbed me and whisked her away, and her mirror ached when I looked in it with my face. I pressed her blouse up to my nostrils for the sweetness of her scent. The hollowness of the wave slaps against the hull had obliterated my sense of smell or taste. My solitary life aboard was mechanical and cold. Only the fact that she had taken a very small bag held the enormity of a promise that she might return.

A week after she left, I was down below, building a chart table where the refrigerator had been, since we had decided upon storing dry staples only. I noticed that I had been tackling the *we* jobs, anything that we had decided together. The slightest sound on the dock made my heart leap. So when I heard a clump on deck, my head snapped up. Gayle appeared in the hatch opening, and squatted with her arms folded over the hatch rails. She peered down at me, and smiled. "Hi, Captain."

She had cut her hair short, and her curls turned upward into the silver bellied clouds in the sky overhead. I didn't dare wink that she might disappear.

"Did you have a good trip, did you go up the Eiffel Tower or...?"

Her eyes searched mine, looking down from the top of the stairs. I never saw anything so beautiful. An angel. How did this street kid from L.A. get into a ceiling fresco in my heart?

"Did you miss me?" she asked.

"Yes. A lot."

"What happened to your finger?"

I held up the blackened fingernail, which I had thoughtlessly smashed planing a tight edge from one of Joya's floor boards, and shrugged.

"I hope you won't be so clumsy," she said, "if we're going to sail around the world together." She reached for my hand. "A deal's a deal, right?"

10
O'Riordan's Hurricane

"The technique you can get from books," O'Riordan had said. It was clear he had something else to impart to us, something he found out there alone in those treacherous walls of falling water, pounding like wind driven hammers over the sea, something magnificent in each moment he managed to survive. He spoke of it as a terrible blessing, and claimed he had never really come home. What an old fox he was, tapping his white cane down to us on the wharf, to teach us how to find him out there. If he were younger, Gayle and I might have conspired to take our mentor with us.

First, he drilled us at the dock. On a perfectly calm day, he had us suit up in our heavy weather gear and harnesses to do sail changes. He shouted directions to us as pedestrians gathered on the wharf for a laugh at a crazy old man with an iron chin in a threadbare sea cap drilling his motley crew.

Then he ordered sea trials. He climbed aboard in his yellow sou'wester gear and sat in the cockpit, huddled under the short roof extending from Joya's doghouse. He glided down river with us, his pipe clenched in his jaw like a finger marking a page. Legally blind his eyes fixed in memory, as cloud reflections ghosted across their blue glaze, and regiments of river reeds seemed to be marching by in review.

"Round up to windward at this bend in the river! Sandbars can shift toward the center of the channel here. Let me know when you see a spit of land at about 120 degrees."

Worried that Gayle and I would drown with O'Riordan instructing us in the open sea, our yacht broker, Alistair, had promised to send over a couple of his clients who were instructors from the Glenan Sailing School in Concarneau, France. The school was famous for its rigorous training in extreme conditions of fog, treacherous currents and rocks, and the huge storms in the Bay of Biscay. Paul and Lad stayed with us for three weeks while they looked for a ship around Lymington. One November day, friends of theirs from the sailing school came to visit, three brawling-shouldered young women who clumped down the floats in wooden clogs and rank wool sweaters. One was chewing a fat cigar. She surveyed Joya from top to bottom, as if our lovely ship was a side of beef. I suppose they were quite fashionable in a frighteningly marine sort of way. Compared to them, Gayle and I couldn't help but question if we were really cut out for this.

Gayle wrote her mom: *Sometimes I think I want to come home where I could go to work, have my own money, independence, and sit down in that nice gold chair, in our nice warm house, in front of that nice loud TV. Aaaaah. But then that would get pretty depressing too.*

"What can they teach you about the sea?" O'Riordan shouted about our new mentors. "If it's a school you want, I can teach you till you beg me to stop."

After the Glenan instructors departed, O'Riordan stepped up our training, without mercy in freezing winter conditions. "Nature is not your enemy. You have to find it in yourselves to survive." When not another soul would think to leave port, he drove us out into the frothing Solent. We reefed our stiff frozen sails in icy winds, our fingers numb as chunks of wood. Techniques that could have been discussed around a table, he forced us to experience. To summon the grit we didn't know we had, at the very edge of what we could endure. There, he said, we would learn all we needed to know.

"Never use a sea anchor to slow your ship," O'Riordan shouted. "You'll drag her down in the water, raise the waves behind you. That's what broke us open in the hurricane. She fell out of that damned wave. Let your ship run free!"

Yes old man, I thought, no attachments to anything, no demands or expectations. Just listen to the sea. We were getting the message.

As we bounded home on another one of those hissing winter evenings along the jaw of darkening clouds, Gayle pointed out that O'Riordan looked tired, slumped in his yellow sou'wester gear in the cockpit. I nudged him. "You should take it easier. We're not planning to sail around the Horn, you know."

He jerked to be touched, as if I had roused him deep in thought. I spotted a slight smile from under the brim of his storm hat, as if he knew that was exactly where we were headed, in one way or another.

To add to our discomfort, our sailing gear was no yachtsman's dream. No expensive high-tech or lightweight wear. It was what we could afford, all from the Navy surplus: stiff black heavy oilskins, black rubber knee-high boots, and scratchy wool sweaters and hats reeking of linseed oil.

Gayle wrote: *I dream of a heated house and 'Mom's stew'. It's so cold and damp every morning it's hard to get out of bed and feel good. It makes me want to cry. To give you an idea, here's what I wear sailing - 1 tee shirt, 3 sweaters, 1 coat, 2 knit hats, 1 knit scarf, 1 pair of thick tights, 1 pair of long johns, 2 pairs of jeans, 1 pair of knee socks, and rubber boots. The army surplus long johns Frank got me are size 38, but I just wrap the top of them around me and zip up my pants.*

11
Taking O'Riordan to Sea

In April, 1974, nine months after I had purchased Joya, Gayle and I waited for a break in the weather to cross the Bay of Biscay to Spain. But the storms grew more tumultuous, shoving the River Lymington backwards, until it flooded over the seawall into town. April stormed into May, and then June. Gayle gulped seasick pills; we were at sea at the dock.

I read over Gayle's shoulder one evening as she signed a letter to her mom. Her writing angled across the page: *Someday I'll write straight again, but it's blowing 50 knots outside and not a stable atmosphere in here. I'd rather have a nicotine fit than go out for cigs. As you can probably tell I've stopped worrying so much. Your last letter said, 'Don't bother to pray if you are going to continue to worry' and that snapped me out of it. But there are still times I just want to forget this whole trip. It seems to be such a hassle, but I'm too involved now. It would be such a waste of time and effort to leave. Sorry for the spots! Water drops keep rolling around on the ceiling and then dripping on this letter. It is slowly but surely aggravating me.*

O'Riordan shoved the fire poker into the coals from his easy chair beside his hearth. Satellite weather printouts for July indicated a large high pressure area pushing in behind the last storm, a fair weather window for crossing the Bay. Gayle had stayed aboard to organize six months worth of stores for the trip, varnishing cans of food so they wouldn't rust, dipping eggs in boiling water then coating them in Vaseline to preserve them, as well as other sailing larder tactics gleaned from O'Riordan and our books.

"I don't suppose you've decided which way you're going?" he asked.

"We've decided to wait and see if the Suez Canal has opened by the time we get to Gibraltar."

"Well, you have survived hard sailing in these waters, a gale outside of Poole....this winter, was it?"

"Yes."

"Some solo trips to the Isle of Wight."

"Yes."

"Still, you have never spent a single night at sea."

"No."

"Well, I suppose you're ready to put yourselves to it by now."

Mr. O'Riordan leaned back in his old easy chair by the fire, nodding his head the way he always did, silently amused over some thought. Then he gripped his armrests. "At least I have given you all I can."

O'Riordan had been a father to me, like I'd never known, and in some indecipherable way an advocate for Gayle. He had become our source of wisdom as we had become his eyes. We had become a team.

As Gayle folded our shore clothes into plastic sacks in the cabinets over our bunks, I tested her feelings about him. "Does it feel right to you, to leave O'Riordan behind?"

Gayle applied pressure to the crease of a shirt, as if it would jump back into the pile, and did not answer.

"I think he would come with us, if we asked him. I know it's crazy, but how can we take the side of the townspeople after all he has done for us. He's not delusional about his age. He's tough and capable."

ISLAND BORN

Gayle looked up. "He is ninety whatever years old. What if he drops dead while we're out in the middle of the ocean?"

"That's a sobering thought."

"Good, let it sink in."

"I don't think he will, but it is a thought," I admitted. "We should get his consent in writing to be buried at sea."

"Perfect I'm stuck with two delusional men making agreements."

"Still it's the right thing to do. Ship's captains can legally perform marriages and burials at sea. Then his relatives would have to respect his wishes."

Gayle folded laundry more vigorously. "I never thought we would be sailing around with such an old codger," she said without looking up.

"Who would have thought a lot of things that have happened? You said yourself that this voyage was a partnership. About doing what's right. No matter what it looks like. Well O'Riordan has been like a father to us. How can we leave him behind?"

"I think he planned this all along," Gayle said.

"I take that as an agreement. To ask him?"

"Do what you've got to do, Frank."

I went back up to see Mr. O'Riordan the next evening, bursting with the news I had for him. He sat stoically in his threadbare easy chair in front of his fireplace. Above him on the mantel was the brass sea clock, pipe tins, and a medal from his service in India. I tested him slightly, before cutting right to my proposal of taking him with us.

"You could fly down and join us in Spain, after we cross the Biscay," I told him.

"Yes. Yes. I could do that. Join you in Spain for a time." O'Riordan looked steadily into the fire.

"Or…. you could just come with us," I said.

"Yes! I could do that!" He stamped his heels on the floor. "I feel better at sea than any place else. The movement of a boat takes twenty years off me. Hmmm…"

He leaned back and sucked on his pipe for awhile as the fire crackled. So be it, I thought. He's coming, and I felt a surge of excitement.

"I'll have to find someone to look after my boat while I'm gone."

The clock on the mantel toned eleven. "Well, it's late," he said. He levered himself out of his chair. I did not offer help, knowing how he would bump into me as if I weren't there. I followed him down the hall past the den where we had worked and visited for the last nine months. I glanced in, but it was dark. He paused at the front door.

"It's the dimness in my eyes that's the problem. Ever since my wife died."

"Don't worry about that, Mr. O'Riordan, we'll be your eyes."

O'Riordan paused for a moment, as if to be certain I meant it. Then a curious thing happened. There was a thud in the living room as if a wet towel had been dropped on the carpet. We hurried back down the hall. There was a puff of smoke hanging in the middle of the room. It must have been a downdraft from the door being held open. O'Riordan gazed into the middle of the room, nodding. It was the first time I had ever sensed the presence of O'Riordan's wife.

He put his hand on my arm. "You go ahead. I'll join you somewhere. When my eyes get better. Maybe Spain, if I can manage it."

The mist was yellow the morning we set sail. It was July 19, 1974. The seagulls had returned to the waterfront from soaring the high winds inland. Joya rumbled out from her berth, reversing through a cloud of diesel exhaust. Our bodies flexed with the buoyancy of our ship coming alive in the current of the River Lymington.

    O'Riordan waved and stamped his feet on the dock. He blew a blast from an antique foghorn, which he'd brought for the occasion. Then several more, as his stout figure disappeared behind a bend in the river. Joya slipped by the river reeds and families of swans in the emerald estuary for the last time, out toward the notorious Bay of Biscay. O'Riordan's racket had eased the silence that lay ahead. Far as we ever were from land, or any safe haven, I would look up and hear him blowing that horn like a madman from the cloud stacks.

12
Bay of Biscay

On our second day at sea, finally on our way to sweet and sunny Spain, long smooth swells rose from the summer haze, and the sea began to spoil. The swells steepened, and their lazy demeanor turned to aggravated jolts. Joya accelerated deeper into the troughs, between ridges ground thin by a rasping wind. The barometric pressure began to drop as the wind increased. By afternoon we had struck our outer headsail, still sailing fast through spray with only our staysail and main shortened down to the second reef line. Anxiety took the place of meals. Our optimism stretched thin as we plunged into a magnitude of forces completely unknown to us.

Gayle sat up in the cockpit with me on my watch, chatting to try and overcome her nausea. "You know I don't feel cheated when it comes to my parents," she said, flexing with the impacts. "I'm even grateful when it comes to Dad. If Mom hadn't met him, she might've met someone with buck teeth, big ears, bushy eyebrows, and fat. And I'd have inherited all those characteristics. Then I would never have met you. Or be on Joya, or be a part of anything that's happening right now."

I wheeled Joya up a steep wave. "That's quite an observation, Gayle."

"I sure hope we've made the right decision. I had that feeling in my gut to leave ten months ago."

"You saw the last weather fax. Stable conditions. High pressure over the bay."

That evening the first galley china crashed to the floor. I handed myself below and stood there, dazed by the change in our home. The contents of the cupboards lurched violently back and forth. The hull resounded with hideous thumps. Fallen items were rolling and slamming back and forth across the floor. I got down and crawled along the cabin sole to grab shifting pieces of broken porcelain, pausing in the midst of gut-lifting weightlessness, then hanging on as we pitched into g-force compressions. Waves crunched at the bow sounding like boots crunching on snow, then the sound of whitewater roaring over the deck.

By the third day Gayle and I had quit conversing. We swayed against each other like exhausted people on a crowded bus. The ocean resembled a vista like the Rocky Mountains at midnight, dark snowy-faced peaks marching toward us through a greenish gloom. In such horrendous conditions O'Riordan had taught us to heave to, by lashing the helm to windward with our headsails (or storm jib) set aback. In this way, with the helm and sails at cross purposes, the ship stalls. She would rise and fall less violently while we waited out the storm.

We heard on our short-wave receiver that the center of the storm was moving directly toward us. We had to keep some sail up to escape the full force of the storm by plunging southward. With Joya's sails reduced to tiny triangles bent like wet steel, we rode up thirty to forty foot walls of water… maybe higher. Who could measure? Some looked higher than our mast, and that was over sixty feet. Nothing I could remember, even as a small child seemed as formidably huge.

We stared out, listened, and summoned what we could from the sea, learning what to do from second to second. If a wave went over the ship, we didn't need to talk about it. If something needed to be done, we did it. If it was time to eat, we didn't ask each other if we were hungry. If a sail had to be attended to, we simply pointed or nodded to each other. Reflexively our legs and bodies anticipated the constant impacts, lifts, and falls. If we ducked a moment late, waves burst over the doghouse, injecting gallons under our chins or up our sleeves.

I crawled through the darkness on my hands and knees to work the deck, tipping my head down and hanging on as the bow shipped white water. Gayle made every move she could on the helm to ease the motion for me. Her helming off the crest of a wave gave me an extra moment to snap on a few more sail hanks. Each suspended second provided an opportunity to adjust a handhold, twist a jar top, scratch out a navigational note, pump a few strokes, pour something, stir, tie a knot. The movement of the ship directly translated into tenderness for each other.

When Gayle's watch started at either 8 pm or 4 am, I made her tea and sat beside her at the helm, until she felt adjusted to the temperament of the sea. We napped, in turns, wedged under the saloon table to safeguard against being pitched out of our bunks. We slept in our damp heavy weather gear. It was too exhausting to wrench it on and off at a moment's notice with one hand while holding on for dear life with the other.

Gayle struggled with seasickness below decks. From my seat at the helm, I heard the main hatch amidships slam repeatedly back, the light spilling out as she heaved on deck between bursts of whitewater. She tried to eat meals to keep her strength. With our butts sunk into a wide nylon strap hooked across the galley, we took turns boiling water for rice or pasta, and heated the precooked meals Gayle had made. That was one of the sailing tips, preserving dinners in canning jars so we could eat properly if a storm made it impossible to cook. We wore a heavy plastic apron to keep from being scalded when food catapulted out of the pots. Even the gimbaled stove couldn't compensate for the sudden and violent movement. Our dinners pitched all the way onto the opposite wall, sometimes sliding down slowly enough with the wall almost horizontal, to enable us to recapture some of it.

Eating together in the cockpit, we tilted our plates back and forth, often vertical in front of our faces to keep the food on them. A very strange ritual that required a timing only known to sea folks. If we misjudged the angle of our plate, our food slid into the wind or plunked down into the cockpit grating. We picked salt-soggy bits of dinner out of the cross hatched grating under our feet, rather than not eat.

"What's that stink?" Gayle yelled from the helm one night, after a wave deluged the cockpit. I looked down by my feet and found a bright red and very rotten octopus that had been flung in. Gayle vomited. After that we gave up even precooked food, for a diet of dry biscuits from a can.

The radio crackled with news of several ships that had been wrecked in the Tall Ships race, which unbeknownst to us had departed from England the same day we had. The ships had been driven upon the rocks of Ashant to our lee. I silently thanked Mr. O'Riordan, for pressing us to put in a hundred mile margin of safety to the west of England, before we headed south for Spain. Otherwise, we would have suffered the same fate.

Storm gusts crowded together until they became a continuous background howl, punctuated by more forceful gusts. Conditions ratcheted up from a near gale to a *gale* to strong gale, then to a storm force 10 on the Beaufort Scale. As defined by the World Meteorological Organization in our copy of *The American Practical Navigator* by Bowditch:

> *STORM: Effects observed at sea: Very high waves with overhanging crests, sea takes on white appearance as foam is blown in very dense streaks, rolling is heavy and visibility reduced; Effects observed on land: Seldom experienced on land; trees broken or uprooted; considerable structural damage occurs; Term and height of waves, in feet: 20-40.*

ISLAND BORN

O'Riordan had coached us to listen "With more than your ears!" he said. "The faintest squeak, vibration, or thumping could escalate into a tangle. Or an untwisted shackle. Then a shroud comes loose! Then you're dismasted. One of you overboard... And worse!"

More than your ears meant to listen to the storm inside of ourselves. That place of reduction, empty of comfort, bravado, security, arrogance, even the next thought - a place empty of hope and fear, where a person is centered in the eye of himself.

On the fourth day the sun broke through. The seascape transformed into blistering blue mountains sheeted with white lace. Peaks tumbled like glistening snow. The curve of Joya's bow burst from the wave summits, then tilted down soaring into the dark belly of the troughs.

We untied our sea hoods. Gayle's cheeks creased and vibrated in the wind, turned pink in the sunlight. She tipped up her chin, her hair raked back with the clouds hurtling overhead. Her hand rested upon the helm as Joya lunged. Gone was any sense of my own exhaustion. O'Riordan's memories were becoming our own, of forces too magnificent not to yearn for them, too overpowering not to dread them.

13
An Old Boot

On the fifth day of crossing the Bay of Biscay, we skidded into relatively calm water and sedate sunshine somewhere along the mountainous north coast of Spain. We had relied upon dead reckoning in the storm, which is to advance a previous known position along our compass course for the estimated distance traveled. Our last known position was days ago near England. We would have to wait till afternoon for a longitude shot. But then I spotted a Spanish fishing boat, and hailed it like someone shouting for a taxi. "Which way to La Coruña?"

They pointed to the right.

"Nice job captain," Gayle scoffed.

"It's still navigation."

That night we motored toward a breakwater in La Coruña. As we motored toward a yacht club noted on the chart, a searchlight flicked on, blinding us. We heard cheering and peered into the glare at the silhouettes of a crowd along the yacht club balcony. Two black-suited Spanish men met us at the dock. We had no idea what all the commotion was about, but I was beside myself with the thought of hot land-cooked food, a clean cloth napkin upon my lips, a scotch, and a steamy shower. We both hurried below while they waited for us. I had already pulled off my sailing gear when Gayle spun on me. "I don't have anything nice enough to wear!"

"Gayle! We just survived a major storm. They don't expect us in tuxedos. Wear anything.... What about the new outfit your mom sent?"

"You go look out there! Not one of those ladies is wearing pants!"

I climbed up and waited with our escorts on the dock, sheepishly shrugging my shoulders as Gayle banged around below decks. She emerged in a pantsuit looking like a ruffled falcon. She clung to my arm as we marched up the ramp toward the grand portal of the yacht club. The sway of the sea was heavy in our heads, and now much worse on solid ground. "Please God, don't let me barf," Gayle whispered.

I sidestepped into a black marbled men's bathroom. The urinal rocked sickeningly. On my way out the door jamb leaned inward and knocked my shoulder hard. Each step collided with the ground, as if the floor were lifting and dropping to trick me out of placing a solid step. Gayle stood holding onto a railing laughing at me as I walked out.

Our escorts led us into the grand dining room of a palatial yacht club of the Franco Era. It was packed with formally attired people in evening dress, black suits and gowns. The drapes hung from cove molded ceilings and were pleated in golden fans on the floor. The room sparkled from crystal chandeliers, silver table settings, and battalions of cut crystal glasses, with waiters garrisoned around each table.

Our escorts marched us through this high pressure system of affluence, as guests rotated their heads toward us like parts of a Swiss clock. We clung to each other's hands to keep from tottering over rows of seated people. The fumes of hot butter, moist smelling flesh (either broiled or perfumed), the toasty scents of pressed suits, and the acidic vapors of wine suffocated us after days of wind-scrubbed air.

ISLAND BORN

At a podium in the center of the room we were instructed to sign a register for THE CUTTY SARK TALL SHIPS' RACE: *Captain's name, crew names, yacht name, date,* etc. My eyes froze on the blank, *Race Participant's Number.* The jowly official watched my fingers twitching on the pen, and withdrew his chin into his neck. Judging from the lack of sign-ins on the register, there were still sailors out there fighting for their lives. We had made it! Hadn't we qualified?

Gayle squeezed my hand, signaling that we should flee. I held her back, and calmly explained to the official that we did not have a Race Participant's Number. But that we had just sailed across the Bay of Biscay, through the same storm as the others. Not feeling he was convinced I added that Joya was a vintage ship, since the race theme was celebrating classic ships.

The podium official reeled his eyes off me, as if he had just pulled up an old boot, or a sliver of inedible fry. He muttered something in Spanish to our escorts, whereupon we were immediately ushered out of the dining room, out the entry hallway, past the gauntlet of gilded framed photographs of impassive-faced club presidents, a dictator or two, and pictures of famous yachts. Whereupon, we were shown the door, as well as the club's dock, which one of the escorts informed me, we would have to vacate as they needed the space. He pointed back out into the darkness and said there was an old fireboat buoy where we could moor for the night.

We motored back out into the dark bay, and I chuckled to remember a sailor named Bernard Moitessier. He unofficially won the first Golden Globe Race, a solo, nonstop circumnavigation rounding the three great Capes of Good Hope, Leeuwin, and the Horn. Unofficially, because after seven months sailing, he turned back just before crossing the finishing line. He then sailed all the way back around the world to Tahiti, 37,455 miles without ever touching land. For us too, the land had turned out to be an old boot.

I snagged the dented fireboat buoy lolling in the shimmering black waters. We sat up on deck under the stars, listening to the gravelly chatter from the club in the distance, a loud laugh ringing out from time to time. Gayle emerged from below with two glasses and a bottle of rum, which we had brought from England. "It's better out here than in that stuffy yacht club, any day," she said.

I raised my glass.

Gayle raised hers. "I guess I can call myself a sailor now, without any reservations."

"You have definitely come a ways from Ships Restaurant in L.A."

"Little did I know."

"You're a certified heavy weather sailor with the Bay of Biscay behind us. No crystal glasses of champagne can add to that."

We clicked our glasses and drank.

"I'll probably always barf. But I am proud of us. We got through the hardest part."

I was more than proud of her. Gayle's hand on the helm those stormy nights had kept us alive. Her hands were hands of the storm itself, finding their way. O'Riordan had seen it in her. Let her think the hardest part was over.

The rum soon melted us down into our bunks. We lay exhausted, still as starfish exposed at low tide, stuck on the flat unmoving surface of our beds, dreaming of flying water and the rushing sea.

14
Running the Gauntlet

"Let's flip a coin," Gayle said, as we sliced the current churning under the monolithic Rock of Gibraltar. "Heads for east. Tails for west."

Gayle had more frequently fantasized over snuggling up in a resort recliner in Barbados with her sandwich and an exotic drink, in spite of it having been the greater unknown that had inspired her to join me in the first place. She saw how silent I became over her enthusiasm for any destination crowded with tourists and hotels, but had just ignored how contrary this idea was for me. I would have dared anything to avoid it, even by heading south to round the infamous Cape Horn into the Pacific, rather than getting side tracked in the Caribbean on our way to the Panama Canal.

At the same time Gayle was my canary in the cosmos. A child-woman she may have been, but I looked to her for a sign. There was no other explanation for waiting till now, throwing up spray beneath the Rock of Gibraltar before deciding which way to go. My wild heart had committed to loving an old wooden boat, an old blind man, the relentless forces of the sea, and a tempestuous young sorceress.

"All right," I said. "You flip."

Up the coin went. It clinked down upon the cockpit grating.

Gayle pounced on it. "Heads! It's east," she shouted excitedly, her eyes sparkling.

I was stunned by how spontaneously Gayle accepted the reversal of her expectations. She never uttered another word about the Caribbean. The flipping of the coin that day put the bar up for me to match this level of Gayle's courage.

Our commitment to sailing eastward around the world would pit us against monsoon headwinds and dangerous weather. *The wrong way around the world*, people had warned. Although an international effort was being made to reopen the Suez Canal, it was still clogged with sunken ships and hundreds of tons of live ordnance from the 1967 Egyptian-Israeli Six Day War. On top of that we'd heard that the Southern end of the Red Sea was full of Yemenite pirates.

Gayle cranked over the helm. I hurried to throw off the running back stays and sheet in the jib. Our ship turned like a needle on our new course, and I picked the fifty pence piece from the cockpit grating. "Give that sucker to me," Gayle said. She had a good arm. She leaned way back and threw the coin out over the sea, grasping my hand before it splashed. "Now our good luck is with the sea," she said.

We sailed through the Straits of Gibraltar in August 1974. The Mediterranean would remain a dead-end street for as long the canal was closed. We holed up three months in Estepona on the Costa del Sol of Spain to make ship's repairs. From there we tried to sail a bee line to Suez, but in the Gulf of Lyon we encountered a mistral, a disturbingly vicious wind from the north. That first night we couldn't carry a stitch of sail. Joya lay bent over under bare poles for three days. On the third day we slouched in the cockpit, black-faced from exhaustion. Steep seas raked over our decks like saw teeth, in relentless succession.

"You told me the Mediterranean would be calm compared to Biscay!" Gayle cried, her face swollen with exhaustion and cinched up in her rain hood. Almost immediately large hailstones began socking our heavy weather gear, drumming and bouncing around the deck like golf balls. Somehow this struck us as insanely funny, and we started laughing till our guts hurt.

"If we make it to shore alive, Gayle, I swear I'll never go to sea again."

Gayle groaned, and crawled into the doghouse cuddy, groveling for our camera. "I gotta take a picture. This way you can't forget your promise."

Making port in Cagliari, Sardinia, we crawled up on a solid wooden wharf with a bowl of popcorn and passed out sharing a bottle of scotch. When we awoke, we were still on the dock, fallen over like mannequins dressed in vintage HMS heavy weather gear, with an empty scotch bottle rolled to the side. Sardinian women passed in black dresses and head scarves, ignoring the sight of us. I came to my elbows actually steaming on a sunny, windswept December morning.

After we developed the photographs Gayle took during the storm, we laughed over my transmogrified face, the swollen unrecognizable me that had sworn never to go to sea again. We laughed at how we had succumbed to fear and exhaustion. How little we knew of our capabilities. Yet how little we still knew was a fact. Pushing on was no laughing matter.

Dear Mom, We are now on our way to Malta, about 400 miles southeast of Sardinia, and have just cut off the noisy engine to give our brains a rest. There's no wind. Frank is cutting my hair while I write. I never got all the vomit and tangles completely out of it. We are just sitting here in the middle of the ocean, listening to music and writing letters. It's moments like this that make the hard times so easily forgotten.

When we made it to the old fortified port of Valetta in Malta, reputed to be the finest natural harbor in the Mediterranean, we found the best equipped shipyard we were likely to find before heading down the Red Sea. In spite of O'Riordan's amusement over my obsession with making strong pieces, I was determined to get all I could get done on Joya before leaving the Western world. Gayle thought I was a real scrooge for refusing to interrupt my work schedule at Christmas. She dragged a scraggly little Christmas tree into the boat and painstakingly decorated it.

After weeks of hard work, I lay upside-down under the front of the engine, fitting an engine-driven bilge pump for an emergency backup. Gayle appeared glaring down at me, with a travel bag slung over her shoulder and wearing her new white jeans.

"I can't get you away from this boat, so I'm going on vacation myself."

I heaved my bilge-spattered face up from under the engine, as her heels levered up the steps through the hatchway.

"Everyone can see how obsessed you are," she said over her shoulder. "You won't even go for coffee, or a beer with our friends. Not even on a vacation with me. So I'm going by myself. To Gozo."

"Gozo? What the hell is in Gozo?"

Without answering, Gayle disappeared from the hatchway frame. I heard her pulling the dinghy alongside, and hurried up the saloon steps. She was already in the dinghy, handing herself along our stern line toward the seawall.

"Go to Gozo. Have a great time. Shit! What do you think I'm on my back down there for? No one in this harbor is going where we are," I hissed. "Across the Indian Ocean and God knows…"

Gayle glared at me as pedestrians strolled along the seafront. I lowered my voice. "I am not like you, Gayle. I don't know how to relax when so much needs to be done."

Gayle turned away, pulling herself ashore again.

"I have nightmares about what might happen to us…"

Gayle stopped pulling and balanced herself in the dinghy to look back at me.

"I didn't want to frighten you, but they are very real."

"What kind of nightmares?"

"Of water welling up in the saloon at night, far out at sea. Our books and floor planks floating around. Or you washed overboard, drifting back in our wake with Joya under full sail. I mean anything could happen, so what I dream feels prophetic and disturbing. Now even when I'm awake, I get these terrible snapshots, so real I have to shake my head to snap myself out of it, before I'm suddenly there. That's why I bought the sheets of lead to make quick emergency patches on the hull. Remember you asked why I went to so much trouble to make the copper handrail around the compass binnacle. I saw something happen…. So whatever I don't do might haunt me for the rest of my life."

"Look Frank, Joya will be fine. So will we. If you can't spend a week alone with me, without the boat, then I'm going by myself." She hesitated looking at me.

"Okay," I said, "I'll come. If that's what you want…"

"It's not what I want Frank. It's what you have to deal with."

We rented a pale blue plaster niche of a place that was mortared into a wall of rock, and reeked of moist lime and fried fish. The sea bashed into the hollows below us and resounded hauntingly inside. Gayle lay in bed mornings in front of the window over the sea, drinking coffee and writing letters

I trudged back and forth to the small general store up on the hill to stock our tiny kitchen. I tried to ignore Joya so firmly anchored in my mind, but I awoke late at night going over every millimeter of her, assessing every part, piecing together a puzzle that defied completion. Somehow my concerns for our safety had increasingly built into another kind of storm threatening our voyage. If I could just get Gayle to tough it out a little further. To Greece where we could take it easier.

"Honey, just because you can't sleep, dawn walks on the rocks aren't my idea of a vacation," Gayle said.

Where is my home? Gayle wrote her mom, *Is everyone slowly but surely forgetting me??? I answer letters I receive. I write again if I don't get an answer. After that I start feeling like I'm talking to myself, then I feel insecure, then I feel lonely, then I feel out-casted, then I feel crazy, then I flip out, then they take me to the funny farm, give me shock treatment, and then they put me in solitary, then I tear my hair out, and then they shave my head. Oh terrible things could happen if you don't write to me soon!*

On the day of our departure from Malta, a Thai woman tied burning incense sticks to our bow pulpit, and Joya rose over the first swells, smoking like an offering. Not three days out from Malta, a howling wind from North Africa called a *Sirocco*, slammed into us. The first afternoon of the storm I heard an echo, a kind of hiss behind me. I looked over my shoulder and saw an opaque green wall as if in slow motion, enveloping the gleaming stainless steel taffrail around the stern. I felt myself lift from the helm and tumble, then slam to a stop against my back.

A freak wave in the Mediterranean! I struggled up from the bulkhead onto one knee. Gayle rushed on deck from below and leapt into my place at the helm, wheeling Joya away from surging downwind into a devastating jibe, as the sea streamed from the decks.

"Holy shit! What was that? Are you all right?" Gayle cried.

"I think so." I reached up to the compass binnacle handrail, and hauling myself upright, looked out at the long slicks between waves charging toward North Africa.

"You said sailing to Greece would be nice."

"It seems there is nothing nice about the sea."

Gayle's pithy remarks were no longer funny to either of us. The never-ending boat work, gales in Biscay, the mistral in the Gulf of Lyon, and now this. How much more of this could we take?

PART II
CROSSING BORDERS

15
Sailing out of a Bottle

We lounged around the islands in southern Greece for months, without any news of the canal opening to the south of us. Neither of us suggested flipping a coin to stay in Greece. Now it was no longer east or west, or even where we were headed, but getting there. Gayle looked at me as if I had lost my mind when I told her my idea of trucking Joya across the desert to the Red Sea. It was already May of 1975. She nodded blankly, struggling to imagine Joya's towering hulk, girdled to the back of a roaring truck as she cleaved her way through the sands of the Sahara. "Are you sure she'll be all right? Not get twisted up or dumped somewhere? How can we trust anyone with her?"

"The idea is too outrageous not to work. There's no other way if the canal doesn't open."

I went to the Israelis but the consulate would not let me in and hung up on me when I called from the concrete phone booth outside the gate. Then I telephoned a trucking company recommended by the Egyptian Embassy.

"Yah, just bring your ship into Alexandria. We can do it.... No, we don't need the size of the ship... Don't worry about the cost.... Don't worry.... Don't worry," the man said.

At that moment Jimmy, a young Greek ship's pilot we had befriended in Iraklion, came hurtling down the wharf, shouting and waving a piece of paper in his hand. A week earlier he had almost gotten me thrown into jail for firing a marine distress flare over a parade of virgins outside a Catholic church. He had insisted on me following him down tiny streets to the parade where he thrust the large canister into my arms and pulled the firing pin. He had then rushed off laughing crazily as a huge plume of red smoke rose directly over me, the red distress flare burning like a sun over the crowd.

Jimmy rushed up shouting and waving a telex over Joya's rail. "The canal is open! The canal is open! You can go!"

The next day, on June 5, 1975, a radio station for the American Air Force Base in Crete confirmed the news. After twelve years, the Suez Canal was officially open. Travel warnings were still posted by the US government: Egypt and Israel had not demobilized their forces; Eritrea was at war with Ethiopia; a civil war was raging in Somalia; Yemen had become dangerously anti-American.

Where you headed? was one of the first questions around the docks. The heads began shaking as soon as we replied, *Through the canal to India.*

"Mediterranean yachties are just scared," Gayle said. "Pirates and white slavery! That's all they've got on their minds. And being safely holed up where they are."

In support of her bravado I purchased an antique double-barreled shotgun and a few rounds of ammunition.

Although the canal had been open six weeks by the time we arrived, an official from the Egyptian Port Authority declared ceremoniously that we were the first sail boat through. A Russian warship blasted its horn as we passed. Rows uniformed sailors leaned over the bulwarks high above, waving down at us. The first boat through!

Gayle wrote home to her mom: *We were greeted by a boatful of seedy looking Arabs in dirty overalls, posing as port officials, demanding whisky and cigarettes. They tried to lead us to a small fishing harbor before we were rescued by a sophisticated pilot boat that escorted us to the Port Said Yacht Club. We had a night of dancing and free drinks. The president of the club, Sammy, had us over for tea the next day at his home. A lot better treatment than we got in Spain, but we had to leave a guard on our boat to keep away the thieves. It was really great, we felt so special, so important.*

Joya slid into the oily canal with a fire-blackened desert and flanks of rolled barbwire either side. We motored speechless past miles of bombed and burned-out ship's carcasses that had been craned up on top of the embankments. The passage through these maritime catacombs left the living world as we had known it irretrievably behind.

At a Quonset hut checkpoint a ways down the canal, I unwittingly went for a stroll to stretch my legs in the dunes. Our white-uniformed pilot whom we had been obliged to hire for the canal journey and who never moved from his aura of bleached spotlessness leaning against the stern railing, suddenly began frantically hissing, as if a shout would have detonated the land mines he pointed out around me. Gayle held her hand over her mouth in horror as I retraced my steps. Fifty yards seemed miles in the distance and every grain of sand a mountain. When I stepped back into the Quonset hut, Gayle grabbed my hand. "I thought you were going to get blown up right in front of me." My legs shook uncontrollably. Land mines! Who would have thought?

Then a little bit further down the canal, angry-faced Egyptian soldiers rushed out of a hut and along the embankment, shouting and waving pistols for us to stop. Our pilot shouted back at them in Arabic and shook his fist. "Army idiots! They don't even know the canal is reopened."

Once outside the southern mouth of the canal, we tied up at the commercial wharf opposite the town of Suez. The empty spaces of bombed out buildings gaped like missing teeth along the shoreline. The streets between were piled with rubble and strewn with trash.

The harbor was foul. Bloated animal carcasses bumped against our boat in a crust of sewage and decaying debris.

That first evening after Gayle was already in bed and I had just finished bathing from the sink with a washcloth, I caught a whiff of the galley trash can outside our bedroom. I groaned and grabbed the bin, climbed naked up on deck to chuck it over the side. Everyone dumped their trash into the sea; there was nowhere else for us to put it. I raised the can with one hand and leaned on the cable railing for support with the other. I had completely forgotten that I had unfastened the cable at one end for repair that day. The whirring sound of the cable running out through the stanchions came too late. I pitched headlong and naked into the cesspool of the harbor, trashcan in hand.

Before my legs could kick upward to the surface, I began to laugh uncontrollably underwater, at the horror of what had just happened. I sank into this last insult, the final composting of Western decorum. In a gurgling paroxysm of bubbles, I struggled to the surface moaning through my teeth, fluttering my feet wildly to keep my chin above the sludge.

Gayle appeared on deck, dancing around in a gleeful fit clutching her bladder. I hauled myself up on the bobstay chain under Joya's bowsprit like an oversized sewer rat.

"Oh, my God! You're not sleeping in my bunk tonight," Gayle cried. "Yuuuuck!"

"Come on. Quick. Get me fresh water and shampoo."

"You smell like a dead cat."

"Gayle! I'm warning you," I said stepping toward her. "Water and shampoo! Please!"

To get to an unspoiled place in the madness of the world, for that journey to stay alive we would have to laugh through our teeth. Only a couple of nights later, lying in bed with stomach cramps and a case of the shits from an Egyptian restaurant named Fil-Fella, that

Gayle called Feel-Awfla, I was startled awake by Gayle shaking my shoulder with her breath hot in my ear. "I hear footsteps on deck!"

Through the crack on the underside of our hatch, we watched a shadow eclipse the wharf light. Gayle ducked under the covers whispering, "Oh shit! Someone is up there. Oh shit!"

Then our hatch cover began to slide back. We slunk down. The first thing I saw was an Uzi type automatic weapon swing down between a pair of outstretched arms in uniform. A flashlight blinked on, directly into my face.

"Hey! In there," a man's voice growled.

"Hey!" a second voice repeated.

Drunken laughing.

There seemed to be several men crowding forward, which disturbed the one with the light. He began cursing in Arabic before breaking back into English.

"You got girls down there?"

Much laughter.

"You got *Playboy*?"

I squinted and tried to shield the light from my eyes.

"No *Playboy* here," I shouted.

Gayle clawed at my side from her hiding place under the sheet.

"Close the hatch," I said waving my arm at the light. "I'm sleeping!"

"Cigarettes!" the voices persisted.

"No cigarettes."

"Soap! You got soap?" a gruff voice demanded.

"American cigarettes?"

"No cigarettes! I told you. Nothing. Go away!"

Our assailants grumbled and cursed, slammed the hatch shut, and stomped back off our deck.

"Shit! No wonder these guys aren't supposed to drink," Gayle said. Did you smell the booze on 'em?"

"I was just watching that Uzi aimed at us every time he leaned in."

Gayle wrote home to her mom: *This place is totally insane. I won't even tell you because you'd worry too much. But whenever things seem too crazy something happens that makes perfect sense. I was sewing on deck in Suez and this little tyke on the dock stands there watching me. He is not very clean and he asks me to sew his name on his T-shirt. So I used red thread and sewed Mohammed on it for him. He rushed off so happy and I think I was proud as he was. He will never forget that and neither will I.*

We set sail down the Red Sea, to the south of Suez and anchored the first night in a bay, surrounded by the most sublime landscape of desert dunes. In the morning I looked with my binoculars and saw that the dunes were honeycombed with camouflaged battle stations. Cannons bristled from them like stubs of black hair. A couple of hours later a man swam out. I dropped the boarding ladder and he climbed aboard in his wet underwear, holding a hand over the shadow of his privates. Standing there naked and shivering, he said that he was an Egyptian Army officer, and asked, "Who is the Captain?"

I stepped forward.

"I am sorry, but you must come with me," he said.

"Where?"

"To my commander."

"Where's that?"

"In the desert," he said, pointing behind him at nothing but sand. "It will only take a few days."

Gayle interjected herself between us, and looked the shivering officer right in the eyes. "He's not going anywhere. We need him on this ship."

He stared back at her for a moment with the shakes, and then conceded, jabbing his finger toward the fortified dunes along the shore. "We have guns. There you see. Don't try and leave here. I will radio for instructions."

The next morning the bay could not have been more serene and lovely. "Do you think they would really shoot us?" Gayle asked.

"I don't know. It seems inconceivable they would shoot a smiling person waving goodbye. Like we never understood. We could just leave."

"Okay, let's go."

We then motored away, waving goodbye while imagining our friendly faces up close in their binoculars. We were not blown to smithereens, but the Western envelope of more or less predictable relations with our fellowman certainly was. Even our European instruments, one by one, succumbed to the sand and salt. Only our magnetic compass, chronometer, and sextant survived to navigate with. Next to go was our English made Perkins engine. It had begun sputtering in the canal, and it soon coughed its last. I chucked the oily injectors into a bucket with the engine manual, and turned off the master valve to the diesel tank.

"Is that it?" Gayle called down from the helm.

I draped my elbows up over the companionway. "We've got juice in the batteries, for the *nav* lights. Kerosene for the lamps. That's it."

Gayle lifted her face up into the desert breeze, her nose white with zinc protruding from under her straw hat. She clutched a cotton sari around her shoulders shielding herself from the blaze of sun.

"Well, I won't miss getting seasick from diesel exhaust."

Joya slipped southward, as if slithering out of an old skin into milky currents of silt. Layers of sand sprinkled over the deck with the wind. The sun blazed through a pointillist haze. A twenty-five foot whale shark with dainty white spots and a three foot wide mouth fell in love with Joya, and nudged alongside like an oversized windsock for most of one day.

Nights, the moon x-rayed a glowing sea of dunes beyond the shore. Our kerosene lantern swayed in its golden light, the only sign of human life on any horizon. I lay in my bunk on Gayle's watch, listening to her sing as if over a cradle, her melodies rising and falling over the wash of the sea.

Gummy salt crystals soon layered every surface of Joya. They raised saltwater sores on our thighs and back ends. Salty clothing only made them worse, so we went naked, cowering from the sun in the shifting shadows of mast and sail. To shade the helm, we hung scraps of material like prayer flags, on a temporary spaghetti network of lines. To cool our drinking water we used the Bedouin trick of wrapping an earthenware jug from top to bottom, with a cotton cord which we kept wet with seawater. Evaporation chilled the jug's contents amazingly well. It was our miniature oasis.

Gayle wrote home: *When we docked in Port Sudan, some young boys started pointing at our yellow quarantine flag, which you normally have to fly when you are coming into a new port. They were pretty freaked out. All the people backed off thinking we had a dreadful disease. Mumbling ooooh and aaaah and what not. Some official must have been explaining that we didn't have the plague or some dreadful disease because these Sudanese women came closer to me. They were dressed in beautiful saris with bright colors that looked really fantastic next to their black skin. They stared at me, a western girl, in slacks and a tee shirt. They laughed and pointed, but seemed very happy to have me around.*

A few days out from Port Sudan Gayle wrote home: *We've been sitting 4 days opposite the Hanish Islands but can't get in without wind. Anyway, there are no people there. An Arab dhow passed us yesterday, slow and spooky-like. A few shady looking figures watched, but no one waved. Since we can't move without wind or a motor, we are taking night watches so we can shoot a flare if an approaching ship looks like it's going to run us down. What I would give to take an evening walk in a town, any town. But there is nothing but water,*

water, everywhere, and these barren desert islands. A Greek freighter from Cypress stopped to fish for dinner this afternoon in the reefs. What a welcome sight! We got some cigarettes, fresh apples, and pears from them, which was great because we ran out of everything fresh a few days ago, but they didn't have anything else they could spare, or sell.

Soon after a breeze picked up from the south, I heard water sloshing in the bilge. A leak? If it was a broken seawater valve, I had better find it quick. I tore up the floor boards all the way up to the foc'sle, and then pulled out a drawer under the bunk. I froze at the sight of a crack of daylight through the hull! Unbelievably, Joya's planks above the waterline had shrunk in the heat. Some were squirting under the pressure of swells raised by the wind. I had been warned that boat planks seasoned in England might shrink. And we had very reluctantly painted Joya's gleaming black hull white in Malta.

Now, we had to sail upright against the wind to keep Joya's open seams above the water. We were well aware if the wind raised larger swells that more water could be injected than we could pump out. To cause Joya's planks to swell tight again and in yet another irony of survival in this part of the world, Gayle and I began drenching Joya's topsides with buckets of seawater to keep her afloat.

16
No Fresh Water –
Hanish Islands

The desert nights made us shiver, but continued baking us at a slightly lower temperature. The desiccating sea wind peeled away anything coating exterior surfaces, but increased the ability to absorb. Shrinking produced strength. Sunbaked things hardened but became brittle. The dull shine of burnished surfaces burned without smoke. Everything became thinner, our bodies, our energy, our tempers. The bones of our voyage shone in the moonlight. There was a hostile and terrible beauty in it all.

"That can't be right," I said, bending over my calculations after a noon latitude shot.

"What?" Gayle clenched the helm, her stomach muscles sore as mine from days of punching Joya to windward, toward the southern end of the Red Sea.

"My sight puts us just south of the same islands we passed three days ago. If this is right, we should be able to see them."

We spun around in unison, squinting back over Joya's stern. Sure enough, barely discernible purplish lumps floated in the frothing blue opacity.

"I don't believe it," I said, slumping back against the cockpit dodger.

"We've beaten our brains out for the last three days for nothing," Gayle said without emotion.

"The currents must have reversed up from Bab al Mandeb. Without a latitude shot in all this haze, how would we know?"

"They must have changed early this year with the wind."

"So now what?"

"It means we ain't gettin through the straights to the Gulf. Not in these conditions."

The wind whistled through our rigging as we sat there, feeling the very palpable collapse of our efforts to reach the Indian Ocean.

"Does that mean we might miss our chance to cross the Indian Ocean this season." Gayle seemed far away, looking out over the dull sparkle of the sea.

"Looks like it."

"I don't need to know what anything means anymore," she said. "Let's just go to those islands, anchor and wait. Maybe the winds will turn around again."

We brought Joya about, and sailed back downwind toward one of the deserted Hanish Islands, Az Zuqur. I had read that the islands were a sanctuary for pirates and gunrunners, a no-man's-land between Yemen and Ethiopia. Who else would be out here in these Godforsaken islands, but renegades with no legitimate business elsewhere? "Certainly not someone who would be scared off by an antique shotgun," Gayle commented, flicking salty spray-soaked crumbs off her plate.

We rounded the lava cliffs into a sheltered cove, with a white sand beach at the end. Swarms of seabirds screamed in protest from their rookeries in crevices high above. I readied the anchor as a sea turtle lifted its heavy jowls from the sapphire waters off our bow. The chain rattle echoed noisily off the cliff face that spilled foaming swells back into the sea.

The next day about noon, we rowed ashore and set out to follow an ashen swale, which cut across a narrow part of the island between mountains of black lava. The heat that radiated from the lava was almost unbreathable, as if from a furnace at over 120 degrees Fahrenheit. Without local knowledge of Saharan Desert conditions, I worried how far we dared explore without risking being able to return safely. There was no sign of life.

At the top of a rise Gayle and I cowered from the torching wind. She had a bandana tied around her forehead. Her face was the color of fired terracotta, budding with water droplets. Her lips were already swollen and cracking. We hesitated looking out over the blackened swale we had followed. It swooped further down a mile or so to an empty expanse of sea and sandy coves on the opposite side of the island.

Before climbing higher, something caught my eye in a pocket of sand, directly in front of me. A human footprint! I stared as if I were facing the barrel of a rifle aimed between my eyes. I quickly looked up to check the surrounding hills and the beaches below for any sign of life.

"What's wrong?" Gayle shouted, catching up all muffled against the wind. I pointed to the single print in a lava cavity full of sand.

"Uh-oh," Gayle said, "Have we got company? Like pirates?"

"Look," I said, squatting and pointing with my finger. "It's fresh! Only a few grains of sand have blown back in over the edges."

We stood and scanned the shorelines again for any sign of a ship. In the distance the porcelain white beaches snaked through the cascades of lava that clawed out into pale green bays like burnt fingers. A chain of small distant islets foamed in the swells.

We followed a few more footprints up the hill, and there, sure enough, Joya came into view on the opposite side. In the squinted eye, she floated quietly as a white swan in her sheltered water, a treasure trove for the taking.

I turned my attention from the point of view of a pirate to my breathing, which had become alarmingly arrhythmic from the heat. I waved and pointed for Gayle to meet me down on cooler ground.

We waited a week for the winds to change, then two. Winds from the north should have been prevailing at this time of year, but the south wind only strengthened, grating up a sea of whitecaps outside the protection of our tiny bay. The heat parched our lips until they bled. We were running out of food but could survive off our staples of beans, rice, and wheat flour. Our water supply was another matter. The fresh water dip stick indicated it was too low to either go back out to sea, or stay much longer where we were.

"We could go to Yemen," Gayle suggested one afternoon as we sat under the shade tarp in the cockpit, munching up fresh bread she had sweated two days worth of water to bake. "It's not far."

"Have you lost your mind? Yemen? You know they're lawless over there. Hostile to Westerners…"

"Look at your ribs, Frank. They're showing right through your skin. We've got to get to land. The east coast of Yemen is barren. They're probably just tribes of regular people. Unconnected to the politics of the world."

I became speechless, talking to myself instead of answering her. How can she be so stupid. It's delusional to make up these scenarios. Where does she get such absurd thoughts? Besides whatever unthinkable horrors they might inflict upon us, sailing Joya into their hands would be manna from Allah.

"I could get a job teaching English in a village," Gayle persisted.

I took a slug of stale, algae-filled water, the last in our tanks, to wash down the hardening glob of wheat bread baking in my mouth.

Gayle pointed over Joya's rail toward Eritrea to the west. "We certainly can't go to that side because of the revolution. And we're not going back up the Red Sea. That's for sure. And we can't go forward. Right?"

I nodded, too upset and numb to speak.

"Someone's going to find our skeletons sitting in this cockpit if we don't get out of here. That only leaves Yemen. Let's make a run for it, while we've still got some water."

That afternoon I made a freshwater still from our aluminum pressure cooker using a length of copper tubing. I attached the tubing to the relief valve and coiled it up so that it cooled the steam to drip into a jar. It tasted like piss from a rusty can, but it was water. Gayle agreed to wait a bit longer for the north wind, but refused to take a turn at refilling my distillation contraption throughout the night. She said her job was baking bread. This she dutifully did, stoking her furnace down in the galley, with her brow melting day after day. When she wasn't baking or flapping salt out of seawater washed sheets, she lay panting in patches of shade on deck.

The preparation of our food and water now relied upon our supply of propane. Less than half of a thirty pound bottle remained.

Gayle wrote: *This is far from a survival trip for me. The hardship has taught me a lot. Sometimes I get flashes of never getting anywhere and spending the rest of my life on this desert island. When I'm sitting on the beach at night and it's cooler, I feel very happy about being here, truly grateful for the little fire and the full moon we've had lately, the warm refreshing sea under zillions of stars, the freshness of the air, and most of all the solitude. I start thinking of how many people would really love to be here. And how proud I am of myself and Frank.*

Staring at the pilot book became a daily obsession for me, as we waited two more weeks for the wind to change. After almost a month in that deserted cove, my eyes fixed on something I had overlooked on the chart. There was a small notation along a stretch of Eritrean coastline that said: *Camel caravan route.*

17
Red Sea Escape

"That's your idea?" Gayle scoffed. Her laugh echoed back from the bluffs, harmonizing with the groaning gulls. "You're going to stand out there? In the middle of the desert? With your empty water jug?"

"The route goes right along the Eritrean coast. I can row ashore when we spot their camels."

"You were so sure they would take our boat in Yemen, now you think these people will give us water and send us along our way."

"If they can't spare any water, then I can hire someone to bring water back to us."

"Going to Yemen is far more practical."

Who was crazier, me sitting in the Sahara waiting for a camel caravan, or her seeking help from grinning Yemenite tribesmen bristling with weapons?

"You want to flip?" I asked.

"We already flipped. Let's just do anything. Anything that gets us out of here, and down to Djibouti."

The next morning we stowed the shade tarps and sailed thirty-five miles across to the Eritrean coast. We waited offshore that evening as the pilot book instructed. The moon rose just as the book said, behind the silhouette of a giant dune which guided us into a desert bay. The sea glittered behind us as we ghosted up into the eerily dark and silent shadow of the dune. Only the *kerplunk* and *splash* of my sounding lead could be heard. I whirled the lead out at the bow as was done in the old days, counting the sewn-in knots on the line as I handed it back in, a knot per fathom. When my fingers felt the weight at three knots on the line, my heart raced. Ahead it was pitch black but we were very near shore, at the three fathom shelf indicated on the chart. I let loose our anchor. The chain roared out the hawsepipe over the bow roller. I threw the capstan brake when Joya had pulled a length out. The main fluttered softly overhead as Joya rounded up hooked against the breeze.

 Gayle walked forward from the helm to help stow sails. We sat in the cockpit silently eating dinner, conversing with our own thoughts, no sound but for the occasional groan of the anchor chain. The breeze flowed softly over us from the smooth desert, empty of scents or spores. It was a famished breeze sniffing at the thin finishes protecting our wooden ship, drawing away microscopic bits of canvass and thread, vaporizing oils in our winches, peeling flakes of varnish.

 We went below after dinner, and I turned on the shortwave. Something I never did. The incessant crackling gave us both a headache. Almost immediately the BBC announced news of war, escalating right here in Eritrea. I sat with my finger on the volume thinking of the millions of listeners around the world, from L.A. to New York, London to Delhi, and not another living soul except us sitting here a stone's throw off that very shore. "It's not a civil war, it's genocide," I said over my shoulder. "The British forced Eritrea to join with Ethiopia. After WWII. The Eritreans only want their independence, but…"

 "Shhh…" Gayle hissed, leaning over me to turn up the volume. *Foreigners are being advised to leave the country immediately…. Two Americans were reportedly kidnapped by Eritrean guerrillas….*

 "So much for your idea," Gayle said as if I had made a stupid mistake.

"Okay, we gotta get out of here. First thing tomorrow morning."

I was up at dawn weighing anchor. Gayle and I shared a nervous laugh as our bow rose to the deepwater swell off the coast, feeling we had escaped too easily.

"What's that?" I said, pointing at a lump of black smoke on the horizon ahead. Through the binoculars I could just make out a green-yellow-red striped Ethiopian flag fluttering from the stern of a speeding naval vessel. "Shit, there's a bloody gunboat headed our way."

A grey steel patrol boat with large white ID numbers surged up to us. As men with submachine guns took cover behind the bulwarks, we instinctively put our hands up like in an old western. They tried to board us, but the overhanging flair of their hull rocked into Joya's rail smashing it to splinters, and then compressed the standing rigging, threatening to dismast us. At that point I forgot myself and ran forward shouting for them to back off, which they did, and then launched a small boat to take me across to meet with their captain.

They took me to the patrol boat, and I sat in the wheel house with the captain. He scarcely looked up at me as he studied Joya's papers. He wore a neatly pressed tan uniform, without a jacket.

"Where is your permit to sail in these waters?" he asked in perfect English.

"I didn't know I needed one."

"You do."

"I don't have one."

"You have any weapons aboard?"

"Just an old shotgun."

The captain wrote in his notes. "We have to be careful of gunrunners around here." He handed me back my papers without looking up. "Thank you."

"May I go back to my ship?" I asked.

"Yes, but we will tow your vessel to Assab."

"What? We're not gun runners. What do you want with us?"

"It's my duty to take you back to my commander. You are in these waters illegally."

The gunboat dragged us south for several hours at high speed, threatening to bury our bow, and tear our windlass off its mounts. They pulled us to a commercial wharf in Assab, opposite a warehouse. Stacks of goods lay fallen over, their contents spilled over the ground. The place looked ransacked. A taxi pulled up and a man dressed in a cream-colored windbreaker and neatly pressed slacks got out. Standing behind him were groups of armed soldiers.

"Hello," he said with oily hospitality. "I am in charge here. I want to invite you out to dinner tonight to discuss how I can help you. For the inconvenience we have caused you."

"I am not going out to dinner with that sow belly," Gayle whispered, as his taxi departed.

"I don't think that was an invitation. We are his prisoners, until he decides what to do with us. You'd better watch your tongue!"

At dinner our grisly host slipped his arm around Gayle's shoulder, opening his jacket over the pistol grips of two 45-caliber US military-issue handguns stuck in his waistband.

"Of course, do your shopping," he said. "Take all the water you need, repair your ship."

Gayle had become horribly silent.

"Americans are our friends."

"They are?" I asked.

"Yes, Ethiopians like Americans. Because they are modern and smart. But they are too friendly. That's their problem. If someone makes trouble for us, that's it!"

I glanced at Gayle.

The next afternoon we went shopping in town. We had just stopped to purchase a cold Fanta, an orange drink popular there, from a sandy haired man with an Italian accent. He was a strange sight indeed, standing barefoot beside his soda cooler, with his huge white feet. No doubt he was one of the dispossessed after the British took Ethiopia away from the Italians after WWII.

Suddenly we heard screaming from across the street. Soldiers were in the process of hogtying a young boy, a child. Then they heaved him into the back of a truck. He couldn't have been more than twelve years old. Distraught family members crowded up against soldiers holding them back with raised rifle butts. The family wept and clawed their faces as the soldiers drove away with the child.

This incident disturbed and confused both of us. There was nothing we could do. Gayle walked back without speaking a word. Her movements were braced as if walking through threatening areas in the projects in L.A. where she grew up, swinging her basket as if defending herself.

That night the situation grew more intense. Dock workers crept to Joya in the darkness. One after another leaning from the shadows, whispering: *The soldiers are drunk... killing people in alleys .... even children... taking revenge for their losses... they took my brother from his wedding... tell your fellow Americans... do something... tell the world what's happening here.* They came hissing to us from the edge of the wharf and finally drove Gayle into our cabin. She closed the door behind her.

The next morning I stood in the galley organizing our market goods, putting veggies in a hanging net in the saloon and fruit in the lower cupboards where it would stay cool against the hull. I heard chain thumping the deck and paused, and then I heard Gayle shouting at someone. I hurried topsides as she pulled chain out of the hawsepipe in a windmill of fists. Apparently she had decided we were leaving, as we kept the anchor ready when we sailed out, in case anything went wrong. A couple of bloodshot-eyed soldiers stood there laughing at her from the dock.

"Why don't you goons shove off?" she shouted again, shaking her fist at them.

"Shhh… Gayle" She shrugged off my arm, but allowed me to hurry her below. She stood there trembling in my arms. I saw that her ankle was bleeding from a nasty scrape. She was right; it was time to leave.

The next morning, for the second time without permission from the harbor commandant or any adieu, I climbed down into our little dinghy and began towing Joya out of the harbor. Gayle cranked up the main, and we floated silently away on a soft desert breeze.

18
On the Brink

Thanks to our abduction by the Ethiopian patrol boat, we had been towed further down into the straits of Bab al Mandeb against the south headwind. Now we were able to tack our way out of the straits. We slid across the Gulf of Aden beneath its sun burnished bluffs, crumbling down into the iron blue waters. By morning a sliver of desert appeared in the distance; the dirty ochre spires of Djibouti poked up through a grainy haze. We worked our engineless boat across light breezes toward this long sought after safe haven.

It was already October 2, by the time we made port. We had missed our chance to cross the Indian Ocean in favorable weather. There was simply no way around the stormy southwesterly gales at the mouth of the Gulf at this time of year. It would be another ten months until September, before the next weather window opened to cross to India.

We anchored near to the so-called Yacht club, a faded bluish building with its walls blasted concave from sand storms. It stood alone at the hook end of a long jetty leading a couple of miles back to town. Across the harbor at the commercial wharf, cargo cranes loaded freighters, clanging and groaning day and night.

The only other yacht was locked mysteriously shut with an overly large and antique padlock staining the white fiberglass door with rust. We heard that it belonged to a Frenchman named Claude, who now worked construction out in the desert. His wife and daughter had left him to return to France, after his daughter's foot had been amputated in Saudi Arabia due to a taxi accident. I wondered how a father could reconcile such a loss with staying on here? The waiting yacht was ominous, not in the failure of Claude's dream, but that his dream had survived. "Creepy," Gayle said.

The temperature increased disturbingly. It was now up to more than one hundred and ten degrees by midday (the pilot book description should be corrected from *"torrid heat"* to *cremating heat*). Walking up the jetty into town was only possible during the early morning or evening. We carried our shopping bags around the labyrinth of dirt streets, lined with ramshackle one-story buildings. A bull or a pitifully bony donkey munched garbage piled against crumbling mud walls. Scraps of filthy material hung aslant over the doorways of prostitutes, who served the French Foreign Legionnaires manning the machine gun bunkers around town, and hanging out at café tables in the main square. Uneasily they joked with street hawkers. Gayle was distant and silent.

We rowed over for dinner at the Club Nautique. Eritrean refugees lined the smudged walls, mostly young boys who stood with their sweaty backs up to the building, kneading a few less degrees into their flesh. Thousands had been sent by their parents to escape Ethiopian troops in Eritrea from towns like Assab where we had been detained. If they survived the desert heat, Ethiopian patrols methodically robbed and killed them. The survivors crawled under the razor wire and gun towers of Djibouti, to starve in the streets. Their emaciated skeletons gathered around the Club Nautique's trash cans, pulling melted sludge up into their mouths as we passed inside.

Upstairs on an open-air veranda, a Somali waiter served us peanuts in a white porcelain bowl with blackened cracks. Some French military officers and local European merchants sat chatting, all with their arms up to catch the breeze as if everyone were at gunpoint.

"A year in this place?" Gayle whispered, watching the Huey helicopter-sized cockroaches crossing the yacht club walls. "I am now truly homesick. I want to go back to L.A. and visit my family."

I doubted if Gayle knew how very far she had come from Los Angeles. All her L.A. clothes had succumbed to the boat rag bin. I held the scraps of her life that had disappeared so quickly in my hand as I worked. The melanin in her skin had roasted to a burnt almond, not like a tan after a summer day on a Venice beach, but a fired tone that brightened the colors of her African headscarf and amber necklace. Her Greek coin earrings flashed at the sides of her face. She had come alive in the desert. Maybe it was the suffering of so many around us in Africa that gave an urgency to her wild and exotic beauty, her eyes seeming a bit too wide, staring a bit too long.

It was risky leaving Joya in such a lawless place. But separating from Gayle seemed to be the greater risk, even if only for a month. A young Swiss traveler agreed to stay aboard as caretaker, and we flew back to Los Angeles. We found ourselves sitting on the floor in Gayle's childhood bedroom when she dropped the bomb. "I'm not sure I'm cut out for the sea." She pawed her stuffed animals. "Being nauseated all the time and vomiting my guts up doesn't help."

My eyes followed the scratches across the aged varnish of her bunk boards, as if tiny childlike nails had dragged across them. The interstices of those scratches configured a destiny. That rusty padlock staining Claude's boat in Djibouti came to mind. How many signals had Gayle received? How many had I missed? That time she left me in England? And would have in Gozo had I not tagged along? And there had also been a man in Malta, I had done my best to ignore. Attraction is normal. But then that suicidal idea of going to Yemen. But I still trusted her judgment. How could I do that, I wondered. There must be something wrong with mine?

"I remember my mom laying me over her knee on my belly," Gayle said, "and swaying her leg back and forth. You don't seem to remember much about your childhood, Frank. But I do. I love remembering things my mom and I used to do."

In that instant, I almost burst out and told her not to come back with me. To stay at her mother's, that we couldn't be certain anything good would ever come out of plunging over the horizon. That she'd be better off in art school, pursuing her God-given talent. I could have lied like O'Riordan, and told her that she could meet me somewhere.

Gayle put her glass-eyed doll back in the drawer. We said nothing of East Africa, or Joya, for the next six months. Gayle stepped right back into her family life, while I languished in L.A.

I went to visit my childhood home and stood on the sidewalk, staring at the stately terracotta colored front door shaded by olive trees across the front lawn, the same trees my brother and I climbed as kids. My eyes searched for a sense of myself as a child, to know where I was headed. But what had once been a huge leap from a limb, or a large step or crack, or window I had dreamed from, now all seemed proportionally so small. It was already June, and in only 3 months we would set sail across the Arabian Sea.

"I would like to be a mom," Gayle said, as we walked up Motor Avenue in Culver City to our parking place.

"A mom? Like all women want to be... someday?"

"Yeah, like that." Gayle gave me a look. "For your information, I'm ready to go back now. I'm not going to quit. Not after we've come this far."

My sigh of relief could have blown away clouds, but I kept it to myself.

19
O'Riordan's Bed

The plane back to Djibouti departed from Paris, so we stopped in England to visit O'Riordan. It was June of 1976, two years since we had last seen him. His phone rang and rang, but I figured he had grown too deaf to hear the red fire bell he had hooked up to it. We dropped our bags in the foyer at Mrs. Bateman's B&B. No one was around, and we left to walk up the High Street to O'Riordan's house. The footpath through the weeds on his driveway had almost disappeared in overgrowth. I pounded the black iron knocker, again and again, listening to the echo inside. We walked back to the same red iron phone box near the boatyard where I first called Gayle about finding Joya. I telephoned Alistair, Joya's yacht broker.

"No, he's in hospital. He had a stroke a few months back."

Gayle began running, and so did I, slowing out of breath in front of the hospital. We held hands as we walked up between the beds of roses at the entrance. Inside the one-story convalescent wing were rows of beds partitioned by white curtains, mostly the elderly sleeping or sitting on their beds. Gayle tugged my arm toward a motionless figure in bed. O'Riordan's face was not easily recognizable on his pillow. His cheeks and eyes had sunken back like a low tide, but his always prominent jaw protruded with a stubble of white hairs on his chin.

I put my hand on his shoulder. "Mr. O'Riordan."

His eyes opened, glanced at both of us, but then he began sliding downward, as if something were pulling him by his feet. His big hands clenched the sheet over his head.

"Mr. O'Riordan, it's Gayle and Frank. From Joya." I rocked his shoulder. "Mr. O'Riordan." I tried to remove the sheet from his face, but he clenched it more tightly.

An old man in the next bed who had been disinterestedly watching this scene unfold interjected, "He thinks he's at sea. Always talking about voyages and storms and whatnot. Doesn't know where he is half the time."

Gayle took a seat on the edge of the bed. I stood by my mentor's shrouded face. The windows beamed squares of daylight across the waxed concrete floor.

"We've made it to Djibouti in East Africa," I said.

The sheet was still taut, but after a moment's silence, Mr. O'Riordan's gruff voice sounded from under it.

"Through the Suez Canal?" he asked in a surprisingly alert and familiar tone.

"Yes. And down the Red Sea."

"So you went east after all?"

"Yes," I replied, gently trying the sheet again, but still coming up against his unflinching grip.

"That's good," he said. "You've proven yourselves now. But what makes me wonder is why you have come back here?"

I told him a little about our trip, pausing, but there was no reply.

I laid my hand over his fingers clutching the sheet, warm fingers still strong as a bronze fist.

"We're going all the way, Mr. O'Riordan. I want you to know that."

No answer.

Gayle stood and bent over Mr. O'Riordan. "Meet ya up there someday, ya old salt."

Our footsteps echoed too noisily down the hallway. Pushing open the hospital door we were blinded by the glare of a summer day.

20
Djibouti and Terror du Mondo

Six months had almost been enough to forget the fragility of our plans, now hostage to the weather and civil war in Djibouti. We stepped out of the customs building at the airport that morning into the desert heat, slowing like sloths as we skirted the wall shade to a vendor's umbrella, scarcely able to breathe.

We signaled a taxi, and crawled along a dirt track back towards town, enveloped in burning orange dust churning off the wheels of trucks and mixed with diesel exhaust. Like drowned things trudging through the poisonous mix, a slow flow of donkey and bull-drawn carts wheeled along, the wrinkled black shoulders of women with pitiful bundles of sticks marched as if to nowhere, and the clean white shirts of office workers cycled through the filth.

In the distance ahead, a pall of smoke lingered over the city, still billowing up forcefully in some places from recent fighting between the Issa and Afar tribes. I turned my head to stare at gutted buildings and incinerated cars flattened without tires.

"Looks like things have gotten worse," I said uncomfortably.

Gayle just stared out the window without replying.

Driving down the jetty road, we sweated keeping our windows halfway up to block the wind from torching our skin. It felt more like wind off molten lava than from the sea. I peered out over the harbor, not at all certain I would find Joya still there. We had not heard anything from Christophe, the Swiss traveler to whom we had entrusted her. But there she suddenly was, almost unrecognizable out in the anchorage. Her hull was coated in harbor scum and stained dark brown beneath her scuppers. She looked abandoned, listing under her sagging green shade tarps.

We rowed out, and found a stinking mess, inside and out. Gayle grunted with disgust as she scooped out rotten vegetables, liquefied on the backsides of the cabinet doors. Flotillas of dead roaches floated in old sink water, and slurped back and forth in unpumped bilge muck. She reeked of the sweet corpsey smell of a roach infestation.

A few days later a new boat, Terror du Mondo, slipped into port. "How could anyone name a boat such a thing?" I asked disapprovingly.

Gayle's interest perked, at the possibility of company, as the faded red hull with peeling black trim lolled into a turn through a steamy afternoon haze. The boat's stern dinghy davits were hung with chicken coops. She resembled a failed pirate vessel, not the lovely Italian schooner with a fine clipper bow that she had once been.

Judging by the crew's skill at maneuvering her under sail through the anchorage, I figured her engine must have succumbed as ours did, some distance back up the Red Sea.

Soon as they dropped their hook, Gayle and I rowed over to greet them. We bobbed alongside waiting to be asked aboard, as pairs of eyes gazed over the rail like crows assessing a possible theft. Finally the gangway lowered for us to climb aboard, as if it was operating itself. No sooner had we stepped foot on deck, I noticed Gayle was engaged in a conversation with a blond, heavyset Australian, leaning confidently back, with walrus-sized arms stretched out along the main boom.

I detected invasive pheromones as snippets of talk whizzed by me. "No, it was a hard trip… aground in Sudan… headwinds (they had made it like us)… leaking… no engine… bilge pump broken….."

One of the crew was a dentist, Bart, newly graduated and taking time off. God knows how he ended up on this wreck. There was Robbie, a red haired and sharp-toothed fox of a youth from England, and an apish girl, seemingly quite fed up with her comrades, and who had been a track star in the States. The boat was littered with baskets of filthy clothes and buckets of parts. Fumes pungent as an Arab *souk* rose up from belowdecks.

Then Gayle was at my side again.

On the raised quarterdeck behind the helm, we were introduced to a hairy mammoth-shouldered man who was cancerously blackened by the sun. He had been paralyzed from the waist down in a car accident in Italy and sat with a dirty blanket folded over his legs. Rather than a wheelchair he had chosen a boat, and I wondered if he had renamed it. He gulped handfuls of pills during our conversation, revealing over a dozen pill bottles concealed in the folds of his blanket.

Gayle began making regular visits to Terror du Mondo. The moment she finished her duties aboard Joya, she fled, under any pretense whatsoever. I attempted to disguise my apprehension for her apparent switch of allegiance. I was sure she was glad for some social life, but I suspected the Australian, named Ted. I made inquiries for the Captain's well being and the safety of their ship, seeking a telltale clue as to her visits. Taking my cue, Gayle fabricated humane excuses to visit Terror, to help the incapacitated satyr, Alex. "They need another person to lower him in for a swim." Or, "He's out of cigarettes, and I picked up a carton for him."

Remarkably, the misshaped merman did swim, with the help of a propeller driven device. Ted and the little fox Robbie wielded him over the side in a sling suspended off the mizzen boom, in the same way cows or camels were loaded off and on local freighters, occasionally plunging into the sea and drowning. His now atrophied legs flagellated in the current behind his monstrous thorax, his eyes bulging horribly as if they had gotten stuck there from the impact of the accident.

Gayle wrote home to her mother: *I am not happy to be back. The sweat just keeps pouring off of us and I feel dirty all the time from work and sweat. I am discouraged from always being sick, probably from the crummy food and bread that always has baby roaches baked into it. But I try to remember your words, 'Take it day by day'. I try! I don't worry about tomorrow. It can only get better cause it's really the shits right now. I often go over to the boat next door for jokes and talks and drinks. The other night I got pissed as a coot. Thank God the next day was Sunday, our day off, cause I had four glasses of water and got pissed again. Sometimes I feel like getting crazy here because of this insane life, but I am not an alcoholic or dope addict as of yet. Life goes on with or without you....*

21
Gayle's Love

The afternoon Gayle went for a sail on Terror du Mondo, she could barely disguise her relief when I declined her invitation to come. She did not ask twice. Nor did Captain Alex bother to invite me after my own visits to befriend him. A man everyone knows is about to have his heart broken is never welcome. So I stayed behind to work on Joya.

As the sun set, I began looking out to the mouth of the harbor, anticipating Gayle's return. I spliced an eye in a new shroud to distract myself from looking up every few seconds like a needle bumping on a scratch on a record. In the bluing dusk, my fingers struggled to splice something that would hold.

By 10 p.m., well after the time Gayle should have returned, the explanations I had been juggling dropped out of mind faster than I could replace them. Sleep was impossible. I lay in my bunk, my mind mercilessly constructing explanations: the unpredictability of the sea, some reason it might have been safer to stay overnight. What could be more innocent than having a great time? They might have found a lovely cove, I thought. She knew how worried I would be. She could count on me to understand that Terror's crew had ignored her pleas to be taken home. She always admonished me, "You need to keep a positive attitude." But neither words nor thoughts could stop the unraveling that had begun. I knew all too well by my experience at sea, that disasters are too often recognized when it's too late to avoid them.

The next morning the bloody red hulk of Terror du Mondo sailed back into port. Gayle was nowhere to be seen on deck, neither was Ted, just the disorderly crew of tanned pot bellies and skinny legs scuttling stiffly about as if all of them were hung over. Not a wave or a glance from anyone aboard.

I forced my attention to retying the boat bumpers with clove hitches over the rail, my fingers working senselessly to keep from glaring over at them. After a moment, I glanced toward the wharf, surprised to see Gayle suddenly there. I peered through the binoculars at her standing at the top of the steps, the thin pretty wisp of her still wearing last night's dress. She dawdled about, not waving, just waiting for me.

I rowed over, and climbed the oily jetty steps, feeling feverish under the monstrous weight of so many terrible thoughts. I squinted to see her face against the low morning sun. Her gaze was cool and refreshing, so womanly. She looked beautiful.

She said it plainly. "I want this affair, Frank. This is my choice. It wasn't Ted. It's what I need for myself."

My voice vibrated, maybe shook, like a net catching the only words racing toward me.

"It's just an affair you need?"

"I'm not sure anymore."

"How long haven't you been sure?"

"For a long time," she said.

"Malta?"

"Even England. I left for France so I could breathe."

"Are you fed up with sailing? All the work?"

"No, none of that."

"Is it me?"

"No, it's not about you, Frank. I was young when we met."

"Haven't we been growing up together? What have we been doing all this time? Keeping secrets? Why didn't you talk to me?"

"I wanted to talk but it was like, you were never available."

"I guess I had it wrong. I thought we were committed. That we were building a life together. I knew I was ignoring you, but I thought you could take it. I made sacrifices too! I did the work that had to be done. I'm in love with you. I thought you loved me."

"Even love can be a trap. The things you do for each other can be a trap. Djibouti's a trap. We live in a trap! I can't do it anymore."

"What the hell. You're going to turn everything on its head. Uproot everything we've accomplished?"

"I'm saying that good things are painful too."

"So pain is part of it. You work through it!"

"I don't know how to work anything out. Maybe I've just grown up. Changed and need some time."

"Time? For what?"

"To be by myself."

"What timing! What fucking great timing!"

"In the overall picture, Frank, you're the man I want to spend my life with. But I need to discover myself as a woman."

"Doesn't a woman…" I said choking back my outrage, "…remain faithful to the man she loves?"

"You seem to know better than I, what you're looking for. Your expectations are too much for me right now."

"What about your expectations?"

"I'm trying to figure them out. They've changed and I don't know right now. You have to trust me, Frank."

Another voice in me spoke up, surprisingly calculating, grasping the opportunity to assess the damage like a cornered crook looking for room to maneuver. "Has this ever happened before?"

"No. It might have. But it didn't."

We stood there in the blast of heat that had already fried the morning activities in the harbor to a standstill. Even the water lay flat as hot oil in a pan. Gayle stood looking straight at me. "You can give me some time to sort this out, or not."

"Let's go," I said, leading the way down the steps to untie the dinghy.

I bent to the oar, rowed my princess home to Joya. She dutifully completed her chores the rest of the day, and cleaned up our cabin nicely before bed. Her politeness, even her kindness, and especially her ease of sleep wrecked my attempts at composure. How could she sleep? I dreaded to think what she might be dreaming. I was certainly too tense to lie quietly down in my bunk, so I stayed out in the saloon, staring blankly at the green vinyl cushions. What constructive thing could I do? A tempest of vengeful and furious thoughts raged around in my head, like a needle painfully stitching a wound without any thread.

Gayle spent the next blistering nights aboard Terror du Mondo. The shape of the black-bearded and crippled captain sat on Terror's poop deck out in the watery dark, swilling painkillers, while I slouched over Joya's bow pulpit, swilling whisky, the two of us like grim lighthouses with our lamps extinguished. I slept on deck with sweat pooling in my belly button, waking me as it trickled down my ribs, with the shadow of Terror Du Mondo to starboard.

Mornings the sun rose blood red on the underside of my eyelids. I turned away until the back of my cranium heated up like a pot in a kiln. I stumbled up to readjust the laundry I had hung on the railing to block the horizontal blast. Even the thinnest cotton sheet for privacy felt like a down quilt in the sweltering heat. I peered out at the obscenity of naked bodies sprawled across Terror's decks.

Gayle returned each morning as she declared she would to work aboard our ship, as if it were a regular job. She had once told me that when she left home and lived on the streets as a kid, she had promised to keep in contact with her mom, so she wouldn't get thrown into Juvenile Hall. Even now I felt that little kid courageously steering her life, the perils of her choices, and how much I wanted to take care of her.

Each sleepless night I writhed upon what felt like a stake hammered into my heart by her absence. I struggled to understand. Her father and his abandonment somehow mercilessly linked me to her unfaithfulness. Some fate had gutted our chance in a lifetime in Djibouti. My own rage flared and had to be constantly extinguished. How could I blame or hate her. I loved her too much not to reach deeper than I ever had before, to feel the current sweeping us toward some other destiny.

At times my thoughts ran away with scenes of murdering him, Ted, and the thought eased me, actually made me laugh out loud. Oh, the sweetness of plotting. There was no law here in Djibouti anyway, no respect for anything decent. The harshness of the desert. People killing each other all around us. Starvation. Only survival counted. Who would investigate?

Better a fight, I thought. I'll do it with my bare hands. My murderer's mind seemed brilliant and exciting in its ability to reason. He was much bigger than I, but he would never stand a chance against the voltage I could discharge. I'll leave him on the shore. I felt the turn of a smile on my face at the thought of it. His bearded head and lifeless body left as a gift for the bills of gulls and fizzling crabs.

These psychotic episodes would then sink me into the depths of despair and self destruction. I saw myself leaping from walls of flame over the black waters of the harbor. My beloved Joya an inferno of broken dreams. But I had no one to talk to, to question my ability to think clearly. I tried forging disciplines to carry me through each scorching day, to be engaged in any constructive activity. Anything that reminded me of life before. Since warriors don't go to market, I savored leftover scraps in the bottom of the cooler, a sweet sweating scrap of Gruyere, a rotten banana, a piece of stale bread. Anything that gave me energy could just as easily turn my thoughts back to killing him. So I occupied myself keeping my clothes meticulously washed and clean, tidied up the deck, scrubbed down the cabins, spliced rigging, but could not help but notice an unsettling and furious kind of strength whenever I lifted any weight.

Tenderness was the last emotion I would have ever thought I could have ever experienced for him, Ted. I watched them through my binoculars, sitting serenely side by side on the jetty rocks like old friends, in the grainy burl of the desert sunset. To my surprise a deep sadness seeped into me because this was a very sad predicament indeed, for him, Ted. Even an honest tear welled up in my eye, for his happiness with Gayle was doomed. Doomed as mine was now. But I knew her well, and knew that she would most certainly keep her promise and come back to me. And then he would suffer. I found a terrible solace in turning away to grant them their few private moments.

The harbor community watched my drama unfold as if I were the first of the whites being butchered on the wharf. We were all caught there in some way, the colonial French and their armies outside their country, travelers out of money, sailboats out of wind, Ethiopian refugees out of hope, and warring tribes of Somalis out of balance. It was one of those places that strips people of their humanity, like empty eyed people at gambling tables, and the desert wasteland, warring tribes, the colonial enforcers, starvation, and the heat were the dealers.

From the shade of my sagging tarp, in the sweet harbor stench of fuel oil, creosote, and diesel, I found a measure of stability watching the French couple on a sloop anchored next to Joya. They ate nicely prepared meals in their cockpit, played music, and enjoyed their boat, immune to the human catastrophes in Djibouti. My eyes, my ever so alert eyes, peered at them from my miserable shadows. In their black slits, I noticed the young French woman smiling at me from across the water. She could have decided to be my friend, I thought. But then when she was sure she had my attention, she turned and bent over straight-legged in very high-cut white shorts, to drape laundry over her skylight, as my heavy eyelids draped over her.

The poor man, her husband, I thought. What a fool for not having left this place when he had the chance. He deserved what he got! I guess in some way we all felt that. That we had compromised ourselves, made regretful decisions, and our fate was this punishing place. At the very least most of us were opened to the bone. At the very best we might escape with our wounds.

The next morning white shorts called out and invited me over for coffee. Gayle had the dinghy, so I swam. Her husband was visibly bewildered when I climbed aboard with my oily webbed feet from the polluted harbor. We sat together in his cockpit, hairy knee to hairy knee, as his pretty wife popped her head in and out of the companionway, handing up cookies, utensils, china, all the while announcing in happy birdsong her progress in the galley. Then she played French pop music much too loud. Her husband asked her to turn it down, and she begrudgingly complied.

The prospect of his wife being unfaithful must have blown a plug out of the Frenchman's mind. He suddenly leapt up shouting angrily at some Somali children who were leaping back and forth in three yacht dinghies, including mine, tied up at the wharf. A dinghy muddied and swamped now and then had been a small price to pay to maintain the peace with the locals. It was common play for the kids. Before I could grasp what was happening, he had dashed up from below with a 12-gauge pump shotgun.

The explosions rocked the harbor, *one-two* in quick succession, over the heads of the children. In the aftershock of the explosions, a hidden army of Somalis raised their heads from over the gunnels of anchored *dhows*, the faces of men and women leaned from scraps of shade ashore, peered over packing crates, appeared from behind every wall and from the shade-dark of every tarped food stall. The entire harbor held its breath.

There had been incidents of Somalis stabbing French Foreign Legionnaires in the back streets if they had misbehaved in brothels. Disadvantaged and outgunned as they were, the locals could exact a price. The next day before I realized what was happening, in the midst of shouts across the harbor, I raised my head to the sound of roaring engines. Suddenly two, then three large Arab *dhows* plowed across the anchor lines of the few yachts there, mangling our ground tackle, and crunching our boats together. I rushed up and down the deck, straining to fend off Joya. I stared into the faces of the Somali men passing in their dhows, dignified faces held high, no matter what this attack might cost them. These were not soldiers but furious fisherman, outraged and proud fathers. Honorable men! And in their faces I saw myself reflected, an occupying colonial, self-expatriated on the wrong side of the sea. Who of us would not have done the same in their circumstances?

22
Coming of Age

By the end of July with onset of the Southwest Monsoon, the spin of the earth seemed to have reversed, and the sands of the desert, the waves, and the whole sky turned around and swept eastward. Joya's shade tarps snapped retorts in the wind. Recent fighting in Djibouti spurred European expatriates to urgent departures. I spoke to the local French dry cleaner at the bar. He told me that he was leaving immediately for Yemen. Our fine sailing ship had been beaten to the escape by a dry cleaning shop!

Gayle felt it too, the ominous impasse with still another two months before the wind allowed us to leave, two months that sealed us up alive in Djibouti with what seemed like two minutes of air left to breath. She insisted on having her 21st birthday party three weeks early. She announced that she had invited her "friends" from Terror du Mondo. Of course that would include him, Ted. Stunned as I was, I turned to thinking on it this way. That this had to be Gayle's ultimate test to accept her feelings, and payback for whatever she felt I owed her. In return I had Gayle's declaration of a lifelong commitment to me. Then there was my brilliance for suffering any humiliation to keep my enemies close at hand, to know their weaknesses, so I could deal conclusively with them when the time came. For instance I heard how desperately they needed to slip their ship for repairs, but I kept a contact I knew to myself. They were after all headed the same direction we were. And even if in some small way, I encouraged the relationship between Ted and Gayle, it was because I knew Ted was their only able bodied seaman and the rest were just travelling riffraff. With a crippled captain and Ted's spirit distracted and hopefully broken, there would be even a less likely chance they would escape Djibouti.

They all arrived on the day, and sat around our saloon table looking bewildered, crowded together like hairy-cheeked possums at their mother's tits. Ted stretched his arms back across the seat in his usual sergeant-at-arms manner. Gayle blew out the candles on her cake, and began opening every present, everyone's except mine. I watched it getting buried in the wrapping trash. She opened a watercolor Ted gave her. I could see it reflected in her eyes, the bleeding sunsets they watched together on the jetty. She was terribly pleased and put her prize in a safe place on top of the books in the bookshelf.

Then everyone started laughing about how Gayle had convinced some of them to take off all their clothes at a party aboard Terror one evening. That was before Ted happened, when I had tagged along to protect my interests. It turned into a night from hell. Gayle paraded around stark naked on deck, dead drunk along with several other of her naked disciples, all male, "to get real," she said. Then she dived off the ship into the blackness of the harbor. I rescued her with a surfboard and paddled her back to Joya, bellowing to her comrades like a distressed walrus.

At the end of her birthday party, Gayle insisted on rowing Ted back to Terror herself. I glanced at the pile of trash that had buried my still unopened present, the antique silver bracelet I searched for in the marketplace, which sparked my hope that its beauty would convey the humble offering of my soul.

"I'll be right back," she promised.

Ted's crewmates had conspicuously left him behind only minutes before. No one knows better than a doomed man with his monstrously accurate intuitions, how perfectly the cosmos has designed his demise. Oh, the agony I suffered watching Gayle and Ted rowing off into the darkness, activating their plan... this final act of merciless betrayal! I went directly belowdecks like the greyest ghost on a grizzly mission, ignoring all the dirty dishes, her unopened present, and through the now sickly glow of the kerosene lights. I jerked open the drawer under Gayle's bunk. In the back corner behind all her cosmetics sat the pale pink plastic case that contained her diaphragm, which we used for birth control. It had been there that day because I had checked it, ratcheting yet another inexorable notch lower, like a fungus feeding on morbidity. And of course, the case was empty.

I sat on the bow pulpit in the pallid desert warmth of dawn, more composed than I had been in months. The breeze picked up, carrying with it the invigorating smell of living things: algae, seaweed, wet feathers, shellfish, evaporating spray. The wharf had come to life in the long shadows of the low sun, but the sight of Gayle rowing back from Terror did not even ripple my blood.

The railing stretched as she tied our dinghy up, and the boarding ladder squeaked with her weight. Her bare feet brushed the deck toward me. She stopped beside me without speaking. It was as perfectly still, as peaceful a moment as I ever remembered between us.

I looked up at her. "You have to leave now."

She nodded, her eyes steady as planets on the desert horizon. She wore a white short-sleeved blouse with some Greek embroidery around the neck and cotton shorts. She had become thin, delicately lovely, a paling rose petal. Maybe it was the low morning light, but I saw again the young lovely girl I'd fallen in love with back in Venice. The one I loved with all my heart.

"I already told Ted last night that it's finished," she said. "I'm going off to travel alone."

Traveling on her own would be best. I knew that she would be all right. That she would grow from all this. That we both would.

"What will you do?" she asked.

"I'll keep going with Joya."

A moment passed. "I'll help you before I leave," she said. "You know. The things that only I know how to do. If you want me to?"

"Thanks, but I can take care of everything now."

Gayle took a seat beside me, gazing off with her chin on her knees.

"But you're welcome to stay here before you leave," I said. "There's no point in being awkward about things now. Whatever's happened has happened."

Gayle insisted on helping out, "for her room and board," she said. I spent my evenings alone in town, eating at a Somali restaurant, or walking around. I coasted my bike back down the jetty late, feeling gloriously free from my previous torment of never knowing if she would be there or not. But she was there, contentedly sewing or writing letters. And my heart lifted to discover it, that she had made peace with herself, that we both had. Those nights after she fell asleep, I lay awake in my bunk, listening to her breathe, her bare shoulder protruding from the sheet, her body gently rolling in unison with mine on the harbor swells.

23
Back to Back

Gayle and I made our way to a hole-in-the-wall mango juice shop, deep in the Somali Quarter. A drunken Somali shamelessly waved a sweating fistful of bills at a very young girl. She looked about ten years old. Amazingly she struggled to accept the money, as her mother tried to beat him off.

Gayle squeezed my hand.

We passed the bony huddled shapes of the young Eritrean boys gathered together in dark alleys. We always bought the boys juice when we came to the mango juice shop. Clusters of them waited outside for the chance to rush in and drink a few drips from empty glasses when customers got up to leave. For this they suffered thudding whacks from a rod wielded by a tall Somali man with a deformed ear, a child's ear that appeared to have stopped growing.

This particular evening, one of them we liked, who was named Michael and from the Eritrean capital of Asmara, shoved himself forward. His head was shaved and pear-shaped, seeming much too large for his shriveled body.

"I will work for you," he said boldly in perfect English. "For free. Just for food."

A bigger boy taunted Michael for speaking English to us. Michael instantly turned on him, and slapped him hard in the face. Shouting and commotion erupted.

Gayle and I dragged Michael back. "Okay, okay, settle down. Come tomorrow," Gayle said to my astonishment. Michael wrenched himself free. "We'll be on the mud flats down at the harbor," she called out over a sea of child's hands waving and shouting for our attention.

I was furious she had involved me in the boy's problems.

"You can use the help," she said to me, as we walked back down the jetty.

"I don't want any help. It's more trouble supervising, than it's worth."

"Frank, you need the help."

"Without you, you mean?"

"Even with me, you need the help."

"No you mean without you. It's going to be me and this little Eritrean refugee. Like a Man Friday. Me and Man Friday sailing the world. A real Robinson Crusoe couple."

"It's the way things have worked out. You might as well accept it."

"Never."

"Not even if it saves his life?" she asked.

"I would rather die before I end up sailing the world with my Man Friday. It's the most offensive and ridiculous story I ever read. And I will never do it. No matter what."

"You don't have to sail anywhere with him. Just get the help you need. And help him."

"No, I will not. He's got his own problems to work out. There are thousands like him. No."

"You are being stubborn. And selfish. Just because of a stupid story."

The next day just before full moon, the lowest spring tides exposed the steamy mud flats across the east end of the harbor. We rowed Joya aground with the dinghy, and buttressed her upright with wooden legs, lashed up under her chain plates, as we had learned to do in England.

Gayle and I sloshed back and forth in the receding water, working furiously to scrape barnacles and tubeworms off Joya's hull. We had only a few hours to repaint her with antifouling paint before the rising tide. The sliced-up worms spattered onto our faces and plopped into stinking piles on the hot mud.

Gayle stood to straighten out her cramped back, her arms outstretched behind her. I laughed at a slice of worm stuck to her cheek. She flung it at me. We wrestled for a moment, slimy, laughing, and threatening each other with hunks of revolting worm flesh, when we heard a scraping sound. I peeked around the back edge of the rudder, and there was Michael, the refugee child from the juice shop, carefully slicing off barnacles with a scraper he had taken from our tool bucket. His face was already splattered with worm flesh. Gayle's replacement had arrived.

I washed the evening dishes, aware of Gayle watching me.

"I still love you, Frank. You are the only one I will ever love in my life, even if I lose you."

I went up on deck and sat, gazing out into the grainy luminescence of dusk over the desert. Gayle followed and laid her arms over the back of my shoulders.

"Where are you going, Frank?"

"There's something out there. I've got to find it."

"But what? Why do you drive yourself so hard?"

"Because I know it's there. Some intelligence. Beauty and harmony on this Earth. That belongs to me. And you too. All of us. I was born to find it. And I will if I look hard enough."

Gayle rested her head on my shoulder and began singing softly in my ear. I loved the delicate courage of her voice, so soothing to me, rising and falling in the waves as it used to during her watches. She sang a new song, *Rhiannon*, by Stevie Nicks.

And the water was closing all around
like the love that had finally found me
then I knew in the crystalline
knowledge of you that drove me
through the mountain
through the crystal
like a clear water fountain
that drove me like a magnet
to the sea, to the sea, to the sea.

"So maybe it's true for you too?" I asked.
"Maybe."

We crawled in bed together that night. It was the first time since her affair. I ran my hand along her naked ribs and up over her hip, feeling the danger, the joy. I gathered her up in my arms and kissed her deeply on her neck, all over her face. She kissed me back. She arched and clung to me, limp as a leaf in my arms. A breathing leaf!

"Shall we try again?" she whispered.

All I could do was disguise the tears falling from my eyes. Her hand slipped around to feel the wetness on my face, and we made love.

24
Fleeing Djibouti

Gayle wrote home to her mother: *Joya is complete and we'll be working fast now to leave by the 1ˢᵗ week of September. My attitude has changed about the boat, as you have probably gathered by my letters. I feel high and alive. Absorbing experiences as they come. I don't believe any longer that I will never change. I have contradicted myself so many times that I feel completely open, and that's a great feeling in itself.*

At least twenty-five hundred miles lay between us and Sri Lanka. The first September weather reports indicated that gales had blown themselves out at the mouth of the Gulf of Aden, and the treacherous banks around the island of Socotra. The tail end of the Southwest Monsoon had arrived. If we did not tear ourselves loose from Djibouti now, we risked sailing in place against the contrary winds and currents of Northeast Monsoon out in the Arabian Sea, with cyclone season moving in.

Gayle and a girl named Ronnie, who had arrived recently on an old hulk of a work boat manned by some young English, made a raid on a "dry" freighter for canned goods. Every large freighter in the harbor was a floating supermarket, and the western style market in Djibouti was more expensive than most boat people could afford.

Our lady pirates departed under the cover of darkness, armed to the teeth with flimsy bright skirts, clouds of perfume, gales of laughter, eyes made up like gangway harlots, and a large basket full of clinking bottles of rum.

Quite late that night well after I had begun to worry, I heard shouts and laughter from out in the darkness of the harbor. The sparkling bow wake of a large aluminum tender emerged, with our girls drunk and howling like game show queens on top of a mountain of supplies, our dinghy in tow.

"This is Billy Swilly," Gayle said, and they all laughed hard. "And that's Kamal who won't put any more juice in his hump." They all collapsed over piles of food.

Gayle and her friend slithered aboard like two entangled octopuses, hanging onto each other for support, not a solid bone in their bodies. I unloaded the ill gotten supplies with the crewmen who had suddenly become more seamanlike again. Gayle had traded a few bottles of rum for 20 pounds of sugar, 30 pounds of flour, large bags of raisins, tea, coffee, cocoa, rice, oats, a case of canned butter, a case of canned cheese, 60 tins of vegetables including canned mushrooms, sterilized milk, and fruit, just to name some of it. A bonanza!

The next day Gayle and I hefted the old blue ice chest off Joya's deck, stowed tarps and equipment, rove the running rigging and sheets through their sheaves and blocks, and pulled out bags of sails. Although the new engine I had ordered from Norway had arrived, customs had demanded the price of it again in duties. We were finally forced to steal it from their storage area, and raced off with it hanging out the back of our taxi. The customs police caught up with us in a Landrover with a siren, but fifty US dollars did the trick. There was no longer anytime to install it, so we bolted it into Joya as freight. I charged our ships batteries to power our compass, navigation lights, and cassette player.

Michael had been working with us for almost two months. We had no idea where he slept in town. He was strikingly handsome, now that he had gained weight and bought nice clothes. He helped us prepare for our departure, seemingly indifferent to the effect our leaving would have on his future. We had almost suggested he come with us, but he preempted the conversation by saying he would never leave Djibouti without documents.

Gayle and I rowed him ashore, and shouted goodnight as he walked up the jetty road into the darkness. We went over to fill our fresh water containers at the public spigot. A herd of camels passed with their hooves gently sweeping the dust like brooms. The wicked thuds of rods striking their hides resounded with the shouts of the Somali herdsman. The camels held their shoe-like heads high, with soft, full lips turned up, as if their long necks would save them.

"You know we're not out of here yet," I said.

Gayle turned the spigot on and held the container under, the water thudding inside. "Yes, we are. We're leaving. And that's that."

"I can't get over the rotten feeling of leaving Michael here. He's too proud and intelligent. He'll get in trouble with the police."

"You've done what you can. It's good you helped him apply for the World Refugee Passport. He'll find a way out of here. Anyway he said he won't leave Djibouti without it. And it hasn't arrived."

"It's like when he socked that kid in the face outside the juice shop for insulting him. No hesitation. He might have killed him if we hadn't intervened. It's a tribal kind of pride. Not to think of consequences."

We took Michael out for dinner at our favorite Ethiopian restaurant in town. Favorite because it was cheap, and I could get a red chili pepper omelet with potatoes and ketchup and a cold beer. While we ate, an emaciated and deformed person of an indeterminable age hobbled into the restaurant. His legs were gouged and discolored like rotting stumps. He supported himself on crutches made from crooked branches, dragging his claw-like feet twisted under him. His head lolled aimlessly at the ceiling as if to hold his milky eyes in their sockets. A young boy led him slowly along.

Africans at other tables gave him money, but as the cripple's feet swung to stop beside my chair, I felt annoyed that the restaurant allowed him inside to beg. There was so much suffering here; I needed a moment's relief to eat. I gave a coin to the boy leading this wreck of a man. The boy looked at the coin long enough for me to register his indignation, and threw it back onto our table. It pinged against my water glass. Michael immediately dug into his pocket and gave the boy less money than my coin, and it was accepted.

The crippled man moved on, and I asked Michael, "Why did he throw my money away? And keep yours?"

"Because you can afford more than what you gave," Michael said matter-of-factly, munching his French fries.

"Let me tell you, honey," Gayle huffed. "That may be African philosophy, but if I needed food that bad, I'd have taken whatever I got."

Michael lifted his eyes directly into Gayle's, not the sort of thing he usually did. He looked angrily at her, as if she had questioned his honor.

Gayle looked right back at him. "I don't want to be the hard core one here, Michael, but we offered to take you with us, without money, without passport, with no conditions whatsoever, and you refused. That doesn't seem too bright considering your circumstances."

Michael acted as if she had not said a thing, just munched fries, one after another.

"He'd be a prisoner," I said, defending him. "He'll never be able to get off the boat. Not without getting arrested."

"He's already in jail here," Gayle shot back.

"I told you I am not coming with you," Michael said. "Not without my papers."

"Your papers could be forwarded," I said.

"Even if he gets this passport," Gayle said. "We don't know which countries will honor it. We're a long way from America. Years maybe, and then what? They've got immigration there too."

Michael got up from the table. "I've got someone to meet."

"Okay, Michael, see you in the morning."

"Good night."

Gayle turned to me, "You and I think differently, Frank. Be realistic! This boat gets small enough as it is."

"What choice do we have?"

"He escaped Eritrea. He can figure out a way to escape Djibouti," Gayle said. "And he knows it."

By the morning of our departure there was still no response at Post Restante, the mail handling service at a post office for travelers with no address. Michael rowed out and helped us pull up our network of anchors and chain, except for one.

The wind peeled up whitecaps across the harbor. Smoke streamed horizontally off the freighters' stacks at the commercial docks, and Joya's mainsail snapped explosively overhead. Joya began to swing her spine from side to side, as if to let us know how easily she could yank that single remaining pair of flukes out of the mud.

We said goodbye to Michael and gave him a few hundred dollars for plane fare, and a pile of equipment off Joya to sell. He said he would *join us somewhere* - the very same words O'Riordan had spoken.

Gayle came up beside me. "He's going to make it," she said, as he rowed away.

Gayle took her place at the helm. I went forward standing over the anchor, and looked back as she leaned from her seat sheeting in the main. I nodded, and Gayle's expression shifted from inward to outward, suddenly alert to everything about the ship. Setting sail is a spontaneous moment that happens when fifteen tons of ship suddenly becomes your own body and life support system.

I nodded again, and Gayle helmed over to fill the sails with wind. Joya heeled and bolted forward against her anchor chain, like a fish with a hook in her mouth. She drove over our anchor, effortlessly yanking it out as I furiously winched in chain at the bow. The sharp crank of bronze gears sounded from the sheet winches, as Gayle stiffened up foresails.

In the distance Michael's arm waved from the dinghy jostling along the boulder stacked jetty. Already the bone white spires of the town faded into the African desert haze as Joya reached back out into the Gulf of Aden.

25
Fire Poppies in the Arabian Sea

I am a citizen of the most beautiful nation on earth. A nation whose laws are harsh yet simple, a nation that never cheats, which is immense and without borders, where life is lived in the present. In this limitless nation, this nation of wind, light, and peace, there is no other ruler besides the sea...
—Bernard Moitessier

We had paid our dues at sea from England to Somalia, and had run the gauntlet of trials by land, culminating in our escape from Djibouti. Our luck had to change, but there would be little or no wind in the days ahead. Our ship rotated in the currents sliding along the North coast of Somalia. There was no one to call for help, no technology that could change our circumstances, not even a motor to turn a propeller, and no doctor to mend us. No one even knew we were out there. I found it strangely settling, even thrilling to be so detached from any other living soul.

Creatures below the surface watched our every move. I watched the smaller ones feed on our waste, and a bit larger ones snap up prey seeking refuge in the shadow of our keel. Before we lost our wind completely, I escaped the unbearable heat by towing myself behind the boat on a long rope. I wove through the sun-shafted void, small fish swaying back and forth under our keel. If I had been a large marine carnivore, I thought, this would be my view looking for a meal.

"You go ahead and troll yourself like bait," Gayle said. "Not me."

The heat was unbearable, and I finally convinced her to sit in the boson's chair suspended off the bowsprit to cool off by dipping her legs. We had just climbed aboard when the shape of something huge glided up to Joya's hull. It was a great white shark! Numbed by how close I was to it just over the side, I stared as it touched its snout to our hull, seeming to test Joya's resistance. It turned away, and by the count of *one, two, three,* it had completely disappeared. But the water visibility was over a hundred feet. I stared, but not a sign of it. We wouldn't have seen it a few meters below our toes.

"It had probably been following us for days," I said.

Gayle would not discuss it. She reversed her tactics. Instead of trying to cool off, she began lying directly in the sun, "to tan," she said. She broiled herself like an oiled fish reading *The Importance of Being Earnest* by Oscar Wilde. How a satire on Victorian life ended up in her hands out in the middle of the Indian Ocean, I had no idea.

After a couple of days, she was overwhelmed by headaches and nausea, clearly symptoms of heatstroke. She resorted to dumping buckets of seawater over her head. The price of a moment's relief was a clammy salt residue that mixed with sweat, suffocates the skin in the heat. After she had sluiced herself for the tenth time that day, I noticed a zig of smoke on the horizon. It was the first ship we had seen, and it had changed course towards us.

Gayle handed the binoculars back to me. "Maybe we can get a cold Coke from them," she said.

A battered ocean going tug pulled up within shouting distance, heaving its weight in the swell. A rusty skinned and barrel-bellied man of Asian descent, with a full black beard, leaned sideways out of the wheelhouse. "Come on over for a cold beer," he bellowed in English.

"Let's go!" Gayle responded immediately. "A cold beer! Someone up there heard my prayers."

I surveyed the compliment of gloomy Middle Eastern minions lurking along the stained rails, and didn't make a move. "These guys look like independents. I don't know what they are doing all the way out here. We can't trust them."

"He said *COLD* and *BEER*. Didn't you hear that?"

"It's too dangerous," I said.

Gayle looked over, and waved back at the captain who was motioning with his massive woman-crushing arm to come over.

"It's way too much trouble to get the dinghy out and inflate it," I said.

Gayle pulled off her T-shirt.

"What the hell do you think you are doing?"

"I'm swimming across if you won't take me. I'd rather get eaten by a shark, than pass up a cold beer out here."

"Don't be totally stupid," I said, "These guys could kidnap you in a second. What's to stop them?"

"I can't believe you are going to ruin this opportunity."

There was no respite from her unpredictability and rash behavior. Even out in the middle of the sea. She made me feel like I spoiled things. A decision as obvious as this one!

Realizing that we were not coming over, the grinning bearded rapist chugged off with his leering crew into the haze. I went back below and unloaded our shotgun.

A thousand miles out in the Arabian Sea, we were completely becalmed, right smack in the Intertropical Convergence Zone where weather charts show the black swooping tracks of cyclones from prior years. For ten days our ship heaved on large windless swells, deep gut-clenching rolls that threw us from gunnel to gunnel, wall to wall, handrail to handrail twenty-four hours a day, the contents of every drawer, cupboard, and locker slinging back and forth in an insane chorus. We raised sails to dampen the motion, but they flogged and gasped like collapsing lungs, till they burst their seams and had to be repaired.

By now it was October. Our British Admiralty book, *Ocean Passages of the World*, directed us south to lower latitudes to avoid the danger of cyclones. South? There was nothing to the South, but the empty expanse of the Indian Ocean between Africa and India. So we turned Joya away from our course to Sri Lanka, toward nothing till Antarctica. We were barely making a fraction of a knot with our wake curling up behind us like settling smoke. A fraction of a knot to where? Nobody knew, not our families, not a soul, not even us.

Huge wool packs of cumulonimbus clouds continued stacking ominously on the eastern horizon, their tops blown skyward over bruised underbellies. Smokey horizontal shards plunged into what appeared to be a celestial x-ray of a shattered body. The sunsets were fantastically bizarre. The light wheeled like spokes through chasms of cloud, splitting into bursts of pastel colors suffused with gold. At night the air grew sodden, our decks glistening like ice under the narrowing band of starlight. We were sinking into a weather crevasse.

I climbed up and down the companionway stairs, my eyes hanging onto the face of our barometer as the needle dropped.

Bowditch on cyclones: *As the fall (of the barometer) becomes more rapid, the wind increases… On the horizon appears a dark wall of heavy cumulonimbus, the bar of the storm…*

Gayle and I stood at Joya's rail, trying to reason away what had to be a sailor's worst nightmare. She had been empty of her usual bravado as the towering thunderheads climbed in the sky ahead, lightning bursts stitching up the horizon as if we were being closed up in the womb of it.

"Is this it, Frank?" Gayle asked, grimly nodding at the dreadful firmament ahead.

"It must be a huge squall," I said, unable to make myself sound convincing. "There's not enough wind. The waves aren't big enough. Not according to the books."

ISLAND BORN

Bowditch on cyclones: *The uninitiated may be misled by the deceptively small size of a tropical cyclone as it appears on a weather map, and by the fine weather experienced only a few hundred miles from the reported center of such a storm. The rapidity with which the weather can deteriorate with the approach of the storm, and the violence of the fully developed tropical cyclone, are difficult to visualize if they have not been experienced...*

We tightened down storm boards over the doghouse windows, battened down anything that could move, and shortened sail, but our movements felt sluggish with the fear we could not express. A lightning bolt struck close off our stern, and I thought I smelled singed atmosphere. It was all so intimate, our hushed purposeful movements, the wind beginning to howl, my skin stinging from rain pelting us like little stones. Gayle and I stood together at the helm, waiting for the moment to strike down the storm trysail in too much wind. Joya's bulk lifted weightlessly off the sea in the blast, skimming the rain-pounded froth like a low-flying wasp.

A huge squall it turned out to be, not our doomsday after all. A few hours later the brooding belly of darkness brightened as if a lamp had to been placed outside of it. Lightning still flashed from the bowels of the horizon. Shafts of sunlight sank down through curtains of pendulous rain drops falling into steamy and confused seas.

"Did you hear that?" Gayle exclaimed, dashing below.

Gayle thrust back the aft hatch which opened under the doghouse and held up three newly born kittens in her palms. We had taken their mom aboard in Greece, when she and her siblings had been thrown into the harbor to drown. Gayle had squeezed water out of their noses like bath toys, and had blown air back into them while I dove for the rest. We found homes for all of them, but kept the loud yowling one, whom we named, Circe, the witch in Homer's Odyssey who lured sailors to their doom.

"Oh, you are sooo cute," she said, holding the kittens up toward me as if they were evidence of something. "Circe's not dumb. She did it while she had the chance."

That she did, I thought. Those nights she'd swum ashore in Djibouti to her tom's call, just as Gayle had done. Then mornings I picked them both up waiting on the wharf.

"Seems there might have been a better time to have a family," I said. "I mean if their survival was at stake."

"You don't understand, Frank. It has nothing to do with survival. The storm is what made it happen."

Like Fire Poppies back home in Southern California, I thought. They only bloom after the hillsides are blackened by wild fires. To be scarified by heat is how they germinate.

The squalls were a blessing at first, fresh water gushing off the foot of the mainsail, filling our water tanks and every bucket and container we had. A good downpour and Gayle dashed below, "I'll get the sheets, and towels."

"Hurry," I shouted holding the washing tub under a torrent off the main. While our self steering system took over the helm, we furiously pounded sudsy piles of laundry on deck. We stood at either end of bed sheets and towels twisting out the suds. As the drops grew heavier and the intervals increased between them, we knew we only had moments to finish. "Concentrate on the sheets!" Gayle shouted, as I tried to finish washing some of my own shirts. Whatever laundry was left to rinse would have to be rinsed in seawater, the salt flapped out after it had dried.

Another week passed. Our celebrations of fresh water turned to cowering in our bunks in torrential rains. We dreaded to have to crawl out for sail reductions, especially at night into soaking gale force winds. The hull oozed water like a permeable membrane. Gelatinous globules flowed across the ceiling and leaned over the saloon table. The mattresses and seat cushions felt like damp sponges. Joya plunged on like a submarine, amplifying the constant sound of moving water, the bilges sloshing noisily no matter how much we pumped.

At midnight on our 38th day at sea, I climbed up into the blackness of the cockpit for my watch. Gayle sat in the dim glow of our compass, wheeling Joya down the faces of large blustery seas. We had picked up a west wind, the last remnant of the Southwest Monsoon after sailing and drifting south for almost two weeks. If the wind had been from the east, we would have turned right for the Seychelles toward Africa instead of India. Out over our bow Joya's twin running sails spread out across booms, like the maroon wings of a giant moth. On either side of us squalls dragged their flaming black curtains across a glittering expanse. Ahead lay some islands no bigger than shakes of pepper on the chart, named the Maldives.

At least once a night an "OH SHIT" rang out from the galley when our food catapulted from pots clamped on the stove. The leading edges of storms flashed over us like oncoming trains. It was my 12-4 am watch, and I handed Gayle a cup of warm tea. As my eyes adjusted, I noticed that she was soaking wet and shivering, her harness twisted to one side.

"You should be proud of me," she said. "A sail-tie got loose on the staysail."

"You promised!"

"It was just a sail tie."

"And with the windvane steering! Down these waves. One big gust and what are you going to do working at the bow! You know how fast she could round up."

"You needed the rest," she said.

"We promised each other not to work the deck alone at night."

"You do it all the time."

"How much rest am I going to get from now on, worrying you might be dragging alongside on your harness? Drowning right beside me in my bunk! I'd never hear you calling out."

"Okay. But it also freaks me out to think of coming up for my watch and not finding you here."

Not finding ourselves there couldn't be possible with only the two us in the universe, it seemed. We sat together at the helm and finished our tea. The stars slowly arced across the top of the mast, and the glow of the compass swayed upon its binnacle post like a hooded oracle.

"Where are we?" Gayle asked after awhile.

"I don't know; I didn't get my longitude shot yesterday. Somewhere out here," I said, laughing.

"What's so funny?"

"I just keep connecting dots on this empty piece of paper. They call it a plotting chart. It's funny because there's no land on either side. It's like our world disappeared."

"You said that last week. What if we made a mistake; the sextant was bent or something, and we're headed out into nowhere?"

"We're here somewhere," I said, pointing at the chart. "With this wind it can't be more than three or four more days before we see something. We're right on a latitude line headed for Male, the main island. I'll get a fix with a longitude shot tomorrow."

Gayle finished her tea, and leaned her body all puffed up in heavy weather gear against me for a hug good night, and climbed below to bed. "Please be careful. Call me if you have to reef. Promise?"

"I promise."

The waves were very steep, and Joya slid down their faces under a full moon. After awhile I spotted the shiny black bodies of a company of dolphins plunging moon-speckled from the wave rows to my right. I challenged them to follow me, veering sharply across a large foamy faced wave. I steered from the forward side of the helm facing backwards, to negotiate the approaching slopes, just as my forefathers would have done. Then I wheeled back across the stars as if I were upside down. The sweeping motions pressed Gayle softly into her mattress, not a bump to betray my madness. The dolphins burst from the waves like mercurial messengers. I chased them and they chased us. Where were they going in their glorious abandon, and where were we?

PART III
PARADISE NET

26
Blooms in Waves –
The Maldives

My charts for the Maldives were originally drawn in 1894, and then updated periodically. Thousands of tiny uninhabited islands were sprinkled in seas of barrier reefs. Some islands had notations indicating *fresh water*, or *high coconut trees visible from masthead*; there were notations of *dangerous currents, submerged islands, wild fruit*, or a *small village*. The largest island ahead, pinched between my calipers on the chart, spread barely across 1 minute of latitude, or only about 1 square mile.

We watched the horizon, or watched each other watching the horizon. Our pencil trail had inched across the coffee-stained chart to the inked outlines of these islands, ringed with x's to mark the reefs. My noon latitude shot placed us just north of the capital island of Male, and my afternoon longitude shot only thirty-five miles out. We hove to that night, so as not to risk closing on the reefs in the dark.

At dawn on October 22, after forty-one days at sea, Joya rose and fell with her staysail backed and helm lashed over upon large waves hissing crisply eastward. I climbed the ratlines up to the first set of rigging spreaders, clinging to the rigging as I heaved across the sky, and wedged myself in for a look.

Vapors of the last squall welled up into the light. A roiling mass of clouds opened a window upon a misty glimpse of blue. A discernible curve brightened into the green shape of an island, ringed with white sand, so small in the distance it seemed as if I were looking down from a mile high. More distant shapes emerged as the sun tore open a frothing vista of iron blue circled by a necklace of palmed islands, each floating in bright turquoise pools.

My feet skidded down the teak rungs of the ratlines, my weight hanging on my grip. Trying to conceal my excitement, I handed my way along the deck to Gayle sitting huddled at the helm against the chilling sea wind. Her eyes were gull-like upon her throne, darkly wild and mute in the glare of oncoming waves. Stopping beside her, I took the king spoke of the helm in my fist. "Climb," I said, pointing to the masthead. "You're not going to believe this."

She handed her way forward in that somnambulant sea shuffle sailors use to walk on waves. She climbed up the ratlines, holding on as the ship tipped back on the swell, and then climbing quickly up a few more rungs before we lay back over again. She draped an arm over the first set of spreaders and held on, gazing out.

She looked shy when she made her way back to the helm. "All I can say is thank you, Lord," she said, looking squarely at the sea. "Thank you, thank you."

We sailed up to the nearest island, where we spotted a channel through the reef, a very narrow dark blue ribbon of water awash with foam. But its location did not match up with where we thought we were on the chart. Excited as we were to make land, the prospect of sailing toward thundering surf, on a bearing through a channel no wider than a pencil lead, would have taken more courage or stupidity than I had in me. Back and forth we sailed, waiting till noon for a meridian shot to confirm our latitude. We watched the humped shoulders of breakers thundering down on the reefs as the midmorning sun hardened their sapphire backs.

Before I got my sextant shot, I spotted puffs of exhaust in the waves as an open native boat pitched and rolled, bobbing in and out of sight towards us. Fishermen, steady as if their feet were nailed to the decks, stared out from under V-shaped hats with heavy white brims. We eased off the sheets to slow ourselves, passing closely by them. I called out the name of the nearby island, pointing off our port bow. They shook their heads, pointing and shouting another name I could not understand. They waved toward the breakers, pointing us through, sawing at the sky with the heel of their hands to indicate what I thought must be a channel.

"We've come too far to get wrecked on a reef now," Gayle said.

I nodded. "Why don't we ask them to tow us? They know the way. The channel looks deep, but it's really narrow. You can see waves rolling across it."

Gayle took the binoculars for a look. "Are you sure this is okay?"

"No. It doesn't look okay at all. I would never attempt that channel on our own."

"Much as I want to get to solid ground," Gayle said. "I think we should wait, till we're sure."

I hesitated also, not taken in by the temptation to make a hasty decision to get into port. "They're sailors…," I said. "We can trust them. They know we're deeper than their boats. And that channel looks deep."

"Okay, Frank, I hope you're right."

We closed upon the bobbing boat and cast them a line to take us in tow. The closer we got, the more harrowing the passage appeared. We slid into a wall of mist thrown over the backs of thundering waves. Whitewater churned over the reef either to side of us as we slipped safely into a calm lagoon.

Our anchor thumped the surface with a splash, planing down into a puff of milky white sand. It lay on the bottom, as clearly visible as if it had been dropped into a fish bowl. We were mesmerized to be still in calm water. A small thatched-roofed village hidden from seaward was now visible under the palms on the eastern side of the island.

The captain of the native boat climbed aboard. He patted his chest, "Asmar," he said. His eyes were as bright as an overjoyed child's. He took my hand in his and held onto it with a broad smile.

Gayle wrote to her mother: *Asmar fell in love with Frank. Here they have no qualms about holding hands if they are friends. He followed Frank all over the boat. Really excited about finding foreigners out in the sea.*

After our welcoming party departed, I dove into the warm nectar of the lagoon and stroked downward to touch the solid world. I dug my fingers into the sandy seabed. When I burst back to the surface, I whooped and flung the wet silky grains over Gayle, cringing in her bikini. She looked so happy. She leapt in unladylike, legs-open and holding-her-nose. Here we finally were, laughing and swimming, hooked upon this bloom of coral, reaching up from the depths for the sun.

27
Illegally Ashore

We had arrived like alien spores on the wind seeking a fertile place, anchored at Turadu Island about fifty miles north of our destination at Male, the capital island. The error in our position was in part due to a strong northerly set of the current during the last night we hove to.

"Is it really possible that after forty-one days at sea, I am not taking my watch tonight?" Gayle asked.

I could only pray that she was right.

I inflated our dinghy, and Gayle stared through the binoculars. "I can see gardens with little fences, banana trees, and a... for sure it's a pomegranate tree. With red pomegranates! Just like the one at my mom's house on Motor Ave."

Before we could row ashore, five elders from the island rowed out to us. They squeezed around our saloon table in an officious mood. Communications relied upon the chart, and plenty of "Ah's" and "Uhm's." Somberly shaking their heads, the islanders made it clear that we would not be permitted ashore. Not at Turadu. They tapped their gnarled brown fingers on the chart over the capital island of Male, another one or two day's sail south.

Not come ashore! We were stunned. "We have to get ashore," I said after they departed. "There's an island named Tiladu, a few hours' sail to the east. The chart doesn't show a village there. It's probably uninhabited. Shall we chance it?"

"Let's go," Gayle answered with enthusiasm. "Maybe we can hole up for a little while before we hit the city on the main island."

"Who said there was a city?"

The next day we slid quietly into the bottlenecked lagoon of Tiladu, lovely and gracefully shaped as if it had been blown hollow from emerald glass. We dropped sail and anchored only a few meters from shore. I tied a rope across the shallows to a coconut palm. Gayle swam and explored the beach, while I flopped in the cockpit with my head hanging over the rail, mesmerized by our braided hawser connecting us to mother earth, lifting and dropping over the water like a marvelous umbilicus. I lay with my arms draped over the rail and cockpit cushion, lulled by the sounds of a crow, the lazy creaks of Joya at rest, the echoing hiss of the shore break in the hollows of the breeze. When I went swimming there were silent squadrons of cuttlefish hovering around our anchor chain. My feet sunk into the fine sand on the beach, and I smiled over the pinch of salt drying on my skin. The smell of green baked in the forest, and wedges of light flashed off the ripples, as I stood watching Gayle collect shell treasures budding in the wet sand.

We went together to gather some low hanging coconuts in the forest, which I knocked down with a boat hook. Gayle stacked them artistically into a pyramid on deck, but they looked disturbingly like a stack of cannon balls. All was blissfully peaceful until the next morning. I was below mixing pancake batter with the last of our sterilized milk, when I heard voices that sounded angry in any language.

I raised my head out of the hatchway as an open native sailing *dhoni* glided alongside, thumping its lateen spar rudely down upon the heap of its sail. An irate islander thrust a walkie-talkie over our rail. It crackled in English, "Hello. Hello, Mr. Visitor. This is customs in Male. You must come for customs clearance," the official shouted, "To Male. You must pay this man for the coconut. And…." The voice faded in static and garble.

"What? Hello, Hello…"

"…rent."

"What? I can't hear you."

"I said you must pay this man rent to stay at this island," the voice suddenly surged out of the box.

"So much for wild islands and coconuts," I said handing the walkie talkie back to the islander.

"What should we do now?" Gayle asked.

"Rufyaa, Rufyaa," the annoying man repeated, holding up 10 + 2 fingers."

"You'd better pay him." Gayle said.

I gave him one dollar, but he dug the air with his fingers for more. I gave him another, and he gave me change in Rufyaa.

"This guy's a regular money changer."

Then he bowed smiling, "Assalam Alaikum."

Soon as the Maldivian rent collector departed, Gayle slapped her thigh. "So if you can't beat 'em, join 'em. Let's hit the city in Male."

"City," I laughed. "Where did you get that idea? Maybe thatched houses with a light bulb. What's the point of sailing all that way south to see a light bulb?"

Gayle darted below, shouting up the hatchway. "Ah come on. Just think of it, movies, restaurants, some shopping. We gotta get customs clearance anyway. What else do you want to do?"

28
Upon a Reef

We were now faced with an unexpected sea passage to check in with customs at Male. It was only a couple more days' sail, but the timing felt like we were pushing our luck. We planned to cross the thirty-mile wide channel to the Male Atoll, and anchor for the night at an island called Kashidou. There was a lagoon at this island with a channel that appeared deep enough to enter on the chart.

The weather felt ominous, with clouds stacked across the western horizon. "God will protect us," Gayle said, falling back upon her Mormon roots. But the sky I watched grew red and angry as we approached the island. The wind strengthened and the sea darkened to purplish. The seabirds had disappeared.

We towed the inflatable dinghy to scout the narrow passage through the reef, but a huge bang sounded from the stern. I rushed back to find that our dinghy had been punctured by the self-steering structure. It was sloshing about like a dead jellyfish in our wake.

"Maybe we should just keep heading south for Male," Gayle said.

"I don't like this weather, Gayle."

The hinges of our cabin door moaned, and I went below to close it. I caught sight of our heavy weather gear swinging out from the storage closet in the head. I cursed, for our late start.

"Let's try and make it into the lagoon," I said back on deck. "It's too late to swim the channel."

"The wind is picking up," Gayle said, wincing from spray over Joya's rail.

"We haven't got time to reef down either. Let's just go for it. We're losing the light fast."

I climbed up the rigging to the mast spreaders for an angle of view that might penetrate the icing-like glare over the water. We were breaking the cardinal rule of never sailing through reefs with the sun at your back. The passage appeared dark, meaning deep compared to the taffy-colored reef on either side. Gayle stood at the helm with her hair blown to one side. Then with only a hundred or so yards to go to deeper water in the lagoon, I saw the first white flash from the bottom. You can only see white in very shallow water. White is sand. We were sailing in fast. A second later more white flashed either side of us before I found my voice, and bellowed down to Gayle at the helm. "Jibe! Jibe! Jibe!" She cranked the helm to port with all her might.

The first impact almost knocked me off my perch aloft. Then another, and another. Each bone and joint-wrenching blow pulverized brain corrals into creamy clouds which boiled up from Joya's keel. By some miracle Joya completed a turn, her weight and solid construction defiantly crushing her way toward the deep water edge of the reef. Then she hit the big one. She rose out of the water, and stalled in a hideous balance, as if the reef were savoring us on its hardened lip before swallowing our ship and dreams. Joya tipped slowly over to her starboard side, vibrating horribly. I clung to the rigging looking down at Gayle. She leaned upright at the helm, still sailing in her heart with one leg submerged in the sea that was flooding our cockpit, not shipwrecked in the middle of nowhere, on a remote island reef.

The dark blue edge of deep water lay only a hundred yards away, but it may as well have been another galaxy in the black heavens. For there was no way in this lifetime to get there. Then a most surprising thing happened. A hard gust of wind put a sign of life into Joya. She pivoted like a fallen leaf and tilted her mast upwards. Her headsails slammed full of wind, and her bow took the lead.

"The mainsail!" I yelled. Gayle threw herself upon the winch. Now with the sun now at our backs, I saw an impossibly shallow path through the giant purple brain corrals. I shouted directions from aloft as our keel thumped forward only inches above the porous brown mat bottom. Thunderous impacts vibrated the ship. Clouds of pulverized corral heads ballooned out around us. Then by some miracle, gracefully as a wounded deer slips back into the forest, Joya slipped back into the deep blue body of the sea.

I charged down the ratlines, leapt below, and tore up the teak planks of the cabin sole. Every scenario of nightmares collated in my head, the details of stretching a sail around the hull to cover the hole, or lowering myself overboard with a large sheet of lead and nailing it over the damage. But the water had not yet exploded in. I waited in the deadly silence, staring at Joya's planks in the bilge, her frames turned inward firmly as the fingers of a mother on her child's wrist, while the sea thudded eerily outside.

Gayle sailed us out toward the relative safety of a blackening horizon. I stood beside her at the helm. There were no words between us. I did not have the energy or spirit to inspect the damage, to hove to while I dove into the dark sea, feeling the hull with my hands. We did not have an underwater light. The blessing of being afloat was all the affirmation we dared to seek for the time being. We watched the islands stretch away and disappear into storm clouds.

We hove to that night as the wind howled into a gale. By dawn the seas were whipped into white froth. Gayle had been feeling sick since yesterday. She had an abscess on her ankle that was getting worse. She hobbled between handholds in the galley. To further mock our horror over this setback, we still had beach sand between our toes. We had no food stores to speak of, except fresh coconuts.

"I'm jumping off the bowsprit if this ship gets close enough," I mumbled, testing the victorious weight of declaring defeat.

By morning Joya bucked her mutinous crew back toward the closest channel on the northeastern tip of the atoll. We could see Monsoon currents churning over the reefs. But it was impossible to make it through the narrow channel before dark, against the heavy wind and currents combined. Each evening we were forced to stand off, and by dawn the land had disappeared once again in the obscurity of storms

By the fifth day, Gayle and I were hardly speaking. The morning was glum. Joya had two reefs in the main and was bucking hard against confused seas and headwinds to get back to the islands. I crouched against the spray at the helm and Gayle sat crouched under the roof edge of the doghouse.

"We should have gone to Male a day earlier, when I first suggested it," she grumbled.

"Someone had to make a decision."

"I felt it in my gut," she added.

"What is this, a woman thing? It will always be my fault for whatever doesn't work out. Like all the sperm that don't get to an egg are wrong."

"That's right. Get it on, Honey, or hit the road Jack."

"That's brilliant. Why don't we make this worse than it already is."

"Travelling is your thing. A woman has other needs."

That afternoon an inflamed perimeter of mist opened around our ship, a molten and silvery circle surrounded by walls of storm cloud, an ephemeral cathedral on the sea. Gayle ignored my calls to come topsides to see. Almost immediately I noticed we were closing on the islands, an unexplainable change in the current. Right before nightfall, this good luck current sucked us through the channel into the atoll with the outward bound sea boiling over the reefs either side of us.

The next morning we awoke anchored at Helengili Island on a gloriously blue and sunny day. I dove to view Joya's damage. Her apron, where the stem joins the keel, bristled with a large porcupine mass of splinters, but she held tight.

On our way to Male as lovely islands slid by, Gayle lay in her bunk like a limpet withdrawn into its shell. She only emerged when I called out that Male was visible ahead. We motored alongside an island family lined up along the gunnels of their boat under the edge of a thatched deck house. They smiled and waved shyly as we slid by. The sound of roaring engines behind us turned our heads. A speedboat, festooned with bare breasted Europeans hollering and laughing sped past, not only exposing their bare asses but then a totally naked man water skiing through clouds of exhaust. I looked back at the Maldivians and their young children staring, dumbfounded by the scene.

"Gayle, I just want to go back to sea. Go find somewhere else when I see that. It's really sad."

"Come on," she said, "this will be good for you. They're just a bunch of dumb tourists. We'll get Joya fixed, and then leave. Let's go eat in a restaurant."

"Those Maldivian kids will never be the same. Did you see their faces? How could anyone explain to them what they just saw? Except that it's the end of their world. That's what it is, Armageddon for them."

"Don't be a hypocrite," Gayle said, climbing back below. "We're tourists too."

"What?"

"Let's face it; your idea of paradise doesn't exist in the world."

"I know it does. It's where it would never occur to a life form to roar around naked in gas guzzling speed boats."

"I hate to be the one to say it, Frank, but after coming all this way, sailing across oceans, all we've gone through… Here we are facing it again. I don't think you're going to find the unspoiled place you are looking for."

"Then we should keep looking."

29
The Land

Male was a bustling metropolis compared to the outer islands, with two banks, electricity, shops, and a few European tourists. Gayle and I strolled the sandy streets overhung with leafy clouds of mango, banyan, and breadfruit trees. After nearly two months of never experiencing speeds exceeding a jogging person, we gawked at bicycles zipping to and fro, and stopped to stare at Male's two or three taxis as they growled from one end of the island to the other in second gear. The treadle sewing machines hummed in tailor shops. We basked in pools of electric light, night shopping from the street. Our noses followed aromas to restaurants. We ate, and shopped, and Gayle was happy.

Rowing back out to Joya was a more dismal reality. The cabins reeked of mildew after our long journey. The deck seams had split in the heat, Leaks from torrential rains pinged and panged into all sizes of pots and pans positioned around the saloon. Not only that, but our anchorage was not secure. The water was too deep and exposed. Storms blew right over and around the few tiny islands protecting us. A good night's sleep was almost impossible with the worry of dragging anchor, awakening to the terrifying sound of surf thundering on a reef, with our anchor dangling in open seas.

In spite of the risk of leaving Joya unattended, we rented a little bungalow with the anchorage in view. Gayle called it "a palace." She was thrilled. Her palace, my watchtower over Joya in the harbor! We had four stone walls, a bathroom with plumbing, ceiling fans, concrete floors, dry furniture cushions, a kitchen with a kerosene stove, a big sink, and sunshiny windows looking out over the sea.

I walked around the island sure that I would find a shipyard of some kind. To my surprise there were no cradles or cranes, dry docks, rails, nothing to pull out a ship of Joya's size and weight. There was only one sandy beach with a few sheds where small local boats were being repaired. We were stopped in our tracks. Continuing to Sri Lanka with Joya in her present condition was not safe. Nor was she safe where she was out in the so-called harbor.

The vigil for Joya's safety fell solely upon my shoulders. I carried binoculars in my satchel, and every thundering cumulonimbus that rose above Male's corrugated steel or thatched rooftops found me anxiously hurrying to the shore. On occasion I had to frantically row out to stop her from dragging onto the reefs.

Gayle, on the other hand, happily scrubbed our new home from top to bottom, pounding the cushions out on the stoop with a rag tied around her head. Maldivians passing along the waterfront smiled approvingly. "And we can leave the doors wide open without the sea pouring in," she said, leaning proudly on her broom, as if she dared not let it go.

I went to see Abdullah Kamaldeen, Minister of the Harbor, a self-assured young man who had been educated in Paris. He was the son of a prominent Maldivian family. I had already spoken to him several times for help to repair Joya, as well as to the shipyard owner, a wizardly white haired old man named Mr. Adam. "I'm sorry Frank, but Maldivian law will not allow any foreign ship ashore," he told me. "But I will see what I can do."

For weeks I visited his house on a quiet section of Majeedi Road. When I arrived he put his arm around my shoulder. "What is wrong, Frank? What is wrong?" He seemed to have gotten the words mixed up with: *good to see you* or *how are you*. Joya may as well have been shipwrecked.

Abdullah told me a Maldivian myth to explain why their people never hunt porpoise. As the story goes, a tear rolled from a porpoise's eye when it had been hooked and pulled ashore by a fisherman. Awakened to his kinship with this creature, the fisherman put the porpoise back into the sea. Now that we had been caught in this Maldivian net of reefs, we were also at the mercy of strangers.

Gayle and I sat drinking *kire du sa*, a Maldivian milk tea, in Red Mouth's tea shop. I called the proprietor Red Mouth, because his lips were stained gruesomely red from eating beetlenut. He relished being asked a question, turning his lips into an awful oval, revealing stained teeth, like a carnivorous fish about to snap you up. His eyes slid side to side keeping watch upon island ladies, who wistfully stroked bolts of polyesters. Children squirmed in their seats, waiting for ice cream.

"I gotta go. My back is killing me, and I got a headache," Gayle said.

"Maybe you should ease up on drinking caffeine."

"I guess you noticed, I didn't have a coffee."

I noticed my sweetheart had been growing bitchy lately, and thought she must have her period.

The boy waiter counted our saucers to add up our bill, when the hulk of a man, much larger than any Maldivian I had ever seen, suddenly appeared beside our table. He raised his fingers to his chest, fingers thick and worn as dredging hooks.

"I, Ibrahim," he said, leaning over us. The ceiling fan wafted down the stench of stale tobacco. His face was pockmarked, eyes bloodshot and worried. He struggled to find words in English. I knew right then, that this was the fisherman in the Maldivian myth, who had come to cast our ship back to sea.

Abdullah casually informed me when I rushed over to his house, that we had been granted permission to bring our ship ashore. A few days later Ibrahim arrived in a dwarf-sized tug, belching grainy black bits into the tropical sky. It dragged us through the harbor entrance, churning up shell fragments and silt over the bottom. Ibrahim looked anxious, his arms stretched across the stern as if they were welded there. Our ship grounded, and Ibrahim could not budge her further.

That evening Joya stood at low tide, supported from falling over with timbers lashed alongside at angles. She was eerily unresponsive to wind driven wavelets or currents rushing through the harbor mouth. She had been dragged halfway to nowhere, neither safely ashore or with any certainty she could get there, nor able to return to the sea. Gayle and I sat in the cockpit in the dark, looking at the stars. She stirred and found my free hand with hers.

"How are you feeling?" I asked.

"Like I'm going to heave," she said. "I don't know why I'm so nauseated."

I felt her head. "You don't have a fever."

She laid her arms over my shoulders. "Maybe you overdid it today. Too much sun."

"Do you love me, Frank?"

"You know how much."

"Do you think anything will ever tear us apart?"

"No. Never. Not after what we've been through together. It's just not possible." I felt the welcome weight of the truth in my words.

"Yes, but timing has a lot to do with the way things turn out."

"Everything is going to be fine for us."

"I love you," she said.

A halo of light arced over the sky from lights in the center of town, and above that, the stars in the dark blue heat. I laid my head against the side of Gayle's, feeling oddly fearful, but glad that the land, what there was of it, had laid claim to the both of us.

30
Congratulations

As a substitute for a Christmas tree, Gayle placed a small coconut palm, still splitting out from its husk, in the front room of our bungalow. Its six fronds sagged under the weight of the colored Christmas lights which we had carried aboard Joya all the way from England, now almost three and one half years ago. Yoon, our next door neighbor, who managed the Korean fishing fleet, had folded origami tin foil animals for decorations. We hung them crookedly on the fronds in the windless glare of the room. But nobody, not even Yoon, celebrated Christmas here.

Outside our window, Joya leaned precariously on the rickety coconut timber supports that were lashed under her chain plates to keep her from falling over at low tide. Ibrahim, our foreman, had still failed to move Joya any further ashore from where he had left her three weeks back. Dozens of men had lined up on long ropes, unable to budge her. Ibrahim had then promised to come with his men and try again the next highest or spring tide, which was tomorrow morning.

I lay in bed as the early morning sun blazed through the horizontal slits of the window blinds, and scythed under the front door of our bungalow. I dropped my feet onto the perpetually warm concrete floor. Gayle busied herself in the bathroom.

"Where you going so early this morning?" I asked.

"To the doctor. I got an appointment."

"Doctor? Why? You didn't tell me you had an appointment."

"I told you a week ago that I had skipped a month."

"You did?"

"I'm late. I gotta go. I'll meet you back here for lunch."

She biked off toward the village center, and I turned toward the shipyard. When I got back to our bungalow for lunch, Gayle had not returned. I waited on the rattan couch in the living room, thinking back on anything that might have something to do with skipping a month. She always had back aches of some kind, but never headaches. And she had been compulsively cleaning. And she complained about Joya's equipment stacked around the house, insisting that I remove it. Then yesterday she had completely surprised me by announcing that she was ready to sail up through the China Sea to Japan. I just stood and stared.

"We can sail back to the States together, alone. Nobody else," she said. "I think that would be the proper way to complete this trip. Just the two of us. It would be quite an accomplishment."

"Yes," I agreed cautiously. "That would make things complete, what we set out to do together."

"You can be the sea dog, and I'll be the sea cat," she said, cozying up to me on the couch. "It can be our 1977 New Year's resolution."

I knew she was dead serious. Privately I balked at the prospect of considering such an arduous voyage. But why would she suddenly decide to face such a challenge, except to force me to the negotiating table by letting me know the risks she would take and the challenges she would face to finally get home. Her courage was always her trump card. And she knew that in the deeper recesses of my boat and weather entangled mind that she was the mercury in my glass, and that I felt it sinking. Something was in the wind. I dared not remind her of waters reputedly full of pirates in the South China Sea, or the distances across the North Pacific. She had thrown down the gauntlet, challenging me at my own game.

Almost two hours had passed while I waited. Bikes and hand trucks hummed monotonously down the sandy road outside our window. I peeked out the blinds from time to time, beginning to worry why Gayle wasn't back. Then I heard her on the landing. She pushed open the front door with her foot and stood before me, cradling her straw market basket in her arms, striped with sunlight from the slits in the bamboo blinds.

"Congratulations, Dad!" she said, walking past me into the kitchen, and dropping her shopping basket with a grunt, onto the concrete floor. She came back and stood akimbo in front of the couch.

That's what Dr. Rashid said. 'Congratulations.' So I'm passing it on to you."

"No…?"

"Yep, already about two months."

"Is the doctor sure? Is there a chance that…?"

"It was a blood test. I'm pregnant." Gayle hoisted her belly with the flat of her hand. "I've got to get something to eat."

Splashes echoed from the concrete kitchen as Gayle dumped a pail of dishwater out through the hole in the wall that served as our drain. I heard the plank door slam behind her as she went outside to the well. I heard scraping on the sides of the well as she pulled up the long-handled well dipper. I lay back on the rattan couch, staring up at the brightest spot between the slits in the blinds, letting billions of lumens beam into my eyes. My inability to understand anything at all eased being blinded by the glare.

Gayle walked back into the room, stood in front of me again, with three boiled eggs on a huge plate of rice, and began eating.

"So what do you want to do?"

"I don't know. I'm kinda in shock. I mean this is good news… of course, but …"

My incapacity to respond made me feel instantly criminal. I sat there dumb, unable to rise from the bog of my own dilemmas, even a bubble of loving tenderness, joy, or support. She deserved it all, and I wanted to express it all from my bottom of my heart. But her announcement cut me a life I never expected, surely as if I were being turned on a lathe by the news. I remembered Gayle at the Rock of Gibraltar. How west became so immediately east for her, with the flip of a coin. How she embraced the outcome. Even at the time I thought it odd, because I knew I would remember that moment one day.

Gayle sat in a chair opposite, lifting her eyes upon me with every bite of her lunch.

"How does a child fit into all this?" I asked as truthfully as I could.

Gayle shrugged, as if my question was of little importance.

"At 4:30 tomorrow morning," I said, "the whole village will be here, to try and drag Joya up on the beach. For the second time. This is our last chance to catch the monsoon to Sri Lanka. If they don't destroy her."

Gayle shoveled in crumbled egg yolks and rice, without answering.

"I'm sorry. Please forgive me, Gayle. I know this is shameful that I can't be instantly loving and happy for us. It's not that I'm not. I'm exhausted, rowing out in the middle of the night every night, wrestling with slimy ropes to keep Joya from falling over. Ibrahim may refuse to try again, if we don't get out this time. This is my baby. And I am maxed out with it."

Gayle turned and marched out of the room.

"I just don't know how to fit baby in!" I shouted after her.

I stepped outside, slammed the front door, and walked out into the blast of midday sun. Joya stood across the road on her supports in the shallows, paralyzed between the land and sea.

Gayle wrote home to her mother: *I waited for Dr. Rashid at his house cause I couldn't understand all the wish wash of the pregnancy test results. I had a cup of tea with his wife, Patricia, who came from Malaysia. She was about 28 and very nice. When Dr. Rashid came back, they both congratulated me, and I felt I deserved congratulations. I felt proud, and in a state of ecstasy over the news. Then I flashed on Frank's face after I'd tell him and thought, Oh no, this is terrible. I went over about 600 ways to tell him, some sad, some happy, some just the facts. I talked Patricia's head off for a half an hour and then zoomed home on the bike with a gleaming smile on my face that I couldn't get rid of, no matter how many people stared at me.*

31
Dragged from the Sea

That night after Gayle found out she was pregnant, we got up at 2:30 a.m. and rowed out to Joya. Ibrahim had already lined up about two hundred men along the tail ends of hemp hawsers that stretched back from Joya to pairs of massive one hundred fifty pound steel blocks, for added purchase. The steel blocks were attached to the black barbs of huge anchors salvaged from freighters, and buried up in the sand. There were no other fixed points in these islands, other than a few banyan or palm trees, no boulders, or any elevation more than a few feet. Muscle and these Zeus-sized anchors buried in the sand were all that could save us from the sea.

Gayle lit mouthfuls of cigarettes and passed them down to thirty or so men shivering in the water. They huddled over the balancing beams on each side of our ship. I dove with my underwater flashlight to survey the eerie spaghetti tangle of ropes cinched behind Joya's keel. I now realized that I alone had engineered this madness to save Joya; everything had been done exactly as I had sketched a little drawing for my foreman, Ibrahim, including the coconut tree trunks at the water's edge to shove under her keel.

"This looks pretty crazy, Frank. Are you sure it will work."

"No, not at all. I never intended Ibrahim to use my ideas. He is doing exactly what I sketched for him in five minutes."

I stood up at the bow, as a fine rain dribbled down my face, and felt Joya's keel began to lift, bumping the bottom in the shallows with the height of the tide.

Ibrahim's voice rose up into the night. It was a surprisingly melodic work song, with all the power and brutish tenderness of the man. A refrain sounded from the men out at their positions in the darkness. In unison the balance-beam-men flung their weight to rocking the ship, breaking friction with the earth and throwing me off balance. I clung to the bow pulpit, as the main boom slammed in its cradle behind me. The long hawsers rose from the sea like ligaments, wringing water from themselves, with the men's backs bent upon them. Joya lurched forward on the first roller, but there was a loud and sudden *bang*. The shapes of men spilled into piles up the beach, as if the earth had shook them down. The rope lay snatched back into lifeless coils in their midst.

I swung down off Joya and waded ashore.

"The boat is too heavy!" lamented Ibrahim, holding the shoulder of an injured man dangling his hand covered in blood-soaked sand. "The ropes is broken. Tomorrow we trying again."

The next evening Gayle and I waited for Ibrahim and his men, but not a soul appeared walking up the dark street toward the shipyard. Feeling desperate, knowing better than to feel or show desperation in a place where a plan is nothing more than smoke, like inhaling a cigarette and blowing it out again, I hurried to Ibrahim's house in town. I shoved open the blue wooden gate on its rope hinges, dragging its bottom across the sand. Ibrahim sat in a walled courtyard, smoking a cigarette, surrounded by family members. He leapt to his feet, and grabbed a chair so quickly out from under an unsuspecting man, that he stumbled into a standing position.

Ibrahim's wife prepared a hookah packed with black tobacco, spices, and dried banana peels. Everyone insisted I have a toke, their palms pumping up and down toward my mouth. I took a long draw on the glowing coals to be polite. Almost instantly I broke out into a cold sweat. If I had opened my mouth to utter a single word, I would have vomited. I clenched the sides of my chair, suddenly aware of the sickening diesel fumes wafting into the courtyard from a generating plant across the street. I have a vague recollection of people talking to me and touching me, but the roar of the generators drowned out everything. When I bent over to breathe deeply, some children crawled up to look up into my face, giggling and making comical expressions.

"Coming to take the ship tonight," Ibrahim said, patting me on the shoulder. "Coming tonight."

True to his word, Ibrahim came before dawn, with more men than before, lined up along even more lines attached to Joya. The men answered Ibrahim's call, and Joya groaned forward. The men cheered. Others dove to wedge more rolling logs under her bow. Foot by foot, Joya lunged into the dawn toward Ibrahim's calls. By sunrise Joya sat on the foreshore, her mast and two levels of rigging spreaders towering over the island with seawater oozing from between her planks.

It took four more days of heaving to pull Joya up the beach, bow to the huge hooks, like a gigantic fish with palm trunks wedged under her curves to hold her upright. The great taproot Joya was for us had been yanked from the sea, as another within Gayle's womb became ever more firmly rooted.

"Now the real work begins," I sighed, as we walked arm in arm back to our bungalow from the shipyard.

"How long will it take to repair everything and get her back in the water?" Gayle asked.

"I don't know. A couple of months."

"Then what? I'll be four months along by then."

"Anything could happen in a couple of months. I can barely recognize our plans, or even ourselves from day to day over the last year. I am at a complete loss to quantify any amount of time for anything. I just don't know."

"Well we now have a new clock in the family to help us with that."

32
Gambling Joya

As Gayle's belly grew and stretched over the next three months, our sailing plans shrank in spirit. She looked down at the mound of our new and unknown life together, and sang lullabies. My inability to respond welled up like a dark tide, where I sank into the brooding shadow of the father within me. I felt threatened by her joy, knowing how much more her mother and family would appreciate her, and how much she must be drawn to them now, especially her mother.

Our plans as they stood put us in India for the birth. That was if all went well with Joya's repairs. India, why not? We had met other couples travelling with young children. I suddenly saw a small village in the shade of Banyan trees and Gayle nursing her baby by the river. I imagined women in Saris, loving hands, sudsy laundry on the river rocks, and soft voices. A place where there were no elevators, concrete halls, wheelchairs, or Doctor's offices with fish tanks.

Gayle and I lay in bed, trying to ignore the moaning porno records from our Korean neighbor next door. He played them whenever his fishing fleet captains were back in port. Late into the night gasping female voices interspersed with the drunken shouts of Yoon's men finally subsided to the kick-scraping sound of the needle at the end of the record. We waited, in the hopes one of the unconscious men would arise to lift the needle. It sounded like rifle shots in the dead of the night.

Finally I got out of bed as I had done many times before, crossed the well courtyard between our bungalows, and climbed the Korean's stairs, stepping over the bevy of sandals parked at the doorway, and over the slack mouthed bodies sprawled all about the room in white underwear, and lifted the needle off the record.

Mornings, Yoon slapped his plastic sandals back across to our bungalow, sometimes handing us a plate of *kim chee*, the spicy pickled Korean cabbage, which we treasured. It was one of the only vegetable dishes we could get in the Maldives. In return for the *kim chee*, it was my job to get Yoon and his sailors out of the trouble that they were hell bent to get into whenever they came into port. I composed letters addressed to Maldivian authorities with Yoon's apologies for incidents such as: *his men are very sorry for breaking out the lights with sticks,* or *chasing Messrs. so and so up the radio antennas…* or *please understand that in Korea if a man grabs the testicles of another man, it is a sign of ultimate friendship. They are called, testicle brothers…*

"Ya Ya, that's good," Yoon shouted.

Gayle had been worrying about a miserable monkey, chained in its own excrement at the bottom of Yoon's drain spout, abandoned by one of Yoon's fishing boat captains. "I don't care who that monkey belongs too," she said. "No one has fed it for three days, except me. I'm confiscating it."

Monkey, as we called the diabolically headed little thing had an alien strength, and screeched wild-eyed with jealousy whenever Gayle and I showed affection for each other. It made short work of turning our bungalow inside out. It was a demon aboard Joya. It fished through drawers and cabinets, relentlessly in pursuit of nothing in particular. Whenever I appeared with its leash, it ran up into the rigging raining urine down on me, or clung to the ceiling fan in our bungalow spraying excrement.

ISLAND BORN

"He knows you better than you do," Gayle said laughing, while the miserable devil pouted vengefully at me in her arms. "You should be nicer too him. He's my training baby."

I spent my days working aboard Joya, grinding, wrenching, filing, sawing, twisting into impossible spaces. Gayle attended to the bright work, patiently sanding and sanding.

Evenings we were too hungry and too exhausted to cook. We walked down a dark sandy alley leading away from the bustle of Majeedi Road, to a little thatched blue plastered hole in the wall place. The room was big enough for a single plank table with a Coleman lantern in the center and a bench. A hefty smiling woman in a black dress with red hibiscus flowers leaned from an opening in the wall and asked, "Cocolo bis?" We nodded, and she turned back to the blue flames wafting up from the rusty burner cans under her brushed aluminum pots.

Cocolo bis is a bluish, corpse-colored egg in a bowl of a clear broth of chilies and coconut milk, the only fishless dish we ever found in Male. Our forks and spoons were completely flat, as if they had been steamrollered. It was like eating with a pair of oars. Hunger and chilies don't mix easily. The trick was to chew lightly so as not to release too many BTU's before swallowing as much as possible whole. We clenched our toes into the sand under the table, and a glass of crimson sugar liquid, the Maldivians called juice, helped to soothe our raw mouths. We joked over whose tongue was more purple from the chili third degree.

We ignored our anxiousness just below the surface as we strolled arm and arm. Pools of kerosene light spilled out from open-sided shops with hand-painted wood marquees. A tailor who was foot-treadling a sewing machine beckoned us. Gayle's hands dragged off my arm as I rushed into his shop, suddenly deciding I had to have a shirt. He had it measured, cut, and sewn together, and then had hand sewed the buttons on, before I had come to my senses to try it on. Gayle waited as if it were taking too long.

We headed back toward the harbor with our arms around each other, following a sandy foot path past old village homes between the main streets. I felt the weight of *what to do* in the damp breadfruit leaves underfoot, the movement of Gayle's finger in my palm as we walked, the star-pricked palm fronds fluttering overhead. The air grew suddenly cooler as we passed under a banyan tree, with its long trunk-like air roots hanging to the ground. I let my hand ride the small of Gayle's back as her Indian bracelets jingled. Her muscles curved prominently into her spine. All her hard labor aboard Joya had made her strong. The folds of her favorite orange sari were bulging over the mound of her new belly. She glanced back at me and squeezed my hand.

"Look, Gayle, I've been thinking. Maybe I have an idea. What if we sail to Southern India? There are small villages with decent harbors for Joya. And wonderful people, living a simple way of life. Family people who I'm sure would help us. Make us feel at home."

Gayle straightened, sliding her arm out from around my waist.

"What's wrong?" I asked. "It might be a great place to have a baby."

"You may think so, but who is going to do laundry? Are you going to do it?"

"Laundry! That's not a problem. Sure I'd do it. But it's India! We can hire anyone you need: a laundress, housekeeper, even a cook.... You wouldn't have to do a thing you don't want to do."

"There are no modern conveniences there. I want modern conveniences. I'm not having a baby alone, while you're off working on Joya all day."

"Come on, Gayle," I said, slowing to face her.

But she kept walking ahead.

"What are you talking about... modern conveniences?" I hurried after her following her butt in that sari, her heels digging like island women carrying the weight of a water jug on their heads. "You haven't had any modern conveniences for years! Why the hell are you talking about them now?"

Gayle stopped in front of a mossy coral rock wall, her eyes moist with anger. "Because I miss them. And I'm not having a baby without them!" She turned, and walked off.

"Jesus!" I said, hurrying after her. "What are we supposed to do? Abandon Joya? Just forget everything, all our plans, all our work, leap out of our life? For a washing machine? A dryer? A toaster?"

"That's right!" Gayle shot back. "I want to go back to Los Angeles and have my baby."

"What!" Just hearing the words *Los Angeles* spoken out loud shattered the distance I thought we'd come. I hurried to catch up, to stop her from saying anything more she might not be willing to retract.

"Look, Gayle, I understand you want safety, being pregnant. A place you can call home. Your family nearby. I understand...."

"No! No, you don't, Frank. You're not going to get your way this time. I'm telling you. I'm going back to L.A. With or without you!"

"Damn! This is my baby too." I thumped my chest so hard my knuckles ached. "At least let me try to come up with a solution. Something that will work for both of us."

Some young men approached from the opposite direction with their shirttails hanging out over their *lungis*. They were holding hands and smirking, in that maddening way painful things amuse them.

After they passed, I turned back to Gayle. "I don't believe we should go back to L.A. Okay? Not after coming this far."

"There's no scheme to come up with, Frank. Not this time. It's gonna be my way! I have slaved on Joya long enough. I'm nauseated all the time. I want to barf at home. I want my mother, my family, a hospital. I want help with this child. Get it through your head, Frank. No!"

We marched in single file back toward our bungalow. It was dark along the harbor front. The ocean wind buffeted us into swerving. The sea chattered over the reef against the breakwater. A navigational light blinked atop a pile of stones at the reef entrance, the only beacon in the Maldives at that time. Then I had it! That's all I need right now, I thought, just one solitary thing to head for. Gayle would just have to accept that we had not arrived.

We stopped outside the pale yellow door of our bungalow, standing on the threshold, the breeze warm and unyielding. "Okay!" I said, "We'll go back. Back to Los Angeles or anywhere you want. But grant me one thing. Just one thing."

Gayle's face noticeably softened with this concession, and a blush of color came to her cheeks.

"What?" she said, hurrying the truth from me, before I had time to think. "What thing?" she demanded.

"Time," I said. "I want time. To see if I can come up with something. A possibility. Something we might not have considered. I don't believe the time is right to make a decision. If I'm wrong... if we can't agree on something else, then you have my promise that we'll go directly back to L.A. I swear. You won't hear a peep out of me. We'll sell Joya. I'll leave her in the Maldives if I have to. There will be no delays. No excuses. We'll get settled in California. That's fine with me. I just need some time."

Gayle stared into my eyes. My promise to give up my ship had stunned her, for me to turn away from everything I had worked so hard for to rebuild the trust between us.

"How long?" she asked.

"The airlines won't let a pregnant woman fly after the eighth month," I said.

"How long do we wait?"

"Till then. Just before your eighth month."

Gayle gave me an unflinching, measuring stare.

"Uh…mm, we'd have to leave by June 15," I said. "That is if we don't have another plan by then."

"By June 15th," Gayle repeated.

"Yes. I promise."

"Okay," She said.

Gayle had now dismissed considering a village in India which lay directly ahead. Our trajectory and my sailing dream had begun to immutably fade along with the spirit behind reaching for such a place, the spirit of transforming our sailing voyage to one of family life. Time was all I could bargain for.

33
Moonless Dark

Gayle and I pushed our bikes toward the market to do our evening shopping. Fishing boats swooshed into port on the cooling breeze. Young boys hurried to ease off their main halyards and drop the patchwork of gray and brown sails billowing out before them. The boats were heavily laden with the day's catch, gleaming a pinkish-silver mound in the holds as they cleaved into an arc toward the shore market. The boys hopped along the gunnels, poling the last distance to the wharf. Tuna was their staple. Every islander peddled or walked home with a fish tied with a string by the tail, swinging from their wrists or handlebars.

We stopped pushing our bikes to watch the sun, sputtering crimson as it sank on the horizon. It gilded the harbor ripples, inundated the beach sand in peach, then wicked up into the plastered walls plumb-colored, and spilled out over the thatched and tiled roof tops.

"Since you're the painter, what exactly is the color of the sky?" I asked.

"Violet," Gayle laughed, "It's the energy of red combined with the expanse of blue that makes violet."

"I am neither good at colors or rhythms, but my sense of direction is true."

Gayle did not answer as the last flickers of the sun cooled on the horizon. Some islanders still made their way home in the molten blue light thickening upon fish scales and human skin. Ashen white shirts dimmed to charcoal, and the market transformed to kerosene glows from every stall and shop. Soon families would re-emerge from the darkness with freshly scrubbed children to shop and promenade.

Gayle never ate fish; she couldn't stand the smell of it. We had been completely vegetarian aboard Joya, sprouting mung beans, and eating grains or legumes such as lentils and soya beans. We strolled past wooden bins stacked with tuna, halibut, mahi-mahi, and the occasional swordfish, in search of anything green among the tables. Men passed to and fro with buckets overflowing with fish tails. A twenty pound mahi-mahi was about twelve cents U.S., and lobsters, which islanders did not eat, sold to tourists for about fifty cents. We peeked into box after box, rank with the warming bodies of sea creatures. We were lucky to find anything more than a stalk of miniature bananas, a bin of dusty coconuts, or a few papayas. Rows of burlap bags contained rice, with a scoop inside. Most of it smelled of mildew. The few small eggs we purchased often spilled out an embryo into the pan. We had to crack them into a separate cup first to keep from spoiling the rest.

There was little else we could find to eat, aside from the precious handouts of Korean *kim chee* from Yoon, or what we could procure from an Indian airline pilot, who had a side business of flying in a few vegetables in his hand luggage. From him we were limited to a single cabbage. It had to be ordered a month in advance. Our only other source of food was a vegetable-loving Maldivian who grew a few leaves of chard inside a high walled garden, as if it were a subversive act. One leaf or two per week was all we could coax out of him. We were the only ones hungry in the Maldives, it seemed. Our meager vegetarian diet did not argue well for staying long, not with Gayle's new dietary need to nourish two.

My promise to return to the States, if we had not reached an agreement by the middle of June, only maintained a shaky truce

ISLAND BORN

between us. Neither of us could imagine a good outcome. Going to sea taught us we had a language in common with sailors everywhere, and now we discovered her being pregnant also spoke directly to islander's hearts. Nothing seemed easier or more natural than family life in the Maldives.

After shopping, Gayle agreed to go for a leisurely ride along the wharf with our market baskets balanced on our handlebars. Along the jetty wall, the outer island boats crowded together, stern to. Cook smoke infused with the aromas of steaming rice and fish stews wafted up from coconut husk fires. Men shouldered heavy burlap sacks across springing planks from their boats to the wharf. Their wide knobby brown feet whitened under the weight. They loaded staples of rice, sugar, and coffee, as well as material goods such as bolts of synthetic fabrics, buttons, and leaf springs to be blacksmithed on island forges into knives, rudder pintles, and fish hooks. Many boats would set sail that night with their cargos, goods more foreign than meteors scattered over their moonlit atolls.

Gayle and I pulled our bikes to a stop overlooking rows of thatched deck houses along the wharf. Men and women squatted at the *dhoni* rails, or leaned on spars to visit. Their voices were soothing tones of affirmation: *ah*'s and *uhm*'s rocking on the swells. I straightened my arms on my handlebars and looked over at strands of Gayle's hair floating on the breeze, reflections of firelight flickering upon her face.

"It's hard to imagine leaving here," I said. "I think we've forgotten what the rest of the world is like."

Gayle mused over the scene, hunching over her basket on the handlebars. I reached over to offer my hand, and she took it into hers. Held it tight. Her hands always felt large and thick for someone so slender and sinewy as a beanstalk. Yet hers were trusting hands, willing as a child's to be held.

"I just can't believe," I continued, "that such madness exists outside of these islands."

"Along with its advantages," she replied mischievously. "But you don't want to know about that."

"No, not really."

"It's where you could never buy a whole tuna for ten cents," she scoffed. "Or an entire swordfish for a dollar."

I nodded my head, looking off down the line of boats.

"It's where fish is damned expensive. That's where I want to go. Where fish is so damn expensive, we couldn't possibly afford it."

She shoved her bike ahead with a wobble of laughter, and several island children trotted along tugging at her clothes, looking up into her face to share the joke.

That night I awoke, restless, and looked over at Gayle. She lay on her side, folded into a ball around her pillow. Ever since she was little she had rocked herself to sleep, curled up on something soft while her father shouted drunkenly on the other side of the wall. "He was Dr. Jekyll and Mr. Hyde," she told me. For a young child, he may as well have been, promising presents that never arrived, outings and hot dogs that never happened, and bedtime stories he never came back to tell. A path of disappointments like stepping stones leading to a ledge. She listened to him shouting outside the house late at night while she rocked herself to sleep.

I reached over and put my hand lightly on her shoulder to comfort her, and thought of how my own father cared for us, pacing the house late at night with his problems, his marriage, his distraught mother, his financial crises. I had listened to the hallway creak outside my bedroom, never doubting he would always be able to protect us. Now it was my turn to wake up and walk.

I quietly slipped out of bed, pulling the sheet over Gayle's shoulder, and made my way through the darkness to slivers of light through the living room blinds. The only streetlight on the waterfront was outside our bungalow. I peered out, surprised to see children standing on the shore, little tots flying homemade paper kites that fluttered white as moths above the light. Not a single adult watched over them. I tipped my watch toward the crack in the blind. It was 3:00 a.m.

    I slipped on my shorts and stepped out into a warm ocean breeze. It blew from a hole of moonless dark on the horizon, carrying the sweet scent of islands and fair weather. The oldest kite flyer could not have been more than seven, the youngest maybe three or four. As if I were invisible, too large to fit into their world, they paid no attention to me. The little kites crackled and ducked over my head, frail enough, it seemed, to be ripped apart in one more knot of wind.

34
Shore Leave

Gayle did not show much of a tummy by March, four months into her pregnancy, but I noticed her belly button had begun untwisting, like a cinnamon roll poking out from the center. She began even more determinedly sanding the brightwork on Joya's topsides, her straw hat bobbing along the rails throughout the whole day. She wore Mao-collared, long-sleeved shirts tailored in the market, to protect her from "blistering like Joya's varnish," she said.

After so many sea miles, our ship had been enveloped in a digestive membrane of salt. Everything that could rot, mildew, or rust had done so. Water tanks, fuel tanks, all her supplies, and such a pile of equipment was stacked on the beach that no one could imagine how it would all fit back in. I rode my bike back and forth, lugging parts salvaged from wrecked ships or pillaged from Gan Atoll, the abandoned English base far to the south: plumbing, electrical, mechanical, cordage, anchoring equipment, outdated sealants and paint supplies. Maldivian shipwrights had replaced Joya's stem smashed by the Kashidou reef with an oversize timber of some local wood, which they had first fitted in place and then handhewn to Joya's shape.

The boat's demands so absorbed my time that I could not imagine how anything I was doing would change Gayle's mind. Had I actually committed to abandoning Joya? I questioned myself. My life's dream! I had never once thought of having a child. My pact with

Gayle seemed suicidal. At the same time being a father sapped my spirit for going back out to sea. I cringed to think of anchoring out in the channel again, the shifting winds and storms, constantly laying and maintaining a web of ground tackle in such a deep anchorage. And then to embrace a seaman's plight again, that safety lay from whence his gravest danger sprang. To run from the land out to the storm is the grist of a sailor's life, anytime day or night.

Gayle suspected my waning spirit to relaunch Joya. I dreaded giving up the relief it was for me to be home in our little house on stormy nights, to stroll down to Red Mouth's for a warm cup of tea. She walked into the bedroom, and stood at my feet at the end of the bed. All my muscles were throbbing after a hard day's work and a warm wash from a heated bucket of water.

"Calling Captain Frank," Gayle whispered mockingly. "Calling Captain Frank… Ibrahim said he wants to pull Joya off the beach. He wants to know why our work is taking so long."

Her words *Captain Frank* percolated sickeningly in my gut. "Can't we discuss this tomorrow?"

"Saw him in Red Mouth's today," she persisted, in a singsong reproach. "They want the space for his father-in-law's boat."

"I know. I know. They're just pestering us about it. They've got the whole damn beach there," I said, knowing we had the best spot opposite the deepest part of the lagoon. "We still have work to do."

"We told them two weeks. Not two months," she sang out again. "It's not right to ignore them. Our work can be finished anchored out in the channel."

I buried my head under the pillow, rather than think of the cumulonimbus clouds that soon would be belly-laughing over us again.

"You're not getting away with it," she said, laughing and digging her fingers into my ribs.

I sprung upright to wrestle her off and smelled that she had been smoking. "You've been smoking again."

"So what," she said defiantly, with that castaway attitude of a teenager on the streets of L.A.

"You've been drinking too. I found a rum bottle opened on Joya."

"Only a little rum with solitaire. Big deal."

"No, we had a deal. No booze or cigarettes. You're pregnant for Christ's sake."

"I need some relaxation. It won't hurt the baby. A tiny little drink here and there," Gayle waved her hand over her shoulder on the way into the bathroom.

So going out to meet the storm at sea was safest for Gayle and me. There was no doubt about it. The land sickened our life together. Now I was certain of that.

I sat up. "Tomorrow, I'll talk to Ibrahim about pulling Joya back in. Maybe we can head out and explore the islands."

"Why don't you get it?" she called back. "I want to be near my mother, not sailing around bizarre villages somewhere. You are always pushing limits. I won't discuss it."

35
Evicted from Land

Ibrahim pulled Joya back off the beach with his men, back to the same giant anchors which had been barged out to positions in the lagoon, with their flukes protruding from the surface like tridents. It was March 28, and there were only about four months left to get our child safely born, somewhere. I was quick to notice that Gayle took charge of managing lines, and then jumped to the helm as Ibrahim's tug dragged us over the crusty lime plateau of the reef, and back into the violet deep.

It was a glorious day, the royal blue swells tufted with white icing. Joya swung her keel weight, whirling eddies and plowing up froth. Her freshly oiled rails and skylights gleamed in the sun. Her white enameled hull sparkled with reflections. Every joint, rib, and valve was shipshape. The native shipwrights had installed our propeller shaft, so now our Norwegian diesel, which we had carted all the way from Africa, thumped us to the uninhabited island of Funidou, directly opposite Male.

To moor her, I trudged underwater in sneakers, lugging armfuls of chain, tools and shackles to loop around the largest brain corals. Then with hundreds of feet of chain I split two anchors off our stern to prevent wind from either side driving us beam on. We had given up our apartment in Male to move back aboard, but I had no expectation Gayle would sail anywhere ever again.

That first night we made our bed on deck in the warm dark. My thoughts drifted among the stars and over the black waters swaying with the sparkle of Male's lights. A wake from a passing boat rocked Gayle against my body; she had fallen sound asleep. I pulled the sheet up over her tanned shoulders and ran my fingers through her hair. Then her eyes opened as if the lids had rocked back upon the dimming embers of her mind. She spoke without blinking.

"I know you don't want to go back, Frank, but I cannot have a baby without any security. We've got to think about what's best for the child now. Do you understand?"

"Yes, I understand."

"There is so much disease," she said. "No clean hospitals."

"It's okay, Gayle." I stroked her head, feeling the lack of resistance. "I know you're right. Go back to sleep."

I looked out across the channel. The distant figures of islanders returned home late, inching along the glow of Male's waterfront. I listened to the approaching *putt putt putt* of a passing boat. Ocean surges chattered their incessant poetics over the reef. I felt the softness of Gayle's cheek, her head tipping on my arm as Joya rocked, our mast arcing across the heavens, and I was glad.

36
Searching Seaward

I awoke late that first morning at Funidou, noting the conspicuous absence of Male's sounds. Here, there was only the windless chirp of ripples over the reef and the clinks in the galley below as Gayle made coffee. The morning sun heated the weathered grain of the teak deck, casting hairline shadows along the seams. The cool ocean air smelled free. I leaned to look over the gunnel. The reef shallows flashed with rainbow-colored parrot fish, black and yellow-striped tigers, electric blue fish, rockfish, and trumpeters. Suddenly a breeze wrinkled the surface and hummed gently in the rigging aloft. Joya's weight lifted her mooring lines, gracefully as a woman unshoulders her slip.

Down below I heard the sink pump in our cabin thumping noisily back and forth as Gayle washed her face. I sat in the cockpit, gazing blankly at the chart. My finger reached to touch a remote atoll on the chart, drawn there like a planchette on a Ouija board. I withdrew my hand as Gayle came up on deck.

She had a load of sheets to wash in her arms, oddly conspicuous to me as this was always her ritual before we set sail.

"So when are we leaving?"

"I didn't say we were leaving."

"Yeah, right! I know you, Frank," she laughed. "Anyway, I don't mind. I feel like getting out somewhere and... Oops, excuse me."

She folded her hands under her now impressive tummy. "I'm getting morning sick.... I gotta barf."

She scrambled down the companionway ladder.

"You've got the whole ocean! Why barf in a toilet?" I called down to her.

"I can't stand the fish eating it!" she shouted back.

The toilet pump handle began to slam up and down, and I looked over the side, at the clouds choked out into the water. The reef fish swarmed to nibble it up.

"They're eating it right now," I called out.

"They can have it," Gayle retorted, climbing back out on deck.

I gestured toward the chart. "Well, there seem to be some nice-looking anchorages in Ari Atoll to the west." I tried to sound offhanded.

Gayle looked pale. She laid her head on the rolled-up cockpit dodger along the rail. "As long as we don't have to go through our typical survival at sea routine."

"Look we don't have to go. If you feel too sick…"

No answer.

"There's an anchorage that looks reasonably protected," I said, "but this time of year… a wind shift…."

Gayle suddenly clasped both hands to the side of her belly. "Look! He's doing his soft-shoe-shuffle. Feel." She pulled my hand over to her. "Do you feel it?"

She had been having Braxton-Hicks contractions for the last couple of weeks. Braxton-Hicks! It made me angry to think that some bearded pipe-sucking medical researcher had claimed part of my wife's body with his name. Who the hell is Braxton Hicks?

A ball bearing smooth rotation of a knee or elbow rolled against my palm. "I felt it," I said.

"Okay, let's go," she said, standing with her washing tub and soap under one arm.

"Right now?" I said.

"Why not? We have enough food for a week or two. We can get by."

I gazed up at the daunting company of cumulus clouds towering over us, harbingers of the Southwest Monsoon and the seasonal battle that would soon develop for dominance over the Indian Ocean.

"By the time we make the atoll, the sun will be setting in our faces," I said, a bit worried and staring at the chart as Gayle went down below. "Like the last time we hit the reef at Kashidou. It would be better to leave early tomorrow morning."

I listened to the familiar clicking and shutting of cupboards and latches, the closing drawers as Gayle stowed everything away belowdecks. "Okay, Okay. Let's just get going."

We left our mooring chains marked with a small red, tar-stained buoy. It was the same one we had dragged behind our ship at sea, at the end of a safety line all the way from England. It had never been much of a last chance, if one of us had fallen over. A seabird had once clung to it for an entire morning, obsessively clutching and teetering on it, with its wings outstretched in bursts of spray. I glanced back as we left this symbol of a *last chance* behind, knowing with some inexplicable certainty that we would never need it again.

37
Relying upon Wind

The morning breeze vanished, and Joya's sails undulated like the wet bed sheets hung out to dry. The sea bubbled in the midday heat. Our anchorage at Funidou Island vanished ever so slowly behind us in the haze. Neither of us suggested starting Joya's new motor. Maybe it was superstition, but both of us felt an absence of worry whenever we were on the wind. The wind or lack of it had delivered us safely thus far. And if it is true that whatever you are seeking is all too often right before your eyes, then Gayle's insistence on abandoning our voyage forced me to stare into the invisible proximity of a solution, one that would save our partnership. I would soon discover that the paternal commitment Gayle wanted from me was not to conveniences at all, but to the often wild and intuitive sensibilities she trusted in her life.

A breeze ruffled the ocean swells after awhile, and sent Joya on her way. Gayle leaned back in the old oak helmsman's seat, her legs kicked up on the windward rail. The helmsman's seat had once been an English office chair. I had removed its legs and secured it with a rotating bracket behind the helm. The irony was that someone had most likely endured decades behind a dreary desk, possibly dreaming of a life that the chair finally got.

I mused that it might not be so bad returning to a place like Santa Barbara in Southern California. We could rent a small house on mountain slopes covered in their rust-green nap of wild oaks, overlooking the windswept Channel Islands. "Lots of sunshine and warm weather. Our families nearby," I said, figuring Gayle would like that it was only an hour and a half drive to her mom in Culver City.

"Santa Barbara would be nice," she said cupping a match, her knee wedged in the helm spokes. Then with her cigarette squeezed between her knuckles, she wheeled Joya across the face of a steep cross sea. It was pointless to start up again, about her smoking pregnant.

"What's eating at me is...," I hesitated. The wind buffeted my hair, the heat of the morning sun softening my face. I felt the water effervescing as it compressed away from the hull. "I want to be the only ones responsible for our child. No one else."

Gayle glanced at me, then back up at the luff of the mainsail, correcting for a slight bubbling of wind behind the leading edge.

"What do you mean?"

"I mean I can't give up all that we've accomplished for someone else to start deciding things for us: a hospital, our parents, or even a doctor. I can't fly back to L.A. for that."

Nudging the wheel, Gayle's focus stiffened. She sat straight in her seat, her backbone following an invisible groove through the sea. The helm seemed to be turning her hand this way and that, holding a precise angle on the wind.

"So what do you want to do?" she asked.

"I don't know. Not yet."

Neither of us spoke further about it. Gayle remained steady at the helm toward Ari Atoll. Blue water splashed over the leeward rail, gushing down the deck and out the scuppers. At some point I thought back upon the glistening backs of a company of whales we had seen when we sailed to the Maldives. I had stood on the bowsprit to watch them make their way across a moonlit sea. They too were simply doing what they were doing, going where they were going in the soundless ordering of their journey.

38
Last Stop

Late that afternoon the haloed mounds of four or five islands rose on the western horizon. They belonged to a tiny atoll named Rasdu, where we would take refuge for the night, before continuing on to Ari Atoll, not much further to the west. After a couple of hours, we cautiously approached a very narrow channel into a hidden lagoon. We glided into the wobbling reflections of heavy limbed banyans, breadfruits and other trees we had never seen. Our mast passed closely under the sun streaked canopy. Dark shapes shallowed and slid back into the depths. A solid shadow suddenly reached up under our keel, and groaned under us, vibrating our bare feet on deck. We slid free, and came into the fiery glare of the sun. We shaded our eyes.

The lagoon appeared a crimson bed of coals, encircled by a wall of black forest. We noticed a cluster of people staring at us from the northeastern shore. There was no village in sight. We anchored, and launched our dinghy in their direction. By the time we pulled ashore, they had vanished into the forest.

The beach was soot-brown and cluttered with uprooted trees and rotting wood, all trapped by the gyre of currents in the lagoon.

"Such an odd feeling place," I said looking around.

"I hope these dudes aren't cannibals," Gayle remarked with her usual sarcasm.

"That's exactly the kind of joke people make before they're never heard of again."

A movement caught my eye.

Gayle noticed. "We've got company."

A small stick of a boy picked his way slowly over the driftwood towards us, like a washed up insect. He smiled nervously, with thin ebony lips and a fine jaw characteristic of his Indian ancestry. We greeted him, and I held up our two empty water containers. He insisted on taking them from me, and motioned for us to follow him.

Once in the shadows of the forest, he picked up his pace, and we hurried to keep up. The path felt soft and earthen underfoot compared to the compacted sand of other islands. We came to a cluster of coral rock houses skinned with moss. All of them appeared uninhabited. I looked at Gayle. She raised her eyebrows and looked around. A few meager gardens with bright red chilies peeked through crooked stake fences. A stalk of pendulous green papayas stood, vertically knife-slit to ripen. A very old wrinkle-faced lady appeared on the path, picking her way slowly in our direction. We smiled at her, but she walked right on past, her crusty pupils unseeing.

"This place gives me the creeps," Gayle said, looking around with her hands on her hips. The spindly boy pulled our water from a well, while seeming to keep an eye upon the edge of the clearing, where I suspected others were watching us.

The afternoon's revelation of what appeared to be agreement between Gayle and me for the birth of our child now presented more confusing problems. I knew the danger land was for both of us, and suddenly how little time it felt we had to fit our plans back into Santa Barbara. In fact any plans we tried to conceive evaporated like ocean spray on our decks.

That night I studied the charts for Ari Atoll where we would arrive the next day. Gayle was asleep in her bunk so I blew out the kerosene lanterns in the saloon, the fumes sweetening the darkness in their poisonous way, and climbed up on deck for one last check on Joya. The reflections of silver-edged clouds congregated over the absolute calm of the lagoon. I went to the bow and peered at Joya's chain. It hung directly downward, slack as if it had never reached the bottom.

The morning heat was suffocating, pressing down on us like a cushion over the sulfurous smell of frying eggs and the drone of flies from the galley.

"Shall we go on?" I asked Gayle. She had been clinking pots and china in the galley in an irritable way.

No answer.

I looked up at the stacks of cumulus clouds gathering, and climbed below. "So what do you want to do?"

"That's up to you." She climbed the steps right past me. From the deck I heard her say. "This is your trip."

"My trip! Of course, why would I think otherwise?" I gripped the edge of the sink muttering to myself. "I can stay out of her trip if that's the game. I'll just unload this bitch into an air-conditioned apartment in Los Angeles with all her fucking appliances and be done with it. Fatherhood and all."

I cursed again at the sickness in my heart, and clawed the edge of the sink. "How can you call the mother of your unborn child a bitch!" I hissed to myself. "Whose terrified little voice is this? Where's your iron to be a man! Where's your love!"

I glanced up the companionway to be sure I hadn't been overheard and finished the dishes, my body glistening in sweat. I climbed on deck. Gayle was hanging a pair of washed underwear on the rail.

"We're almost there," I said. "So let's just go."

Gayle brushed right past me to the helm and began to organize her things in the cockpit, her two shawls to keep from getting sunburnt, one to cover her legs and the other for her shoulders, her book, glasses, and zinc for her lips, and her sunhat.

I went back below, threw the compression lever over on the engine head, and cranked the flywheel handle till it started popping. I weighed anchor by myself on the foredeck, handing down loops of wet chain into the hawsepipe, noting how smooth and composed my movements were.

Gayle took the helm. She sat there silently sweating, like pink ice in the heat as we made the open sea and wind filled our sails. When I finished my deck work, I took over, and she went to the foredeck and began shampooing her hair from a plastic bucket. Then as the melancholy beauty of the Rasdu Islands slipped away in our wake, she began manicuring her nails, then her feet. I couldn't remember the last time I had seen her do that. Out in the middle of an empty ocean with porpoise silently skimming our bow wave, she preened herself as if she were going out on an imaginary town.

A few hours passed before the first scraggly-headed palms of Ari Atoll poked up over the horizon ahead. We had not spoken a word. As we entered the channel to the atoll, I climbed the ratlines standing on the first set of spreaders, wedged between the opposing tensions of the rigging wires, calling out directions of so many degrees to steer port or starboard. With the sun high and slightly behind us, the deep blue passages showed clearly through the reef. We followed the sandy white floor of the channel and wound our way through vertical walls of coral, undulating with luminous plants and flashing with reef fish.

We were passing a submerged island, resembling a wedge of kiwi fruit awash in sea foam, when suddenly a huge shadow caught my eye to port. Gayle saw it too, a giant black-winged manta ray soaring over the surface of the lagoon. Completely air born, landing with a thunderous "KAWUMP."

We turned to each other in amazement. The experience wiped us clean of the morning tensions, as the kinship with whales or porpoise somehow brings us back to our own magnificence in nature. The wind tugged at our sails, and we slid past empty thumbnail-sized isles, ringed by lagoons and palm lined beaches. There was no sign of habitation. I made for the clumps of two brotherly isles ahead, where I hoped to find us a safe anchorage.

39
Island Siblings

We eased off the main sheet in the protected water between the two islands, nearest to the smaller one. The last puff of air carried us into the rippling reflections of a huge banyan tree and a forest of palms. On the larger island opposite, the burnished gleam of several thatched roofs shone from the forest, pitched over white coral rock walls. The small dark shapes of children dashed down the beach to stare at our arrival. The larger shapes of some adults gathered behind them at the forest edge, their bodies barely distinguishable from palm trunks.

As the depth shallowed to about twelve fathoms between the islands, I pulled the slip knot on our kedge anchor. The chain roared out from the hawsepipe, twirling down into the deep sun-shafted blue. I turned and let go the foresail halyards, and the bronze piston hanks on the foresails hummed down the wires. My arms burned as I gathered up the sails, stiffened by sunlight and salt. Gayle left the helm to help me tie them up against the life lines, as Joya rounded up slowly by herself, grumbling her connection to the earth, the chain twisting taut, groaning, and flipping its links on the steel bow roller. Then all was silent.

We stood together in the cockpit, a stone's throw from the smaller island, named Kuda Fulidu. The forest beside us rose in a fountain of green, seeming fixed in a cascade back toward the lagoon. The narrow beach curved in lacy shadows under the palms that leaned over their watery mirror. The occasional fin darted across the surface making slurping sounds.

At the south end of the little isle, a pale avocado lagoon lay against the beach. There was no sign of life other than the inhospitable squawks of crows echoing from the tops of palms. Their black bodies sailed across the sky and melted into the orange corona overhead.

Gayle interrupted my musing. "Looks like we've got company."

Two small boys rowed a boat crabwise across the current from the bigger island. An old man stood stoically in the stern as if he were an arriving pharaoh. I braced myself to be ordered back out to sea, as when we first landed in the Maldives. The old man glided alongside, and his boys shifted the oars inboard. He wore a brimless cotton hat, collapsed on his head like a sunken biscuit. His hair had whitened like the shag end of a rope, and his mouth folded in where his teeth had once been. He looked at us in glances, piecing together the puzzle of our visit. Joya usually fascinated the islanders, compared to their simple coconut wood boats with lateen rigs, but this man kept his attention only upon us.

I invited him aboard. He declined, raising the flat of his hand. So I held out mine to shake his. "Frank," I said, pointing at my chest.

He extended his hand abruptly across our gunnels, as if this were why he had come, to show us he knew how to shake hands. His arm was stiff as a stick. "Mosabe," he said, pulling his arm quickly back to touch his own chest out of respect.

I squatted and looked into his face, relaxed as an old sail bent to its spars. He stood comfortably swaying with the movement of his *dhoni*. Gayle leaned back against the doghouse while we all took in the silence. Then suddenly at the top of his voice, as if so much blue sky could suck away the sound of a man, he started shouting something in Divehi. Seeing that I didn't understand, he nodded over at the sun, and slid the flat of his hand down his chest, his palm twisting vertically away like a fish toward his island.

I took this to mean we were invited for something, and thanked him. He pointed at the sun and dropped his finger. Again I guessed, he must mean after sunset. To avoid our usual embarrassment about being vegetarian, having to refuse eating a generously prepared marine delicacy, it was better to tell him straightaway. "Noon mas," I said in Divehi, waving a no finger in front of my closed lips.

He stared at me for a moment, and then barked at the boys to row him home.

Gayle went below without comment. I leaned down into the companionway hatch. "Looks like we're going out for dinner."

"You go ahead," she said.

"Ah, come on, Gayle. Don't be like that."

"I wouldn't mind spending some time alone, Frank."

"You're snubbing their hospitality. What other way can they take it. It's not polite. Not only that, it's odd."

"Maybe so. But I still want to be alone."

"Is something bothering you?"

"Nothing is bothering me. Just go ahead."

An hour before sunset I untied our dinghy from Joya's stern. I was about to climb in and row over to the old man's island, named Bodu Fulidu on our chart, when I spotted a boat in the channel. A large native *dhoni* with six oar positions stroked towards us.

"Looks like they're coming for us," I called belowdecks.

Gayle emerged wearing a clean blouse, and carrying her shore sandals. That just felt like a huge decision for her.

"I'm really glad you're coming."

She sidestepped past me along the edge of the cockpit coaming to the stern pulpit where I had lashed a little house for monkey. She lifted the flap door.

"You're not bringing Monkey?"

"He's not like Circe, she said. "He prefers the land. And anyway he's my date."

Monkey looked at me and began his awful chattering. Gayle had sewn a miniature blue vinyl heavy weather outfit for it, complete with a hood. Out at sea he stood atop his little house like a shrunken and hooded apparition chained to the seas.

The islanders of Bodu Fulidu had never seen a monkey, most not even a picture of one. Other than a few domesticated chickens, rats, and land crabs, there were no other land-dwelling animals we ever saw, not even cats. In fact, the Maldives could scarcely be called land at all, not in the usual sense. There was no soil, rivers or lakes, to support land life. The largest island was not much more than a square mile and the rest were much smaller, and supported only one small village each. And that was only if there was potable water underground. Few islands had it. Only about two hundred of about twelve hundred were inhabited, with islanders living off fish and coconuts for the most part. The islands were nothing more than lily pads upon which these seafaring folk raised their families.

As the boatmen rowed us ashore, sharp eyed children spotted Monkey pacing Gayle's forearm. Circe's kittens had not stirred up any more interest on Male than would an unusual but inedible fish. As I leashed Monkey upon a tall shrub on shore, all the children crowded excitedly around. Some dashed back home, returning quickly with coconut shell dishes of sweetened milk tea, banana, coconut meat, and bits of fish. Monkey grabbed at everything and ate until his eyes began to droop.

The setting sun streaked the root-mounded paths as Mosabe led us to his house. It was just one room with a sand floor, crowded with bare-chested men wearing sarongs, and women in faded cotton smock dresses. Mosabe singled out a humble man in his forties and introduced him as "Veriyaa," which we later found out means chief. We were seated in the only two chairs in the room, as younger children peeked shyly around the legs of their parents.

A wick flamed in a dish of coconut oil, and flickered into the thatched rafters over banyan root spars, some breadfruit lumber, and bundles of stained canvas sails stored there. A narrow wooden bed platform stood in the corner of the room with a hand mirror and some effects on a single black hardwood shelf. Behind Mosabe's pillow a dark wooden box was locked with an aged padlock.

The islanders served us curried squash, egg pancakes, and some unidentifiable morsels, along with steaming rice smelling of mold, but all prepared with great care. A meal without fish probably seemed crazy to them. It would be like refusing water as that's all they had to eat out here.

After dinner, a young girl performed a dance with drumming accompaniment, while I endured the pain of some kind of flesh-eating louse in my chair. The undersides of Gayle's legs were protected by her sari. I cooled the burning lumps with spit on my fingers as secretly as I could, but everyone noticed. Gayle and I were the only ones sitting so I got off my hot seat and squatted with them.

When the islanders led us back to the boat, the forest danced in a mesmerizing beauty of flashlights and kerosene lanterns. I invited everyone to come see us aboard, with a sweeping arm gesture out toward Joya, and waved good bye.

Back aboard Joya, Gayle stabbed her toothbrush in and out of her mouth over the small oval of our porcelain sink. "Why did you invite all those people back to Joya?"

"It was a gesture of hospitality. In return for tonight."

"How would you like me to invite a whole village over to visit, without talking to you first?"

"It seemed the obvious thing to do. That you would have done the same."

"I told you I needed some time alone."

"Yes but..."

"And you invite the whole village. Like I'm not even here."

"It was the right thing to do."

"Right for you. Not for me."

"Don't worry, Gayle. You're getting all bothered for nothing. They're not going to come. No one probably understood anyway."

Gayle boosted herself into her bunk, and turned away toward the hull, with the sheet cinched up around her neck.

I climbed back up the companionway and poked my head through the hatch, breathing deeply. The fragrance of night-blooming plants drifted on the air as Joya slid across the currents, as if she were working her way upstream to spawn, seeking her memory place.

40
Hospitality

I heard it first, then again, the hollow *thunk* of an oar-strike against the hull of a wooden boat, echoing from across the channel. Then I heard distant voices, a lot of them. I looked over at Gayle, lying in her bunk, absorbed in her book. I stood on my bed casually, and slowly poked my head out the aft hatch, squinting against the glare through a thin overcast. I saw one boat, then the shapes of several more behind, and still more being launched from the beach at Bodu Fulidu. *Oh my God,* I said to myself. I reached for the binoculars in the doghouse and peered at what seemed to be the entire village, more than a hundred people dressed in their Sunday best, packed into an armada of boats heading our way.

"Gayle," I whispered.

No answer.

"Jesus, you're not going to believe this. You better take a look."

She poked her head out the hatch, shrugging away the binoculars, and groaned a long groan as she sank back. "Frank, I'm not ready for this."

"What should we do?" I asked.

"I don't care. This is your party."

"You're just going to lock yourself in your cabin?"

"Or take the dinghy out to sea," she replied quite seriously.

"After all their sweet hospitality last night!"

"Look, I'm nauseated. Like I'm going to barf. They're always staring at me, especially the women, and shouting because I can't understand what they say. It makes my head pound. You are going to have to deal with it."

I scarcely had time to pull on my shorts and start boiling pots of water for tea, when the first boat arrived at our stern. Gayle closed her cabin door with a solid *clunk*.

I helped everyone aboard, little girls wearing bangles, pierced earrings, and island-made dresses. Some of the boys even wore shoes. Babies were handed aboard, their eyebrows connected with charcoal dust like the wings of a crow. More boats arrived. Each group handed me a gift: a few eggs tied up in a scrap of cloth, a bundle of coconuts, papayas, shells, and so on.

Gayle's emotional honesty was painful for me. In my family people put on a good face, no matter what torture any of us were going through. My father was mute as a tar pit full of sunken dinosaur bones, and my mother had a kind of pioneering spirit of not relying upon or involving others in personal matters, not even herself in her own it seemed. It was not altogether a bad trait. Her indomitable state of wellbeing, health, and eventual longevity argued somehow for whatever she concealed. Gayle's transparency was threatening to me because I didn't know how to rely upon it.

Islanders peeked into her room from time to time, as there weren't any locks, but then backed their heads out as if a cobra had hissed at them. No one seemed to mind though. Most were too respectful or fearful to even sit on our saloon seats. But they could not help gawking at our equipment, their mouths in an astonished oval over the stainless galley sink and pumps, our jars of spices, the varnished cherry cabinetry, the shelves of books, the stacks of navigational charts. The women were especially dumbstruck by the propane oven and stove.

I dashed up and down, welcoming or sending off each load of visitors. Surprisingly, Gayle emerged and helped me collect and rewash tea glasses. She shoved in some music cassettes, and demonstrated the stove burners, but her noticeably dispirited effort was obvious to me. She had her reasons, but I couldn't help but feel unworthy of being either the islanders' guests or their hosts.

Several women gestured to Gayle's stomach, looking warmly and inquisitively into her eyes. "Maaban'du, maaban'du," they said touching their bellies and nodding to each other.

Gayle turned away and disappeared up on deck through the foc'sle. She took up a position on the end of the bowsprit, far from everyone as she could get.

I concentrated on some men admiring Joya's topsides, tracing scarf joints with their fingers, poking their nails into rubbery seams of synthetic deck caulking. They marveled at wire splices and other work I felt proud to have done. I too would have expressed my appreciation for the sea-kindly grace and superior simplicity of their coconut-wood boats. The deep shine of acknowledgement in their eyes and in mine was for the passion sailors share for the sea. They never made me uncomfortable over our unimaginably more expensive and sophisticated boat. What they had was enough, and they knew it.

Just then, my glowering and fearsome figurehead wrenched herself off the bow. She clunked past us like a piece of carved wood, down the companionway, and repositioned herself below in her cabin.

Mosabe and his friend, Abdullah, gathered around me like worried mothers, not a sign of being offended. Abdullah had been one of the men who rowed us back from dinner last night, a muscular but Lilliputian sized man. His forehead crinkled and worried, motioning along the direction of Gayle's splintery trail. Mosabe nodded nervously in agreement, his cheeks sunken even further into his toothless spaces.

In a short conversation of mostly gestures, and expressions, they asked if she was sick. I said no, that she was pregnant.

"Aaaaah, maaban'du, maaban'du."

Then they asked if she missed her home. I said a little with my fingers in a pinch. They knew I was lying, and motioned firmly that I should go take care of her. I hesitated but they patted me on the sides of my arms, kneading me like a piece of raw dough toward the hatchway.

Just then Gayle reemerged, and went back to her position on the bowsprit. She sat with her chin on her knees, gazing forlornly seaward. Of course, the islanders must have understood that the stakes were high, for Gayle to be so far from home, pregnant. If they wondered why we had come, they only tried to make us feel more welcome.

I went forward and put my arm around Gayle's shoulders. They were tense.

"Are we going to be good parents?" she asked.

"Yes, of course. It's all going to work somehow."

Gayle laid her head on my shoulder. I sat there till my arm would break, not daring to move, as the last of the islanders slipped into their boats, waving silent goodbyes.

41
The Agreement

The next morning Gayle and I rowed over to explore the uninhabited island next to us. Gayle plunked her basket down under some palm shade. Vines with pale yellow tubular flowers, sweet-smelling as honeysuckle, reached out over the bone-white sand. She had insisted on bringing a mosquito net with her in a large straw market basket.

"Who the hell brings a mosquito net to the beach?" I said amused and shaking my head.

"Don't worry! You brought your snorkel and mask, I brought my mosquito net."

Gayle always made me laugh. She went to shore and turned, waiting for me to plunge in first. Then Gayle cleaved in backwards like a ship being launched, the bulb of her tummy raising a wave.

We drifted over a forest of corals, mesmerized by such a forbiddingly beautiful garden. Eden it was. Valleys of white sand, wrinkled like skin by ocean currents and weaving through brain corals oozing reds and purples into the undulating light. Reef fish flashed their sides like brush strokes on liquid pages, before dissolving back into their sea camouflage. We snorkeled over creamy plains of antler corals, which shallowed to the plunging hard blue edge of the reef. We descended over the vertical face, skimming over giant clams crowded along ledges, their luminous purple-black lips agape in shafts of sinking sunlight.

The enveloping warmth erased the boundaries of my own flesh, as I bobbed up and down like a translucent jelly. Suddenly, something violently seized my leg. I knew it was Gayle, but my body was already shot through with adrenalin. I spun around as gleeful bubbles burst from her facemask. She kicked furiously to escape, but I caught up quickly with fins and sank my teeth into her pumping rump. I heard her scream from underwater. I apologized back on the beach for the force of my bite, but the bluish impression of my teeth below her bikini elastic was pleasing.

Gayle walked up the beach to check on Monkey's water under a palm where she had leashed him. I flopped face first onto the sand, flat as a sand dab with one eye up. I pulled warm sand to my chest and dished out a hollow place with my jaw to lay my cheek, just as I had done growing up in Southern California. My body had melted into bliss, when Gayle declared, "That's it, I'm gonna hang it up. I just heard one."

I groaned, getting to my feet to help her suspend the mosquito net she brought. It drooped from a palm frond like a snagged piece of blue synthetic refuse that might endanger wildlife. "You can't tell me you're going to sit under that thing. You can't be serious?"

Paying no attention to me, she scooted her towel under and crawled in. Her shape inside looked like the smoky organs of a beached jellyfish. "You know there's a point when you must give in. Become part of your surroundings. Even if you get mosquito bites."

Gayle jabbed her leg out from under the edge of the net to display the silver dollar-sized scar on her ankle from a staph infection. "That was a mosquito bite. Remember?"

So that was how it started that first day, me lying beside my blue veiled mummy on the shore of tropical paradise. It wasn't long before mummy began to bake in her windless oven. I suggested exploring the island, and we followed a man-made path through a dense tropical forest leaning in from either side. These paths sheared across the head of many islands in north-south directions are what the islanders called wind roads, which allow the monsoon winds to cleanse them of mosquitoes.

We followed the beach scallops back around the west side. Gayle had an uncanny ability to spot cowry shells budding in empty stretches of shoreline. She dashed from one to the next, twisting their shiny patterned surfaces over in her sandy palm. Crowds of pinkish land crabs divided in our path, fleeing into the forest and down the beach. Overhead the squawk of crows echoed in the sky, and our feet slipped into the sand like the softest socks.

I stopped on the shore realizing that not a scrap of man-made things, not even a splinter could be found to remind us of where we had come from. But oddest of all was that on the very brink of our relationship crumbling, the sweep of these pristine sands felt full of promise, newly born themselves and beaconing Gayle and I. Here was a simple truth, no matter what mankind could conceive of or destroy, this beauty belonged to us. Standing there I felt that just maybe, maybe we were on the threshold of everything we had fought for. What a terrible twist of fate, I thought, that this island was likely to be the very last stop in our voyage together.

Before we rowed back to Joya, Gayle posed for a picture. I had grabbed my corroded old Pentax 35mm as we disembarked for the island, which felt unexplainably noteworthy at the time. We had taken so few photos in all our travels, and taking this one had an official feel to it. In the background over the shore bushes the distant white sliver of Joya floated on a silvery horizon. Many years later I would look at this photo as if in the moment again, Gayle cradling Monkey and clutching his gray whiskered head to her breast. She looked back at me as if through time, the significance of where she was standing so alive in her eyes.

We motored away. Gayle stroked the deck with the tip of her finger, maybe feeling the engine vibration, maybe feeling the pain of giving herself a blister. There was a scramble of reefs ahead and I needed to check the chart. I pulled the throttle back and stepped over to the chart table in the doghouse, too dispirited to even ask her to take the helm. Joya bumped on some swells coming in over the barrier reef, and our eyes met. I could not turn away, nor did she.

The helm spokes flicked back and forth with no one to take hold of them. My heart was knocking crazily. My neck suddenly ached. Something I had to say was unknotting itself from deep within my tissue. I went over and sat in front of her on the deck.

"Gayle…" But the words did not come.

She tilted her eyes up again, peering at me from over the top of her knees tucked up under her chin.

Then it came, words solid as stones from my throat. "I want to have our baby on that little island," I said. "Just the two of us."

Gayle's expression did not change. Her eyes steadied on me.

What I had said now ricocheted back into my head like gunfire. I had taken myself by complete surprise. The truth had just sprung out. I felt suddenly horrified that I had now fully divulged how alienated I was from her. How irreconcilable were our differences. I had denied her humblest wish, a few modern conveniences to have her baby, and her family nearby to care for her. A girl who never had anything, and I had turned my back on the one most important thing she had ever asked of me. Now it surely seemed the chance to be a family and raise my child was lost.

"Where would we live?" Gayle asked.

She said it as simply as that! Without laughing out loud. I might have even laughed with her. Having a baby on an uninhabited patch of sand, barely mapped in the middle of an ocean! Absolutely nothing there. Even I could laugh at the insanity of that. But she had asked, *Where would we live?* And even crazier, I knew the answer. The whole thing came to me in a stream as if I had already planned everything.

"The islanders over at Bodu Fulidu Island could build us a house. Just like theirs. Corral rock walls. A thatch roof."

"And would you deliver the baby?"

"Yes! I'll figure it out. Just like everything we've done. We can get books from the States."

The sun seemed to swing around us as Joya idled into a wide breathless circle. Gayle bent her head, sitting perfectly still. An errant breeze combed sunburnt strands of her hair across her face. The main boom thumped as the untended mainsail seized a puff, but then sagged back into an empty pocket of canvas.

She looked up. "That's what I want to do."

"You really do?"

"Yes," she said. "I think having our baby on that little island, and you delivering it will make us all very united. Very quickly."

Thrilled was hardly the word for what I felt. I could scarcely grasp what had just happened. In only seconds the months of crisis over what to do had been resolved; our destiny, invisible till now, had suddenly appeared. I dared not think for a second. Gayle shaded her eyes to look back at the island, and turned back to me.

"Before I have this baby out here," she said, "I want a proper medical examination. To make sure everything is okay."

I saw a mature woman in her eyes suddenly, vulnerable and strong, seeking more than I knew how to give, more than I could have ever hoped for, seeking the father I yearned to be. I would do anything for her.

"Of course, we can go to a hospital. Anywhere! India or maybe better we go to Singapore. Anywhere you want, Gayle."

"I would prefer Singapore," she said.

"That's fine. We'll also need supplies, all our stuff for the birth."

The tangled shadows of spars and sails shifted back and forth across the deck, reminding us that we had been idling around in a windless circle. We laughed. Gayle jumped up and grasped the helm.

"You should probably know now, Frank, I considered going home alone. Your mother offered me a place to stay with her and Homer in Santa Barbara."

That was news! Unbeknownst to me, my own mother had tried to save Gayle from her son's wits, which she had joked were "half baked" when I was a kid.

"But my decision," Gayle said, looking down at her tummy, "is based on what we know is best for this little guy. I can tell he approves of this idea."

We set our twin running sails that spread like red wings across the blue. Gayle and I had found our home in the sea. That was the most glorious day we surged back to the capital island of Male.

42
Stepping Ashore

The huge presumptions we had made to have a baby on this uninhabited island, seemed nothing more than details in the exhilarated state we were in, not the least of which was our assumption we would be able to obtain permission to live there. Uninhabited islands, as we had discovered upon our arrival in the Maldives, are well accounted for.

Then there was the fact that not all islands had fresh water. I already figured we could collect and store rainwater if necessary, as we had done aboard Joya. But without the help from islanders across the channel, we would never be able to build a native house in time. I could not imagine how they could they refuse us.

Then there were the logistics of getting a medical checkup and supplies in Singapore. Absolutely every single thing a family would need to survive and have a new baby on a deserted island would have to be determined, purchased, and shipped a couple thousand miles across the Indian Ocean to the island of Male, in only three months. That would be Gayle's eighth, which was the last month an airline will allow a pregnant woman to fly.

Once back in Male with all our supplies received and our house built, we would load everything and ourselves into a native boat bound for our island. Let people think we were off our rockers. No matter how outrageous the journey, it now felt self fulfilling, a solid plan.

Our plan also assumed we would find a solution for Joya. Leaving her unattended was not an option. Too many things could go wrong. Hiring a delivery captain to come from the West posed the inconceivable burden and expense of arranging her care somewhere else in the world. There was no way around it; she would have to be sold. But who on a moment's notice would travel halfway around the world to remote islands, to buy a ship they'd never seen, a ship in deep water – in the midst of a long and challenging sea voyage?

I remembered that the Glenan Sailing School instructor, who had stayed aboard with us in England, had asked me to let him know if we ever decided to part with Joya. I felt contempt for him to suggest such a thing at the time, just as we were beginning our voyage. Yet I had wedged the scrap of paper with his address in an old filing folder. When we got back to Male, I sent him a telegram.

It was the second week in April, about three and a half months until Gayle's due date at the end of July, and only a two and a half month window in which the airline would allow us to fly back to the Maldives from Singapore. Gayle and I checked in with postmaster, Rashid. He gathered up three letters, including a brown envelope that looked like a telegram. He clutched them back out of reach.

"You will sell your boat?" he asked, obviously having read our telegram back from Paul.

"Yes, we are."

"Where will you live?"

"Ari Atoll."

He looked out the postal window over the lagoon and turned back to us. "But nothing there," he said. "What will you do with the monkey?"

Rashid was clearly not going to give us our mail until we resolved this matter. He adored Monkey, who usually rode on our shoulders into the post office. He had confided in us that his two wives were always jealous of one another, saying, "Too much trouble all the time in the house. I will never marry again. But love your monkey. I do." He dared to say that with sad seductive eyes. I looked at Gayle. She nodded her approval.

"All right, you can have him."

Astonished, his round, well-fed administrator's face snapped awake. "This is a great honor." He hurriedly pushed our mail into our hands. "I promise you, I will treat your monkey like my own child."

We walked out staring at a brittle piece of brown folded paper covered in ornate Maldivian seals. It was the telegram from Paul in Florida that we had been waiting for.

"Open it! Open it!" Gayle demanded. She read over my shoulder. *Will come immediately to buy Joya. Best, Paul and Marion.* Gayle jumped off the ground. "We did it. We did it." She dragged me off, skipping like a kid along the street to the airline office. We booked a flight to Singapore.

As we walked back to the harbor, rows of white flags fluttered hard atop the walls of the mosque. The midmorning prayers broadcast from speakers hung in clusters off the minarets. All vehicles and pedestrians stopped to bow their heads. We stood with them until the last lilting pitch of the Islamic prayer had been sung.

"I am afraid the islanders might not accept us," Gayle said as we continued.

"Don't worry. They're family people. Like we are. Mormon or Muslim doesn't matter here."

"I was raised Mormon, but I don't consider myself any religion."

"Well I think Maldivians are islanders first. Women wear bright colors. No veils or head scarves. We never saw anyone kneeling to the east out in the islands. Not even a structure used as a mosque out there. There's none of the religious fervor found in other Islamic countries. Why would they object to us?"

Gayle studied my face, blushing to try and think of why she might be rejected by the islanders. "I don't know. Would our baby be a citizen?"

"I asked Abdulla Kamaldeen. He told me our child has to be raised a Muslim for seven years to be a Maldivian. He'll be an American because we are, but there's no way of getting him a passport here."

"So when he's born he'll have no nationality?"

"No American agency will even know he exists until we walk into an embassy with him one day. He won't even have a birth certificate. He'll be the very first Kuda Fuliduian."

43
An Elder's Decision

A few days later we sailed back to Ari Atoll to ask permission from the neighboring islanders to live on Kuda Fulidu, and if they would construct a native style house for us. This time we took a translator, cricket-like Shareef who had worked odd jobs for us while we repaired Joya up on the beach in Male. Mostly he lay in the cockpit reading books from our library. His disheveled black mop of a head popped up bright-eyed, always cheerful no matter how annoyed I was to find him taking time off again. I would have fired him, but Gayle defended his shameless claim to free time.

The Bodu Fulidu islanders recognized our ship approaching from seaward. Through my binoculars I watched them drag Mosabe's big *dhoni* down the beach, gripping the gunnels on each side, their knees splashing across the lagoon shallows. We dropped anchor in the same place between the two islands. Mosabe's two young conscripts oared the old man out, stiff and erect as a statue in the stern. Gayle made *kire du sa,* nice and milky and sweet with evaporated milk, the way islanders make their tea.

Mosabe climbed the boarding ladder in his faded persimmon and white checkered sarong. His white cotton shirt was frayed, and his brimless cap sat like a squashed muffin on his head. I caught a whiff of stale urine as he stepped past, and sat opposite me on the straw mat I had rolled out on deck. The young boys at the oars remained in his *dhoni* to fend it off Joya.

Mosabe cleared his throat, testing the tea Gayle served him, but it was still too hot.

Shareef asked him who owned the island.

Mosabe indicated that he did. Then in a high windblown voice he explained that he had been the medicine man for the last Sultan, and had received the island in return for his cures. Shareef translated.

I told him in English how much we loved the little island, how at home we felt there, and that our baby was due in about three months. I paused for Shareef to translate, but he just smiled dumbly, as if he had forgotten his job and wanted me to finish telling my story.

How could the old man not understand, I thought, with Gayle so pregnant? The urgency of getting settled had to be obvious. No islander would ever think of having a baby on a boat. "We want to ask for your permission to live here and have our baby," I said, pointing toward the little island.

The old man's speckled eyes turned to Shareef, who came out of his trance to translate. He went on and on, well beyond the time it should have taken to convey the simple meaning of my words, even with some embellishment.

Gayle and I glanced at each other. I could have kicked Shareef to stop, but Mosabe was listening patiently. Then Shareef stopped talking, and there was a long silence. Joya swayed back and forth like a metronome in the currents.

Mosabe stood.

Gayle and I stood with him.

He solemnly muttered five or six words, then "Salaam," with his right hand held up prayer-like, he turned and climbed directly down into his boat. He barely glanced at me. It did not look good. For all we knew he made his decisions by which direction the wind blew the threads on his cap. We waved goodbye.

Shareef leaned back on the doghouse roof, as if making or breaking a deal were all in the course of a day's business for him.

"What?" I asked him.

His dark intelligent eyes sparkled. It was impossible to guess his mind.

"What did he say?" I demanded.

Shareef shrugged. "The old man said, 'It's okay.'"

"That's all?"

"Yes, it's all okay, everything you want to do."

"They will build the house?" I asked.

Shareef broke into a slow, mischievous grin. "Everything," he said.

I turned to Gayle. She sat quietly on the doghouse roof. Her eyes looked soft, watering in the breeze. I jumped up to sit beside her. She took my hand and clung to it.

"Are you worried?" I whispered.

"A little."

"Why?"

"There's only two people in the world I trust," she said. "That's you and my mom. At least I have you. So I guess I know everything will be all right."

Early the next morning Gayle, Shareef, and I rowed over to Kuda Fulidu to scout a building site. I hopped into the shallows on the southern shore. My toes dug into the warm wet-sand to drag the bow of our dinghy up the beach. Gayle slipped a sandy arm through mine. "I can't believe this is our new home! Do you think the old man will charge much for rent?"

"My bet is that he wants to help. And the money he wants will only be a little for us, but a lot for him." Gayle pulled me toward a shady clearing overlooking the lagoon, the same place where I had photographed her cradling Monkey ten days earlier. "This is where I want our house," she said.

"Don't you think we should check out the north end?"

"Nope. This is the spot where I want to have my baby."

"The islanders on Bodu Fulidu built their village on the north end. Probably for a good reason." I looked out through the palms for a bearing on the sun.

Gayle stood on her toes to be certain Shareef was at a distance, and dropped into a squat to take a pee. "Now I've marked it." Gayle wiggled her bottom and reached up for my hand.

Shareef emerged from between some bushes, fussily unsnagging himself like a town-boy.

"What do you think about this spot?" I asked. "Will our house get blown away by the Southwest Monsoon?"

"I don't think so." He rolled his ping pong ball eyes away unconvincingly. It crossed my mind that the services of a would-be con man or an idiot are the most readily available to a foreigner. But we had to trust Shareef. In fact we had to trust almost every opportunity and person to accomplish so much so quickly.

"Okay. Let's sketch it out."

Gayle and I dragged sticks through the sand to draw the outlines of a little two-room house. It had a 20 by 20 foot bedroom-living area, and an 8 by 16 foot kitchen with a back door. We needed something to mark the foundation corners but there was nothing, no rocks, or fallen limbs, not even a stick that wasn't rotting. So I drew a treasure map, pacing off the corners of the house from easily identifiable palms, one that curved up like an elephant's trunk at the southeast corner, and a tulip cluster of three on the southwest corner. At worst, if Shareef simply positioned the house under the only huge banyan tree on the south end of the island and faced the lagoon, the setting was stunning, a dream tropical paradise that was real.

The next day Shareef firmed up the details with Mosabe. The rent the old man decided to charge was the equivalent of twelve US dollars per month. Period. No adjustments for inflation or periods of bad fishing for the rest of our lives, simply twelve dollars per month. We would have to agree not to cut wood or pick coconuts. These things belonged to Mosabe. (I had already found it physically impossible to inchworm up a coconut tree.) Shareef said the islanders had agreed to build our house, but that we must provide a boat to ferry workers back and forth from Bodu Fulidu, as their boats were needed for fishing every day. The total cost of the men would be a few *rufiyaa* for their food or about 1 U.S. dollar per day, for all of them. The coral rock and thatch would cost nothing, as these were resources easily gathered from the island. If we wanted glass windows or a cement floor, we would have to bring these materials from Male. Mosabe said he could supply coconut beams for rafters.

Shareef told us he would speak to his uncle in Male, who had a boat and crew we might be able to hire. I made it clear to Shareef, once again, that all our plans hinged upon him and Mosabe. That by the time we returned to the Maldives from Singapore, our commitment would be irreversible. Gayle would be too pregnant to be permitted to fly anywhere else. We would be committed to having our baby in the Maldives. Our house had to be finished.

Shareef gave his little cricket nod, far too slight a nod for the size of the task facing him. I looked over at Gayle who was closely studying Shareef. Joya lay serenely at anchor in the lagoon. Our entire stakes were on Shareef.

"Don't worry," Shareef said. "I promise to have your house ready by the time you get back."

44
Joya's Sale

The very day we anchored back at Male, a launch made its way out to us. It bounced over unusually turbulent gray water hurrying in from the west. A panoramic dark stain wicked up from below the horizon, darker in the bowels, and unstretching itself overhead.

Someone hailed from the launch. "Joya! Joya!" A lanky, bearded figure with a crop of blond hair leaned out in a yellow sea coat. "Joya!" he hailed again.

It was Paul with that big seaman's smile that could conceal any disaster or hardship. His appearance had scarcely changed in the five years since he'd stayed aboard with us in England. He must have left Florida the same day he telegrammed us. A woman and her eight-year-old daughter hung on beside him, huddled up against the wind and looking seasick. I waved back.

They climbed aboard and we embraced, all talking at once with excitement. Paul instructed the driver of the launch to wait alongside. We went below out of the weather and gathered around the saloon table. Paul's eyes were smaller and rounder than I remembered, his nose narrower and lumpier, his manner more anxious.

Marion appeared to be about ten years older than Paul. They wore matching designer looking sea coats, and expensive jeans. She was pretty, physically fit, with brown shoulder length hair, cut professionally. The first smell of perfume in our ship somehow eliminated the distance they had travelled.

She sat bolt upright, going over the terms of the sale she must have worked out at her kitchen table in Florida. She told us her second husband had recently died of a brain tumor. She put a stack of travelers checks on the table. She wanted every detail of the sale in writing, including guarantees, such as Joya's hull being sound, which we narrowed down to being free of teredo worms. Gayle and I shared a look over the absurdity of guarantees as Joya pitched uncomfortably in the swell. Marion and her daughter might be hanging onto their stomachs. Paul knew it too, and enthusiastically pointed out all the meticulous care Joya had received to bolster Marion's confidence.

I remembered how O'Riordan tapped his cane down to his ship on the river. I'd find him sitting alone in one opened corner of the cockpit tarpaulin, smoking his pipe. As I signed the sale papers, it meant nothing to me that Marion could not pay all the money, that we would have to wait a year for the balance until her husband's estate had settled. This was the first time O'Riordin and I had parted ways; I would not be growing old with my ship, and dreaming of a voyage I would never take.

Shafts of sunlight broke through the darkening clouds and slashed down through the main deck skylight, landing in a square beam upon the saloon table. The rocking glare and shouldering sea gave Marion an inquiring pause. Her features had settled into middle age without ever having been uncreased by wind. Yet some kernel of wildness had taken root. She took her turn to sign the documents with an obvious determination to overcome her queasiness.

Gayle looked up at me as if to say, *this woman has no idea what she's in for. She's not in her right mind bringing a young child out here.* Paul stood behind Marion with his hands on her shoulders, impatient to leave.

Marion suddenly fixed her eyes on Gayle. "How is it living aboard a boat?" she asked. "How is it to be at sea?"

The question was so awkwardly placed, coming upon the heels of just purchasing Joya, in the middle of an ocean. Even Gayle was momentarily at a loss to respond. "You'll get used to it," Gayle said, in an encouraging tone. "You'll just have to hang in there."

"We should be getting back," Paul said. "The launch is waiting." Turning to me, "I want to leave on the Northeast Monsoon for Sri Lanka as soon as possible, and we have a lot to do. How soon can you hand Joya over to us?"

"We can pack a few bags and give her to you anytime. We're not taking anything. We're leaving it all for you. Spare parts, tools, basically everything."

"How about in three days?"

I looked at Gayle, and she nodded.

Paul stood, but Marion paused for Gayle to stroke her daughter's hair. That was the last time I ever looked Paul closely in the eye. He turned to climb the companionway ladder, the same ladder he would someday run up, shouting for everyone to abandon ship.

45
Parting Maelstrom

Late that night after we sold Joya, I felt my skin pulling against the mattress. Our ship surged over unusually large swells in the lagoon. The hull creaked with the strain. The hoarse howl of an old wind sounded somewhere high above the deck. It was not the sound of the usual squall. Not the prancing chatter of a mischievous wind, or a solid good blow that makes for a wild and strenuous ride, or an angry wind that makes sea life miserable and sometimes frightening. No, this wind had a pernicious tone that made me shudder in my sleep, a force with deadly business.

My eyes opened in the groaning cabin dark. High above a raspy whistle shredded the night. I sat up and peered closely at the bulkhead clock. It was 4:30 am, the *hour of the wolf,* the hour before dawn when people for ages have believed that demons are about, when most people die, and most babies are born.

"What is it?" Gayle asked from the darkness.

"I don't know. Whatever it is, it's just beginning."

I climbed from my bunk feeling that familiar claw in my gut - that nausea of apprehension for sea duty at its worst. I dragged my heavy weather gear and sea harness from the wet closet in the head, and wedged myself in the cabin doorway to tug on my sea pants, stamping my heels down into my boots. I grabbed the companionway ladder, my arms and legs feeling almost too weak to climb, and threw back the deck hatch. I jerked my hand back remembering how my fingers got smashed once in strong wind as the hatch floated on its rails from high interior pressure.

I pulled myself up on deck. The blow shoved me aft against the doghouse. I locked my arm over the main boom, jerking in its cradle as if it was possessed. Only a half mile away, where the lights of Male should have been it was pitch-black, a howling obscurity. My eyes burned and my cheeks vibrated in the chill.

I bent and handed my way forward to check our anchors. Midway I clung to the rattling shrouds. The storm was gathering force quickly. Had a cyclone dipped south? Waves should never be breaking in the lagoon. White water swooshed past as I crouched down to check our anchor lines. The oversized main braided anchor rode and the smaller secondary rode were cinched hard as steel cables around the windlass. They stuck into the lacey faces of the waves like tendons pulled out of the muscle. I stared, numb and bewildered over what to do, as Joya bucked crests throwing plumes of spray back over the ship.

I tried to reason out our predicament. There was no chance of running for the open sea, not through the surrounding reefs. Our anchors would never hold, of that I was certain. I put my hand around the hawser of our main anchor to feel the tension. It was bone hard. At the moment there was no vibration to indicate that the anchor was dragging on the bottom. For an instant, my ear caught a roaring sound off the stern. I lifted my head and could hear large waves thundering on the reefs to our lee. Escape was impossible, even if Joya were wrecked and we took to the life raft, we would not survive the surf. And beyond that, there was nothing for thousands of miles, just the raging void of the Indian Ocean.

I handed my way back to the cockpit and flicked on our decklights shining down from the first set of rigging spreaders. Air born foam bolted through our hollow of light as Gayle appeared at my side. She peered out from the cinched oval of her heavy weather hood and seized my arm. The monstrous shape of a freighter emerged in the smoking opacity of our decklights. Its stern slowly swung towards our bow as it dragged anchor. The liferaft! But the words never came. There wasn't time. The dented black plates, the lumpy iron welds and barnacled red blade of her leviathan rudder raked over our braided nylon anchor warp, just missing our bowsprit.

The warp exploded with a loud bang at the winch drum and slithered out through the bow roller. Joya staggered back upon her one remaining anchor with the freighter sliding closely to port. The silhouettes of its crew members raced frantically back and forth, past the illuminated pilot house windows as the old engine sluggishly thumped and groaned to start.

I rushed forward to peer over our bow again. Our remaining anchor warp hung slack in its roller.

"WE'RE ADRIFT!" I shouted to Gayle.

Grabbing the helm spokes, Gayle laid Joya over under bare poles to reduce our speed to leeward. I handed my way aft along the guard rail, feeling absolutely sick in my guts. The dreaded reality now was that our lives were quite in danger. I plunged down the companionway ladder into the oddly serene and crypt-like cavity of our home, its single kerosene lamp rocking in its gimbal. I frantically tore away the side boards to the engine compartment and began cranking the flywheel. There was nothing I wouldn't have sacrificed for the solid thumping of that piston. The sound of the engine starting brought me out of shock.

Gayle and I gripped the hand hold around the compass binnacle, staring over the side, praying for a fraction of a knot made good. The wind began to ease and the smoky wicks of Male's lights flickered to port. Amazingly, Gayle had kept us in the center of the channel.

With first break of the soot-gray dawn, Joya heeled hard over as we bucked our way a mile north to the lee of a small island. We crowded in with several Korean fishing boats and a small freighter. I dropped our only remaining anchor astern. Then I loaded the dinghy with mooring equipment and dove over the reef, walking on the bottom underwater like someone without gravity on the moon, lugging armfuls of shackles and short lengths of chain to secure our bow to giant brain corals.

Gayle was seasick and exhausted, her mood sullen. I found her crawled up into my bunk. I leaned over the bunk boards with my swollen palms resting lightly on the side of her tummy and felt our little one kicking around in his own sea. My hands were nearly too swollen by rope and chain to feel the thumps of his little heels and elbows.

Nature's indifference when she bellows brings a quiet into a man. From every boat, captains' heads could be seen peering out from the misty glass, as mine from Joya's doghouse. All the energy within us would be summoned as if we owed it back to the wild that lent it to us. Breaking waves soon wrapped the headland and charged into our refuge with northerly blasts amidships. Joya swung directly onto the reef, slamming up and down as if to pile drive her mast through the base of her keel.

Gayle screamed and leapt out of bed.

I plunged into the water with my facemask peering through clouds of pulverized coral to see which direction to winch Joya off the reef.

Bursting to the surface I shouted, "We've got to get a line over to one of the other fishing boat anchors. It's our only chance."

Gayle stood at the rail, trembling with cold and fear. "Please don't drown."

Oh what a man might do, O'Riordan had prophesied. I stripped all the rope from Joya's running rigging, crippling her for the wind. Then, with almost three hundred feet of rope coiled over my shoulder, sinking me under its weight, I swam to pirate the anchor of another ship. I grasped the nearest boat's anchor line and pulled myself down the murky curve. When my lungs seemed they would burst, I dizzily threw a series of clove hitches over the links and,

ISLAND BORN

clutching the *bitter end*, headed back up to the wobbling and silvered surface.

In my private gasping world I felt a surge of joy to see Gayle in the cockpit searching for me with binoculars, for the joy of saving each other, and for this courage we found together that never came into question. Here we were alive and in harmony with each other.

I searched the Maldivian faces in launches that braved the storm whenever possible to help stranded boats. Paul's owlish white face never appeared with the others who brought badly needed food and equipment out to the ships in the storm, and especially for us an anchor and a huge coil of rope of a diameter used on freighters. I had expected Paul to come to our aid the very first day, especially as we were saving his ship.

The moment there was a lull in the weather, we made a dash for the safety of a tourist island lagoon, about three miles to the northeast. An ugly gash in the charcoal wall over the leeward reefs displayed several fishing trawlers and a small freighter lying belly up like bloated carcasses. When we dropped anchor in the lagoon, I knew its splash would be our last, that our sea life was over for now.

A couple of days later a motor launch lurched and tossed its way toward Joya. Marion, her daughter, and Paul clamored nervously aboard. Gayle and I unceremoniously embraced them and silently deboarded. I couldn't look back at first. We had left our life aboard Joya for someone else to climb into, a cosmology of energy and love that she was for us. Knowing the difficulties they would face, I hadn't the heart to take a single thing they might need. I turned away from my sextant and chronometer, our library of carefully collected sea books, the handcrafted fittings, and all the painstakingly chosen equipment for any step of a journey. With nothing but our clothes and a few odds and ends in duffle bags, Gayle and I braced ourselves in the stern of the launch. It pulled away pitching as weightlessly as a box of stick matches. My legs took to the sea, but my fingers sought

Joya's firmness in a handhold. Instead I found Gayle's shoulder and held on as Joya slid away over our wake.

"You're not going to take me to some crummy hotel are you?" Gayle asked.

"We've got some money now. We'll treat ourselves. You've earned it."

"I suppose that includes a hot bath?"

Gayle leaned her head against my shoulder. A sea of lifeless debris uprooted by the storm tossed in the silvered light over the waves. Shards of clouds hung from the sky like soiled rags. Joya stood majestically in the seesaw glare. We watched her until the rake of her mast stood like a sliver on the horizon.

PART IV
ISLAND EXPEDITION

46
Unnatural Worries

Gayle wanted to know where she would be taken if she had a medical problem during birth on our island. She decided to have a checkup at the local hospital in Male before we left for Singapore. We walked up a palm-lined drive to a single-story whitewashed building. A sari-clad old lady stooped at the waist, sweeping leaves out front with a handleless broom made from sticks. We walked up some steps and down a gloomy dark corridor without electric lights. A family waited on a bench, a woman with a thick braid of black hair hanging down to her waist, her husband, and small daughter.

"Doctor?" I asked, pointing at the door.

The man nodded, sliding over to make room on the bench. I played peek-a-boo with the little girl in a candy-pink dress. Her mother ogled Gayle's belly with an incredulous leafy-dark expression. Probably Gayle was the first pregnant white woman she had ever seen.

A very bony and barefooted old man in a khaki uniform appeared beside us. He held a torn scrap of brown paper with a pen pressed to it. "Name?" he whispered in English and scrawled whatever he understood when I told him.

He led us to a room with a rusty-legged exam table upholstered in brown vinyl. There was a privacy curtain, and a barren metal desk up against the wall. "If they bring me here hemorrhaging, or God knows what, they'll probably bury me here too," Gayle whispered.

An East Indian woman entered the room, wearing such a gleaming red and blue silk sari that our spirits brightened. "I am the doctor. How can I help you?"

Gayle bumped me to explain our plans to her.

"And what do you want from me?" she replied rather abruptly after I had explained.

"Advice," was all I could say.

"Well, my advice is if you want a natural birth, just do it the way islanders do it." She waved the back of her hand dismissively. "We have very few births here in this hospital." She stood reaching for her papers. "There is no maternity ward like you have in your hospitals."

Due to my insistence she checked Gayle over, took her blood pressure and urine sample.

We walked away from the hospital feeling very alone with our decision to be alone. Kids peeked at us from over the coral rock walls and ran along under the palms giggling.

"Anyway," Gayle said, "I can get a checkup in Singapore, before you drag me out into the woods to groan like a wild animal."

"That's what my mother believes. That I want to torture you without drugs, deprive you of the scalpel."

"She was much more positive after I wrote how committed we were."

"Don't let her fool you."

"I told her about Scandinavian countries," Gayle said. "How they have the lowest mortality and C-section rates with midwife assisted births."

"Listen, in my mother's world, statistics don't matter. Anyone giving birth without everything a hospital can throw at them is doing something subhuman. Bowing to science is a moral issue for her. Statistics won't change that."

"Well honey, let me tell you. My subhuman wants to walk on a real sidewalk, and go shopping for something other than bananas. Eat real food in a restaurant. And smell some good ol' exhaust."

"Just don't expect much support from the medical establishment, Gayle."

"You just don't want to go to Singapore because you're afraid of having a good time."

"You're right; I am. I don't completely trust myself. I'm feeling strong and clear headed out here, but I guess we'll have to take our chances. I know you're dying for some fun. And you deserve a break."

Gayle squeezed my arm as we walked in the shade of palms curving over the road toward the shortcut back to our bungalow on the harbor.

"It's just that seeking help from the very system we're stepping away from feels... what can I say, unsound. To them having a baby on an uninhabited island undermines their own beliefs."

"I still don't know why anyone would care what we do out in the middle of the ocean?"

"It's like we are putting ourselves in the hands of the enemy not bowing to technology. But it's not really even about technology or statistics. It's simply that if we don't accept dependence upon fear mongering systems and institutions, it is a kind of cultural heresy. And there's the rub."

"You don't have to worry about me, Frank. You're the one who gets so worked up about all this. I'm committed to our island. Nothing is changing my mind."

47
Singapore

We arrived in Singapore, May 22nd. The countdown was six weeks before Gayle's eight month when she would not be allowed to fly back to the Maldives. We took a taxi to the towering Central Bank to pick up funds we had wired from the US. Vaulted ceilings and columns towered like a cathedral above us, echoing with ringing telephones, the tapping sound of calculators and typewriters, the clicking of ladies heels up and down the marble steps. The institutional grandeur all seemed suddenly marvelous. How absurd our plans would seem to anyone ensconced in all of this.

"Go ahead; ask someone. Get a reference to a gynecologist or an obstetrician." Gayle nudged me toward some Asian women hurrying back and forth in their business suits.

"It's a little weird, a guy asking a lady for the number of her gynecologist," I said. "Maybe you better do it."

"You knocked me up. You find the gynecologist."

A good looking Asian woman stopped beside us to look for something in her purse. Gayle bumped me again with her elbow.

I put my hand up politely by way of getting the woman's attention, but she shook her head as if I were a mosquito buzzing too near her face.

"Excuse me," I persisted, leaning a bit closer.

She pressed her lips together trying to ignore me.

"We are new here, and my wife is pregnant."

She must have noticed me inhale her nice perfume because her face went blank, maybe a bit pale. I quickly asked, "Could you recommend a gynecologist?"

On the mirrored wall opposite I noticed our reflections. Our faces were deeply tanned and sinewy compared to her powdered cosmopolitan appearance. Our Maldivian tailored clothes now looked very homemade. "We've just arrived from out of town," I added humbly.

She scribbled down a name and telephone number on a note pad pressed against the gold metal rim of her purse. I thanked her as she hurried off without a word.

The gynecologist she recommended had a cancellation the next morning. The moment we walked into his office up on the thirtieth floor of a polished high rise, we felt like wet dogs in the house. A fit looking Chinese man about fifty, wearing a grey tailored three-piece business suit, ushered us into his office. I had scarcely begun to tell him our plans, before he began fidgeting noisily with his pen on the glass-topped desk. His face grew inky colored like an agitated squid.

"You should reconsider doing this," he interrupted, ignoring me and focusing on Gayle.

"We have made up our minds," I said, trying to protect her.

He turned and glared at me. "Do you realize the death of your wife and child may well end up on your hands? I can't give you my help. I can't have any part of this, not even talking to you about it."

We hurtled out, hand in hand down the neon-lit and lilac-carpeted hallways, down the elevator, and into the fumes of downtown traffic. The revolving glass doors buffed the air behind us. Gayle looked at me sadly. "I guess we should try somewhere else?"

I hailed a cab, feeling the sting of exhaust in my eyes. "A hospital," I told the driver. "Where's a good hospital?"

"American Hospital." He pointed up the street. "American Hospital."

"Okay." I waved him on.

A poorly maintained asphalt driveway led past a sign reading *Seventh Day Adventist Hospital* and on to a compound of planked buildings that looked as if they had once been an army barracks. The receptionist exuded heaven on earth friendliness, and said she was from Iowa, when I asked. We took a seat at a picnic bench under a covered walkway. Very shortly a tall Caucasian man waved to us from down the hallway.

Dr. Steele was either an immediately terrifying vintage piece of mooing Americana with wire spectacles, a red bow tie, crewcut, and red socks with white diamonds over the ankles, or too weird not to trust completely.

"So what can I do for you?"

And I went over our plans again. He clasped his hands together as if in prayer, his finger tips straight up forming a steeple under his chin.

"You know, my daughter just had a cesarean birth. Her pelvis was too small for the baby's head. I never would have expected it. She is not a small girl."

The phone rang. He answered it, opening a world atlas and running his finger around till he found the Maldives. I glanced over at Gayle to coordinate another escape.

"No, bring her directly here," Dr. Steele said into the receiver, while looking directly at us. "That's right. What time does the plane arrive?" He jotted down some notes on a pad and hung up the phone.

"There you are. That was a call about an American girl in Bali. She hemorrhaged during delivery. She's being flown here. To this hospital. This afternoon."

Both Gayle and I gripped our armrests, our plans shrinking to a painfully claustrophobic size.

"You see," he continued, "only a modern hospital can deal adequately with serious complications."

Gayle squeezed my hand. I shifted my weight forward to stand. "We're going to the island. We just wanted some assurance that Gayle and the baby are in good shape."

"Settle down now," Dr. Steele said, motioning me back into my seat. "I know something about natural childbirth. I was a flying doctor in Canada. I've delivered hundreds of babies out in the woods without any serious problems. I have done it on old newspapers."

Everything next happened in less than an hour. Steele got Gayle up on an exam table. It felt odd for her to become our training dummy, but then I realized she had seized an opportunity to size me up, along with Steele. He showed me how to rotate my finger in Gayle's vagina to deal with an umbilical cord around the baby's neck by slipping the cord over the upper shoulder and birthing the baby through the loop, and also how to cut the cord if it was too tight. He showed me where and how her perineum could tear. He referred to a book with pictures to explain suturing.

Then Steele whisked us through a door into a medical supplies warehouse. He gave me a large pale blue plastic sack to hold open, while he walked down the aisles dropping stuff in: Pitocin, Novocain, syringes, sutures, the antimicrobial betadine, and heavy flat sacks of a saline solution.

"Saline solution in an intravenous drip will help keep Gayle's blood pressure up if she hemorrhages," he explained. "That's your only hope if you have to sail twelve hours to a hospital."

He chuckled, tossing into the sack several jaw-like devices to clamp the umbilical cord. "That's just in case you can't find a shoelace on your bare feet."

Gayle did not laugh.

"Seriously, I wish you both luck."

He showed us out a side door in the warehouse, and we found our way back down to the street.

"Can you believe that? Wow, he gave us everything we need. No charge."

"These are stolen goods," Gayle said. "I feel a bit dizzy."

48
Medical Grip

Freedom is not an abstract philosophical concept, but the vital concrete possibility for every human being to bring to full development all the powers, capacities, and talents with which nature has endowed him, and turn them to social account.
—Rudolf Rocker

Back in the neighborhood of our Chinese hotel, Gayle and I strolled down a street cluttered with food stalls. Gayle had been eating impressive amounts. The sizzling woks of Singapore were nothing less than smoking treasure chests of Chinese cuisine after fantasizing about vegetables for so long in the Maldives. Bok choy, chard, mustard greens, and Chinese broccoli hung clothespinned on wires around a table or two.

We joined a greasy-chinned customer who slurped away at his bowl tipped vertically up over his nose, chopsticks twitching like mandibles at the corner of his mouth. Blue flames roared up around a huge wok. We pointed at the freshest-looking vegetables. It was all thrown into a vaporous meltdown of ginger and garlic, whirled around for a few seconds, and scooped out into a shiny green mound on top of a bowl of rice. A meal soon to be consumed only in our imaginations.

Our hotel was a faded green plaster building with wooden roof beams turned up at the ends into the shape of flames. It turned out to be full of Indonesian smugglers. Four levels of wooden peristyle catwalks ringing an interior court were almost impassable for the packing straw and cartons of electronic goods. All day and late into the night men hammered and ripped strapping tape.

Our bedroom wall had a conspicuous number of small crudely-bored holes over our bed. Most were plugged with matches or wads of paper. I pulled one out, and sure enough, you could see right into the hallway. "They're peeping holes," I said astonished.

After our first night some of the wads had been pushed out.

"Have the peepers been peeping?" Gayle asked.

"Looks like it."

"I'll give 'em a black eye with my belly button tonight."

That night the peepers witnessed the strangest of sights. Namely me, crawling around the floor with an ache in my back, groaning and arching up as if I had been shot with an arrow. I thought it was a spasm from swimming the anchor lines through the waves in the Male storm. By the third day I was incapacitated with pain, sliding my cheek on the floor slug-like, under the blur of the blue ceiling fan.

"That's it," Gayle finally declared. "I'm not gonna be a pregnant widow. You're going to the doctor. And that's it."

Back at the Seventh Day Adventist Hospital the urologist gesticulated with his fingers over the ghostly illumination of my Xray. A hard white spot had lodged in my urethra beneath my left kidney which was swollen almost twice the size of the other. A kidney stone! How stupid, I thought to myself, remembering the white rocks in Maldivian tea kettles, which they had purposely boiled out of the water.

Gayle stayed with me at the hospital during the next three days, not daring to set foot alone in our bandit hotel full of peepers, not even to retrieve some clothes. Doctors unsuccessfully shoved a kidney stone crushing claw up and down my urethra for two hours. My first pee was like the birth of the universe through my penis, the suffering of all life emerging in rivers of flowing lava. That's the way it was for the next several days, as I hung onto a wall pipe over the toilet. After that, I almost cried with laughter when they recommended surgery.

"I can pass it myself. Don't worry," I assured Gayle.

I was packing up my things when the doctor entered the room. "I feel obligated to let you know the danger of not removing that stone," he said.

"Are you sure about this, Frank?" Gayle asked.

Positive. Men have been pissing stones for millennia. Right Doc?

"Some die trying."

Gayle put her arms around me. "Let's go."

If freedom is making the choice to be whole rather than safe, then Gayle and I laughed for the glorious freedom we felt that day as we walked out of the hospital. Another step had been taken on our expedition to our island.

"Okay, we have to make this official," Gayle stopped to face me. "You have to promise, Frank Burnaby, not to die on our island."

"Okay, I promise. But you have to promise, too."

"I do! I do! You said it too. Now we can get married," she laughed. "Like your mom told you to."

I embraced her and whirled her off her feet, around and around in circles in the street, until she begged me to stop crushing her stomach.

49
The Map

More books on childbirth arrived at the Singapore Post Office from my brother and sisters. Gayle was seven months and a week pregnant. Back at our hotel she scanned a few pages of each text before falling asleep. Books lay propped up around her tummy like paper houses on the side of a volcano, the pages vibrating with the tremors in her belly. Soon enough I realized that the practical knowledge needed for delivering a child by ourselves was in the omissions, always labeled *consult your doctor*. It was maddening.

"Consult your doctor if it's more than 2 weeks overdue! That's all it says!" I slapped the page.

"We'll probably know what to do when the time comes," Gayle said uncertainly.

"Here they're instilling fear for placental insufficiencies. There's actually a greater risk being killed by a domestic dog. What happened to the value of a woman's God-given ability to give birth naturally?"

"You are getting kinda hysterical, Frank."

"Overdue! Babies don't grow like pears in bottles!"

"What are you talking about, 'pears in bottles?'"

"A pear tree covered in bottles. Like hair curlers. I saw it in an advertisement for some French liqueur."

"Why don't you stop spending all your time reading these books, if they're driving you so crazy?" Gayle said. She looked out our hotel window over the street bustling with vendors and food stands. "Let's go check our mail."

The clerk at the central post office handed us a packet of letters. Gayle snatched one from her brother on a Mormon mission in Avellino, Italy. On another I spotted the return address from my sister, Dina in West Los Angeles. For an instant I was lost in the image of her Tudor house on a hill with a swimming pool, shaded by huge oaks and avocado trees, with my blond nieces and nephews taking turns roaring down the black asphalt driveway in a red wagon.

Then I noticed the corner of a small postcard protruding from the stack in my hands. I pulled it out. On the front there was a picture of two Maldive islands, ringed with white sand in a blue sea.

"It's from Shareef," I said, and flipped it over. Gayle leaned over my shoulder.

Your house is finished. Come back to the Maldives soon. I am waiting for you on Kuda Fulidu Island.
Your friend,

Shareef.

I felt the weight of Gayle's chin on my shoulder, as people shoved by us. The words were scrawled in light gray grooves from a knife-sharpened pencil. Words that trailed off the bottom corner of the card leading our eyes and our hearts like a map.

"He did it," Gayle said, cinching her arm tighter through mine. "Right on time."

50
Last Errand

It was June 4, 1977, and the sooner we were able to fly back to the Maldives, the less likely we were to have difficulties with the airlines. We had accomplished a lot in two weeks, but we still had to purchase all our supplies, and get it shipped in time. I tried to envision every scenario of our daily life while pulling things from shelves: utensils and containers for cooking, basic ingredients for meals, bedding, clothes, a washboard and laundry buckets, materials for repairs, tools, medicines, and of course everything a newborn baby would need.

We loaded up on staples that would keep without refrigeration like rice, flours, grains, legumes, nuts, as we had done for voyages aboard Joya. Canned food was too expensive and bulky for shipping in large quantities. Street by street we searched through small local shops with signs in Chinese, and proprietors who spoke no English, seeking something familiar in baskets of dried seahorses and bats, bottled reptiles, piles of antlers, and dried fish bundled like kindling. We even found a can of pearl powder. There were mysteriously pickled or dried fruits and vegetables, and a basket of animal parts that Gayle would not touch, that turned out to be dried mushrooms. Dried onions were also a great find. Some things were unidentifiable, and we had to take chances. I convinced Gayle to let me purchase a case of pickled bean curd in beautiful burgundy vases with wax plugs and roped handles.

Back and forth we went, lugging our cargo through the sliding planked doors of our shipper's warehouse. Disgruntled taxi drivers waited in the street with boxes stacked to their felt head liners. Our shipping agent, Eddie Wong, watched from his office window, peering over thick black rimmed glasses. It made no difference to him if we were gun dealers or desert island dwellers. Everything was freight to him.

I suggested to Gayle that we could take seeds with us, and make soil with compost on our sandy isle.

"We can grow flowers," Gayle said.

"I was thinking vegetables. Food to survive on… if anything were to happen."

Gayle narrowed her eyes. "Like what?"

"You always ask that question. Like anything. That's how I think. Anything is always there; we just don't know what it is yet."

Our search for seeds led us by taxi to a fenced and planted area under a freeway overpass. We walked along a bamboo fence repaired with strips of cloth, wire, and string. The bamboo staves were hung with hubcaps, reflectors, and pieces that had flown off the overpass that droned with traffic overhead. A very old Chinese man leaned on a spade next to a wooden handcart piled with fertilizer. He peered at us like a basilisk through slits of wrinkled skin, his feet planted under him in rubber boots. When I spoke to him, he waved his hand to indicate he spoke no English. I opened a bean pod and pointed at the seeds. He led us to a lean-to where he lifted out a drawer filled with containers of seeds.

Here surrounded by high-rises, in the concrete understory of overpasses shuttering beams of sunlight over these gardens, we had the odd feeling of having found an old wizard. I watched his stained and cracked fingers working ever so slowly, folding our seeds into little squares of newspaper. I had never grown an edible thing in my life, but he pressed each packet firmly into my hands, as if his seeds had latched onto us by some design, the way seeds hook onto the fur of passing animal or get carried in the belly of a bird. The old man walked away without uttering a single word, and we carried off our auspicious packets of seed.

One last errand had not been checked off our list. My mother had written us back in the Maldives, how concerned she was about having an illegitimate child in the family. *Your beliefs are your own business. But it is not fair to subject your child to them,* she had written.

What nonsense! How could we call ourselves parents without being true to our beliefs?

Eddie Wong at our shipping company gave me the address of the marriage bureau, and as we waited for a taxi out in front of the huge green sliding plank door of his warehouse, I grumbled about it. "Getting a marriage license feels like an annulment of the commitment we already have."

Gayle laughed haughtily. "Even with my big belly you'll still have to beg me to marry you. But I'm not sure I want to anymore."

"Wait till my mother stirs up the moralizing winds in the empty souls of her Victorian henchmen. Then you'll be able to guess what their chilly reserve means."

"So we'll just have to get married then. Come on daddy," she pleaded. "A ring wouldn't hurt, not with my big belly and all."

"I don't have a ring."

"You can owe me," she shot back.

"Okay, how do I do this? Will you marry me Gayle?"

"Yes," she said, laughing and throwing her arms around me.

The taxi pulled up and I swept her off her feet and chucked her in the back seat.

We arrived at an aluminum trailer with a whirring air conditioner dripping on the side of it with a sign that said, Singapore Marriage Registry Office. We took a place at the back of a long line winding around the corner. We distinctly heard the English word "turtle" in a wave of giggles from young couples that had soon lined up behind us. It was smoggy and hot, and Gayle was in no mood to be made fun of.

"Just laugh with them," I said, trying to maintain the peace. "It's funny, you have to admit."

We climbed up the steps of the trailer, and the door spring squealed and banged the door shut behind us. The room was freezing and whirred noisily from the air conditioner protruding from the wall. The magistrate sat behind a rosewood desk across a dark blue carpet. He waved us forward, raising his spectacles to view the prodigious mound of Gayle's belly. He looked back down at his papers and whispered hoarsely that he would bypass the rule requiring a six-week wait for a marriage license.

"Where are your witnesses?"

"Witnesses?"

"You must have two witnesses."

"Can I go find some now," I asked?

He agreed I could, and Gayle followed me out.

"I'll get a taxi to the packing company," I told her. "Hold a place in line."

Eddie Wong listened to my breathless explanation and then yelled out into the straw-smelling dark of the warehouse. Two sweetly dumb Chinese boys with large biceps emerged from between the crates. Their names appear as witnesses on our marriage license #4132, Tay Ser Tee and Ong Poh Ohua.

51
Back to the Maldives

On June 25, five weeks before Gayle's due date, we boarded a plane to Trivandrum in southern India, and switched to a small prop plane back to the Maldives. That's all there was then. An English lady sitting across the aisle cast bewildered and unkindly looks at Gayle's stomach, clearly too large for her to be on vacation. Then she eyed the small clay pot I carefully held in my lap. It contained a pure strain of yogurt starter culture I had searched out from a small dairy in Trivandrum. We would make yogurt from powdered milk on our island, probably the first yogurt ever made in the Maldives. I also hand-carried our precious suitcase of birthing supplies from Dr. Steele. The shipping company had promised that our food stores and other supplies, that were so crucial to our birth plan, would arrive in two weeks.

The turquoise reef of Hulule Airport tipped into view as we banked for an approach. The tiny runway stretched to each end of the island. Islanders in local sailing *dhoni* dotted the sea, heaving broken hunks of reef overboard to extend the runway for big jets. Time was running out.

Monsoon winds buffeted us as we stepped out under the immense skies, surrounded by the sun blistered seas of the Maldives once again. Whitecaps hurled the wind from the southwest. The heat was infused with the perfume of wood and green shrubs. No officials checked our baggage or gave us a visa under the sunburnt thatch of the customs hut. We passed through one door and out the other. Maldivian faces, with their credulous brown eyes and wind-jostled hair, remained innocently perplexed as to why tourists continued to come.

The airport launch dropped us at the wharf in Male. The same shipwrights who had worked on Joya's reef damaged bow, climbed down off the *dhoni* they were building and walked up to us. The head shipwright peered out from under his white cotton fishing hat, curious as a sea bird with his mouth pinched to smile. I could have embraced him and swung him around in circles for my joy to be back.

He wagged the back of his hand in the air, a Maldivian gesture for, *What's happening?*

I explained we had traveled to Singapore, which was to them an unimaginable Shangri-La of the modern world. I quickly added that it was *sock-er-eye*, which is Dhivehi for something lousy, very bad. I said the Maldives were much better.

They looked at me for a moment as if I was crazy, and then we all burst into laughter.

Things seemed to be going well, until the first week of July when Gayle began to swell. We had rented a bungalow in town on Majeedi Road, in the shade of a large breadfruit tree. I had arranged for a fishing dhoni to take us to our island soon as our supplies arrived. The swelling of her fingers and then her ankles could have been normal symptoms of pregnancy. But then one morning she sat up with sunken hollows for eyes, and her face was featureless as a balloon.

She stretched and yawned. "What are you staring at?"

"Can't you feel it?" I asked, calmly as I could without frightening her.

"What?"

"Your face. It's swollen. Very swollen."

She got up and looked in the mirror. "Oh my God!"

We went directly to the Male hospital, where our Indian lady doctor confirmed albumin or protein in Gayle's urine, a forewarning of toxemia. She prescribed plenty of rest.

Back at our bungalow, I dove into our books while Gayle lay with her swollen legs bent up over a stack of pillows. She looked like a tipped over easy chair. I read out loud: *Preeclampsia may or may not turn into eclampsia. It rarely does, and its incidence is decreasing. Eclampsia comes on suddenly, and consists of convulsions and coma. The mother may die from heart failure, edema in her lungs....*

"Okay! Okay! I got the point!" Gayle interrupted. "So what can we do?"

I looked around our room. In the kitchen our red clay yogurt pots sat along the counter, working up our first batches of yogurt with the starter I carried on the plane. The breeze pulled back the sunlit curtain, and leaf shadows from a mango tree in the courtyard spread across our concrete floor. I sat resting my hand on Gayle's belly.

"Plan B could be to have the baby right here," I said. "We have all our birthing supplies. Our food should arrive soon. We've got a good bed, a bathroom, a nice walled garden, and the Male hospital down the street. The airlines won't let you fly, so this may be a blessing. Our best compromise."

"No."

"What do you mean, No?"

"I don't want to have our baby here! I want to go to the island, Frank!"

"We will. But we promised each other, 'One red flag, and we won't go.'"

"I feel fine," she said, wiping away a tear.

"Why are you crying?"

"I don't know."

"Are you scared?"

"No."

"What, then?"

"I just hope our baby will be all right, that I haven't done anything wrong if I have toxemia."

"Like what?"

"Well, how do we know? Maybe all the traveling. Maybe the lack of protein, like you read."

"So we'll get protein."

"Maybe you should bring me some fish."

"Fish! You hate fish."

"If my test improves, we can go. Just bring me any fish with white meat. With no smell or taste."

I borrowed our landlord's bicycle, tied a basket on the handlebars, and spent the next days weaving around Male in search of food. I fought like a cat at the fish market for swordfish whenever one came in. Often I could only get tuna. It was darker and bloodier, and Gayle gagged on it, but she held her nose and choked it down. When she refused to eat another boiled egg without salt, which we had eliminated to reduce water retention, I found jars of wheat germ at Red Mouth's tea shop. I mixed it all with our homemade yogurt, and Gayle gulped it all down.

Finding vegetables was almost impossible. I circled the neighborhood homes like a crow scavenging for food. I found on man growing some chard, probably the only Maldivian in the archipelago, and negotiated a leaf or two whenever I could get him to come to his front gate. Our landlady showed me a delicately thin tree with tiny edible leaves. I inched out on smaller and smaller branches like a human-faced caterpillar, leaving the poor thing finally bare.

Gayle munched ice all night to soothe her heartburn, lurching into sitting positions with the onset of contractions, or suddenly heaving herself out of bed, and thumping her heels into the bathroom to take her hundredth pee for the night. The heat made her so miserable in her swollen condition. I kept the windows closed for the first part of the day to hold in the cool night air, just as my mother had done when I was a kid during summer heat spells. Soon enough, our bungalow reeked like urine from our yogurt production, all our clothes, hair, everything. Then add in the smell of frying fish, and only a sea otter would have been able to breathe comfortably in our den.

I was thankful that Gayle had not thought to inquire about the arrival of our supplies from Singapore. It was already mid July, and I had been secretly checking customs daily. One late morning after returning with my marketing, Gayle sat holding a hand mirror below her belly button. She was red faced, and pushing with all her might. I dropped my basket in the doorway. "Are you in labor?"

Gayle exhaled a big breath and said calmly, "It says here that if I push, and the baby's butt is below my navel, then my pelvis is big enough. And it is. Isn't that good news? The baby's head must be engaged."

"That is great news," I agreed.

One evening I proudly stepped in the door with a jarful of goat milk, hoping to help Gayle's preeclampsia symptoms. A family milking a goat for their child with a medical condition had generously agreed to help.

"You drink it first," Gayle insisted. "It smells like pee."

"Well, it was a very old grandma goat, she might've leaked a bit when she was letting down. A few trickles only. Pee is supposedly sterile anyway. Nothing to worry about."

Gayle turned away with a grimace. "Very funny."

"It's good milk!" I said, holding out a glass. "You need it. I worked hard to get it for you."

She flicked me away with her fingers from over the back of her shoulder.

"Okay, I'll take a swig first, to test it. Then it's your turn. All right?"

I took a small swallow and my throat spontaneously constricted, shut tight as a vault with my eyes bulging, the same reflex people experience drowning. I fled outside to retch in the bushes.

Gayle howled with laughter, her head lolling in the spasms. "I can't believe…," she choked, clutching the underside of her belly. She got control of herself long enough to deliver her assessment. "I can't believe you didn't figure that out. There's no grass on this island. They feed that old goat fish, I swear. The guts… all the rotten stuff."

I gulped glasses of warm, metallic tasting water, which we now boiled like the islanders, crystallizing white clumps of minerals in the bottom of the pot.

On July 22 I received a note from Male Customs that our supplies had arrived. I hurried over to Customs on my bike, but they would not release the goods.

"You must have Bill of Lading. I'm sorry."

"The shipping company never gave me one. But the crates are addressed to me!" I said, waving my passport at the officials. "My wife is having a baby any day. We have to leave for Ari Atoll. Please can't you make an exception?"

"We would like to help you, Mr. Frank. But we cannot release these goods without a Bill of Lading."

Back at our bungalow Gayle said, "Don't worry Frank. It's going to work out. The Bill of Lading will arrive."

"But it's the shipping company's mistake. There's no time to wait any longer. I have to figure out a way to steal some of the most important crates we need. At least then we can leave if your tests are negative."

"Just wait till after the weekend, before you do anything rash. See if it comes in the mail next week."

On Wednesday, July 27, four days before Gayle's due date, I received the Bill of Lading at the post office. I rushed to customs with several hired men and handcarts. We stacked boxes to the ceiling around every wall of our bungalow.

Gayle had tested for albumin twice and failed both tests. She was better but not completely free of the toxemia threat. On July 29, two days before the baby was due, Gayle told me she wanted to test one more time.

We went back to the hospital, and sure enough, she tested normal. Not only that, but the Indian doctor thought Gayle's condition was excellent, and that the baby's head was fully engaged.

The moment we walked out of Male's hospital, we were so elated we almost ran down the street.

"Oh my God. I did it," Gayle exclaimed in amazement. "We can go!"

Gayle stopped and bent over with her hands on her knees to rest, breathing hard. The wind blew the back of her pants against her legs and her white cotton caftan up over her back. At the end of the road the sea glimmered blue in the blustery conditions.

"We should go, like now!" she said.

"But you could go into labor any second. You are due the day after tomorrow."

"It's Okay." She stood with her hands on her hips. "I'm not going into labor on the boat. I recalculated my due date last night."

"What?" I said.

"My periods are about thirty-five or more days apart, instead of twenty-eight. My due date should be around August 5th instead of the 31st. So we can still leave."

"That's like not believing your gas gauge, Gayle. What if he comes early?"

She leaned on my arm, and smiled. "Let's go. It's going to be all right. I'm going to make it. Don't worry."

52
Our Island

The first boat I could arrange to take us to the island was on August 5, exactly on Gayle's recalculated due date. There was nothing that would stop us now. It would have been like changing your mind in the middle of a pole vault.

In the windy predawn darkness, several islanders arrived and helped me carry our supplies to the waiting boat. Gayle would not sit down and relax. She handed boxes to the men from the doorway of our bungalow. Thunder boomed in the distance. I walked in a line with the men, following their footsteps and dark bodies hurrying through the palm shadows. Raindrops began to plunk noisily onto the cardboard boxes hoisted onto our shoulders.

We were all anxious over the weather. Stars disappeared and reappeared. Gusts of wind flailed the leaves and rocked me off balance. Up ahead through the palms, a sea of whitecaps shuttled the sea across a black horizon. Waves sounded hard on the shore, reminding me of the heavy slap of the manta ray upon the surface of the lagoon when we first entered Ari Atoll, an omen we assumed was of good fortune for us.

The native boat was heavily loaded with our crates. It pitched and rocked, against the coral rock jetty. Several crew members heaved their weight upon poles to fend it off. The tarpaulin over the crates billowed up in the blasts like an enormous black wing and threatened to capsize the boat, or tear it away to seaward without its crew.

The captain met me on the jetty, shouting excitedly in Dhivehi, wagging both hands at the wrists for me to stop loading more boxes. The boat was too heavy, he indicated. Both of us leaned a shoulder against the wind, facing each other.

"We cannot leave our supplies," I shouted back in English. "We have to take it all!"

The men paused with their loads, awaiting the outcome of our standoff. Twilight had by now peeled a layer of darkness from an eerie frothing sea, which seemed to plunge like falls over a horizon still black as night. I turned my face up to the hallowed shards of clouds hanging down from the soupy dark.

The Maldivian captain and I stood opposite each other, buffeted by the wind like branches that won't tear away. Almost imperceptibly the blow eased, if not in strength, certainly in its voice, as if to mediate. The *dhoni* captain sensed it too. He relaxed his shoulders and gazed away to seaward. The men understood and resumed handing boxes down to the boat, shouting directions to each other with their legs straddling the jetty.

I walked off for the next load, but stopped at the forest edge to look back. The captain still stood alone, sniffing the wind, listening to the low moan in the distance. He turned towards me again, but this time the decision to leave had been made.

Gayle bent over repacking the jars of Chinese pickled bean curd. She straightened, pushing up with her hands on her hips, rocking back to balance the weight of her stomach. "My back is killing me. I've got to sit for a minute."

"Just relax, Gayle. I'll pack up the rest of it."

"How are things going?"

"Fine. Everything's fine."

"These guys look a little tense." Gayle glanced at the islanders pulling boxes from the last stack against the wall.

"Yeah, well there's a bit of weather."

"A bit?" Gayle looked fixedly into my eyes.

"By the time we are loaded up, there's a good chance it will clear."

Gayle smirked and shook her head back and forth slightly, one of her *you're not fooling me* looks.

"These guys have local knowledge," I added. "We'll see how it is at dawn."

Gayle turned back to packing. "Is everything going to fit in?"

"Yeah, that's the other thing. The boat won't take much more."

"If we have to leave anything, leave this pickled bean curd." She gave the box a kick. "I'll bet you never eat it."

I looked at the glazed burgundy jars, but couldn't give them up. "We'll get everything in," I said. "Don't worry."

"I'm as unworried as I can be, sailing nine months pregnant into stormy weather! With guys that have that same demented look in their eyes that you get before you do something crazy."

"We won't leave if it still looks bad."

"Spare me, okay? We're leaving. So go. Keep loading. Before these guys take off with our stuff."

When the time came, I escorted Gayle out to the boat. A morning chill caused her to shudder; the air was damp from low night clouds lingering overhead. The squall had settled down to a well exercised sea, that flipped up luminescent whitecaps, with spray feathering off and vaporizing in the dawn light.

The islanders had reserved a royal seat for us on top of the engine cover, the only superstructure on the boat apart from the mast. Gayle had suited up in her heavy weather gear, but a crew member gently folded a shredded piece of orange tarpaulin on the wet wood for her to sit on.

With everything loaded and battened down, the men chattered back and forth as they poled the *dhoni* away from the breakwater. A man jumped down between our legs to crank start the old diesel. It hammered under our seat as we motored out. The captain squatted behind us, his arm draped over the tiller. He leaned outboard, tilting on his heels to see ahead.

I prayed for a safe passage, trying not to imagine Gayle's discomfort for the next twelve hours in an open boat. In our wake my little sailing *dhoni* trailed on a rope. Asmar from Turadu, where we first made our landfall in the Maldives, had custom-made it for me. He had brought it to Male only a few days earlier. It careened along behind us, up one side of the wake and then back across to the other. It would be swamped and surely have to be cut loose in strong wind.

The six man crew settled down, wedging themselves between stacks of boxes. No one spoke. The boat surged into the wave troughs, throwing spray. The silence of setting out to sea was all too familiar to us, the hollow stomach sinking over the first waves, the silence that dismisses the chatter of land, the gnaw of adrenaline tightening our grip, the chill of going to sea that is more than being cold. There was also the irresistible urge to sleep upon the threshold of a passage.

Gayle and I gripped the engine cover against the rolling motion, thankful for a scrap of tarpaulin to hold in front of our legs against the chilling dawn spray. So much could still go wrong, but this little boat pitching across the sea was the last link to Kuda Fulidu Island.

The seas mercifully calmed, subdued by a bright sunny day. Our sodden little boat smoked with steam as we ploughed over the now smooth undulations. Gayle did not feel well. She held her head crunched down toward her stomach. "It's the contractions," she said, breathing deeply.

"Take deep breaths." The swells pushed her against me with my arm around her waist. I prayed these were just the usual Braxton-Hicks contractions.

To the man, the crew kept their eyes on Gayle, the frayed brims of their sea hats lifting from time to time over their salt-encrusted arms. Nature could not be so cruel as to start labor now, I said to myself.

"Don't worry," Gayle said under her breath as if she heard me, "we're not having a baby on this boat." She leaned on my arm to sit upright. "But I hate to tell you, Frank, I have to take a pee. I just can't hold it any longer. I'm going to burst."

"A pee? I can't believe we never thought of that," I said.

Gayle began to writhe uncomfortably in her seat.

"Wait, wait… let me think a second." My mind raced, how would she be able to hang her butt over the stern in her present state?

As I studied the boat for a solution, the captain climbed forward, softly patting his bladder. I nodded, and he pulled a mangled yellow and oil stained plastic bucket up from beneath the engine, and handed it to me.

Gayle sank slowly down over it into the bilge, to conceal herself from the men. I braced her shoulders against the roll of the boat. When I looked up, all the men were wide awake, every eye upon us. The boat rolled deeply from side to side, and the curve of the hull was slippery. I gritted my teeth.

Gayle handed the bucket back up to me. It was empty, but I carefully turned it over the side, with all eyes upon us.

The threat of the morning cleared into the sunniest blue day imaginable. Gayle's bilge gymnastics improved along with her spirits. We settled into the pleasant trance-like monotony of the bow wash, cleaving up and splashing white lace patterns of foam out over the surface of the sea. On the distant horizon, I kept an eye on thunderheads marching up from the west. I checked my pocket compass. Yes, it had occurred to me to bring it, just in case we needed to know which way to swim.

By midday the sea had turned a glittering royal blue, with icing-tufted crests. The crumbs of islands appeared on the distant horizon ahead, bobbing in and out of sight.

I turned and smiled at the captain.

He nodded back.

"We're not far from home, Gayle," I said, pointing out over the sea. "That's the eastern edge of Ari Atoll."

Gayle straightened and peered ahead, her face already browned, freckles reddening in their own little archipelago across her cheeks.

I put my arm around her.

"How much longer?" she asked.

"About three this afternoon is my guess."

"I can't wait to see our house. I just didn't believe at first that Shareef would manage."

"He's a smart guy," I said. "Maybe he just never got a chance to do something like this in the government job he had. Think he was a clerk."

We entered the north end of Ari Atoll into a blazing glitter of afternoon sun. Wind driven currents rushed like river rapids over the barrier reef as we followed the shallowing channel in. The white visors of beaches protruded seaward as we passed the first uninhabited islands. Then over on the western edge of the atoll, the larger of the two islands, Bodu Fulidu, came into view. Our island destination lay concealed behind it.

"I'm nervous," Gayle said. "I'll feel a lot better when I see an actual house."

"Seems like yesterday we were here measuring the foundations with Shareef."

"It's been three months," Gayle said.

Our island slid into view from behind the north end of Bodu Fulidu. The captain steered with his broad foot curled over the tiller, the diesel thumping us toward the southeastern end of the reef. The crew dislodged themselves from crannies between our boxes and stood along the curve of the coconut wood gunnels peering out, casting puzzled glances at us. Even if the Captain did know what we were up to, he would not have said anything. That was their way.

I stood on the engine compartment as we turned around the reef, paralleling our beach. Every head craned for the first sight of something, anything other than the palm forest or empty stretches of sand ahead.

PART V
OUR NEW VILLAGE

53
The House

Our *dhoni* motored westward along the beach where our house was supposed to be. Gayle and I held our breaths. There was not a sign of anyone, or any structure. No footprints or the grooves of boats having been pulled up on the beach. Nothing. The island looked as if it had never been touched by human beings. Our boat bumped the sun-glazed swells that had blown across several thousand empty miles from Africa. Tall skinny palms stood above the forest, their heads raked back by wind.

I braced myself for the unimaginable. I knew exactly where we had told Shareef to build. Shapes and reflections leapt from the shadows, competing with each other for my hopes, any telltale glint of sun in the forest, fronds creating triangles, or glimpses of surfaces with a man-made texture. At this point anything unexpected spelled disaster. I stood on the engine compartment, knowing I should have seen something by now, and I felt a dreadful knot developing in my gut.

Past the point we should have spotted something, the unmistakable sheen of new thatch caught my eye through the trees. I steadied myself with a hand on Gayle's shoulder. "I see something, Gayle! A flat surface. Yes, it's a roof. Look! Definitely the triangular peak of a roof! Can you see it from down there?"

"Where?" Gayle craned her neck.

"Over there" I shouted, squatting down beside her to point from her eye level. "It's our house! Right there!"

Her shoulders stiffened like a current had run through them.

"Now, you see it!" I laughed.

In a few moments we caught glimpses through the shrubs along the forest edge of white coral rock walls laced with palm shadows. I glanced at Gayle, her mouth open in awe. I glanced back at the captain, and his leathered lips broke into a big smile.

Our boat turned into the small channel through the reef into the lagoon, crossing over coral heads mushrooming in every hue of red to blue. We skimmed over bone fields of antler coral as striped, spotted, or marbled reef fish flashed out of our way. Up on the beach a group of islanders began trekking diagonally toward our landing spot in the turquoise shallows.

One of our crewmembers heaved an island-made grappling hook off the stern. The faded poly line tightened and groaned in hairy turns around the sternpost. The captain threw the gear box into reverse with a loud clunk, and revved up the diesel in a noxious cloud of exhaust. I jumped over the side into the water with the crew, curling my toes into the sand to help hold the boat off. The heat from the sun flashed off the sea onto my chest as all of us strained against the weight.

Some men rushed up from shore to help, and I spotted Shareef among them.

"Shareef!" I waded up to grasp his wet hand, and held it as Maldivians do when they feel close to one another. He gave me his big white-toothed smile, but his eyes flickered away from mine. As I peered at him, the other islanders greeted each other, calling out comments and laughing, sharing news. I turned and reached up for Gayle, to ease her down by supporting her under her armpits, but she was too heavy. She slid down my front side like a boulder, splashing ungracefully into the water.

Shareef nodded respectfully to Gayle, "I am happy to see you," he said uncertainly, glancing at her formidably huge belly. "Come up and see the house."

We walked up the beach with the men. The breeze was sweet and fresh. Palms fluttered high up in the blue overhead, higher even than I remembered. The sand pressed under our feet, soft as crushed feathers. I put my arm around Gayle's waist to give her some support. Islanders gathered in the tree shade up near the house as we approached.

"Is everything okay?" I asked, looking back over my shoulder at Shareef, who lagged behind us.

He cleared his throat before speaking. "Well, yes. I tried to write you, but I didn't know if you were still in Singapore."

"We've been in Male for the last month, staying at Rashid's on Majeedi Road. Is something wrong?"

"There have been some delays. Nothing serious."

Mosabe emerged from the woods, greeting us with a grunt and nod, wringing his hands like an old woman, not at all like the self-confident village elder of our first visits to the island.

Gayle squeezed my hand for support as she climbed the last of the sand bank, her belly slung low in her sarong. We stopped short of the house, our entourage tripping over themselves to avoid being an inch ahead of us.

No one spoke as the situation came into a mental focus. The grounds were littered with construction debris. The house was no more than a shell with gaping holes for windows and doors. Inside, there was no floor, just piles of broken antler coral, which islanders use in place of rebar. The house was uninhabitable!

"I'm going to check it out," I said grimly. I left Gayle, and picked my way through the rubble to the back doorway of the kitchen, praying to find the well. We might be able to manage if we had fresh water. But where there should have been coral rock walls mortared around a ring of fresh water, there was nothing. Just sand and green leafed vines trailing out from the forest edge. That was the final blow. Not only the house, but the island itself was uninhabitable.

I turned to Gayle picking her way around the coral rubble in the dimness of our bedroom. She leaned on her thigh with one hand. Her contractions had been coming every eighteen minutes at times, but not in a regular rhythm.

"How is this possible?" I muttered.

Gayle motioned toward the boat. "You might want to consider stopping the men from unloading, Frank. We can still sail back to Male."

I looked over at Shareef standing beside us and he quickly gave an order to a young boy who dashed down the beach.

Gayle straightened slowly from leaning on her knees, and wiped the beads of sweat from her brow. "I gotta sit down."

Mosabe had already made a seat for her from a *dhoni* sail folded on a box on the front porch. I leaned out from the porch to see if the men had stopped unloading our things from the *dhoni*. They waited, holding the bow off the beach, with some of our crates stacked about in the sand. House workers gathered around us, their hands white with coral rock dust and hanging at their sides.

Shareef's big overripe eyes seemed to have lost their sweet glint of optimism. Suddenly Mosabe became quite agitated with Shareef, shouting at him in staccato bursts.

I withdrew to sit next to Gayle on the porch. The house would have been perfect if finished, with its lofty thatched roof, its windows looking out over the lagoon. Staying up all night to pack, and the long *dhoni* ride to the island, and finally this, had done us both in. I felt feverish and weak. I worried a bit about the outbreak of hepatitis in Male before we left. Almost overnight, everyone we'd passed on the street had bright yellow eyes from jaundice. Gayle thought my eyes looked all right.

"Frank," Shareef called, motioning me over to a gathering of the men. "Mosabe says the house was more work than they thought. But he says they will work day and night until it's finished." Mosabe wrung his hands in front of me. "In three days,' Shareef said, 'they will be finished.'"

"Three days!" I exclaimed glancing over at the shell of our house, trying to reassess how that could even be possible.

Mosabe stepped forward, speaking more loudly in Dhivehi, pointing to the side of the house facing the forest.

Shareef translated. "He says, he will fix a good place under the tree."

Mosabe interrupted in commanding tones, jabbing his finger at a spot under the large banyan tree.

Shareef nodded dutifully. "Mosabe says, you will be very comfortable over there."

"But we have no water, Shareef!"

Shareef translated to Mosabe, who replied quickly staring straight at me.

"Don't worry about that," Shareef said. "The islanders will bring you all the water you need."

I hesitated to even tell Gayle what they were suggesting. Old Mosabe looked beseechingly into my face, as if it were a matter of personal honor for him to make good on our agreement. None of the men dared look over at Gayle. They only addressed me. And I too was as suddenly eager as the rest of them to make the situation good.

Gayle was completely alone, not another woman in sight to advocate for her. I went and sat down again beside her, dropping my feet into the sand over the edge of the porch, grinding my toes down into the coolness below. I took a breath looking at our boat waiting down the beach, with the men holding her bow. After a few moments I looked up at Gayle. "What do you want to do?"

She gazed into the forest where Mosabe had indicated setting up a temporary campsite. Then she leaned back to ease her stomach, which was bulging alarmingly. Her breath was short as she spoke.

"I'm not having my baby in the jungle."

"Of course not."

"Surrounded by these guys, with no privacy…in the pouring rain."

I cringed at the thought of being in any way responsible for that. "No. We can get back on the boat," I said. "Right now. Maybe that would be best, Gayle."

My sincerity still did not suppress the thrill in my gut at the prospect of another leap beyond all reason. But this decision had to be made by Gayle alone, uninfluenced by the huge effort and goodwill of the islanders, or this amazing house which was almost completed, or even by her courage to stay the course, for now there was a new life to consider over all else.

I glanced up at Mosabe. He looked perplexed, bewildered even. But not for the reason I first thought, not for his failure to meet timelines for us, but rather over our hesitation it seemed, after all they had done for us. These people don't think like Westerners, I reminded myself. I was sure that Mosabe just could not understand how we could retreat from the heart of deal we made. And where could we possibly be going from there?

Then we heard a *clunk* of an oar out in the lagoon which resonated deeply from the body of a boat. We all turned at once. A *dhoni* slid into view, listing to port under the weight of a tall load. The rowers hailed. Our bed and furniture the islanders had made for us arrived.

Mosabe and Shareef trotted down the beach with the other men to greet them. In a few moments they had pulled a king size bed frame, and a dining room table off the boat. Last they set a carved wooden cradle on the beach. Shareef looked back at us, beaming. All our furniture had been made with hand tools from the dark wood of the breadfruit tree. It stood on shore as if it had been exposed by low tide.

Gayle turned to me, "What about the rain?"

I could have bitten off the end of my tongue for the chance to protect my wife from the rain. "We can rig up *dhoni* sails in the trees. Plus we've got some good tarps in our supplies."

But my voice sounded too eager. I gazed up at the sky over the top of the palms. Blue not a cloud.

"Weather looks clear, for now," I said.

Gayle did not look up, but continued staring at the spot under the banyan tree where they planned to put us.

"I'll rig the mosquito net over the bed," I said. "Make a temporary kitchen, and stack our supplies around for privacy. But it's completely up to you."

Gayle turned to look out at the furniture on the shore.

"I'll make sure you are comfortable. The islanders will…"

"Okay go," she said with a smirk. "Join your buddies."

"You're sure?"

"Positive."

I dashed down the beach to help carry our furniture and boxes of supplies. The men saw me coming and understood. With great energy, even jubilance, we carried everything up and placed our bed under some large limbs at the base of a banyan tree. Mosabe and some men constructed the overhead shelter from *dhoni* sails.

We had crossed the moat of our last fears. We were now on our island as our island selves, and there was no turning back. I hurried off down the beach, the soles of my feet counting our blessings in every grain of sand.

54
Jungle Camp

Throughout that first night I escorted Gayle with a flashlight to take a pee in the woods, deep into the tangle of shadows and limbs, so there would be no smell around our camp. In the morning I opened an overtired eye upon the gauzy wall of our mosquito net with forest trunks and bushes surrounding us. The *clop, clop, clop* sound of carpenters' mallets rose and fell in the wash upon the shore. Reflections of sunlight off the sea wobbled on the underside of the palm fronds. Gayle awoke when she heard workers hailing a boat. She moaned and pulled the sheet over her head.

I swung out of bed and pulled on a pair of shorts, my head aching and my joints sore. The islanders had left several earthenware jugs of water standing outside the low wall of boxes stacked around our campsite. I lit the kerosene stove under a pot of water for coffee. Some workers, who apparently had nothing better to do, gathered around to stare at me as I cranked open a can of honey-baked beans. I tried to shoo them away so Gayle could get up and dress.

"These guys are not going to leave us alone," I called back to her. "Just pull a sari around yourself and come have breakfast."

"I have to take a pee," she said. "Get their heads turned long enough so I can sneak off."

I looked back at my audience. There were four or five young boys, the smallest levering himself up and down with his toe on a box corner, a dumbstruck man standing straight as a post, and a leather-faced old woman standing back with a huge machete stuck in her cloth belt.

I rattled the frying pan on our tin kerosene stove to get their attention. Fumes of petroleum and sizzling butter quickly enveloped our camp. "Okay! Okay! Everyone look over here." I held the frying pan up and shook the can of honey-baked beans into it. The crowd pushed forward, and Gayle slipped out the far side of the bed and slunk into the trees.

"That's right. Push on in for the chance to taste the treat of a lifetime." I held out a spoonful of beans with melted canned cheddar cheese. "Who's first?"

The crowd recoiled from the sight of the organ-red kidney beans in yellow slime.

"Come on! Don't be shy."

I tipped a spoonful of beans into my mouth. The crowd grimaced at the sight. The older boys tried to shove a small kid forward, but he violently fought them off. I heard Gayle's voice behind me.

"Having fun, Frank?"

"They're terrified of beans."

After I cooked breakfast, a hardcore contingent would not disperse, laughing like goons at every move we made.

Suddenly Gayle began to laugh, locking her lips together to hold her food in her mouth. "Not exactly what we planned… eh, Frank? Not…." Tears welled up in her eyes.

"Come on Gayle, they'll think you are being rude."

"Rude…." She slapped her hand on the table and looked at me, her cheeks bright red, lungs about to burst.

The truth always amused Gayle, even when it was at her own expense. This was the most wonderful farce of our own making. When I looked up at the crowd which had grown to about fifteen, they had suddenly become dead still, and staring at Gayle almost rolling off her seat. Some of them averted their eyes out of respect. One by one they drifted away. Gayle's laughter was a mighty moment. She could put the unknown into the hearts of complete strangers in such a way that they respected or feared her.

Excited to get up to the activities at the house, and needless to say feeling blessed that Gayle's labor had not started, we hurried to clean up our makeshift kitchen after breakfast. I washed the dishes with fine sand and seawater at the shore, and Gayle secured our campsite against land crab and crow attacks before we walked up to the house.

Gayle stopped at the front porch feeling shy, maybe of exposing the men to the fearsome tremors men have over a pregnant woman needing a nest. They were working mightily at their jobs that day. I tugged her in. We were greeted with bows, and soft voices. "Salaam Alaikum. Salaam Alaikum..."

Incomplete as it was, the house was already a palace under the palms, coral rock walls plumb and true, a thatched roof that extended out over the front porch, and our very own emerald lagoon lapping at the beach a few steps away. We stood there stunned, as these first glimpses of what we had created were becoming clear.

"Nobody would believe this," Gayle said incredulous. "Not even my own mother."

Workers bustled about as we stood listening to the clinking porcelain sounds of coral rocks being chipped for walls, the ring of adzes grazing hardwood beams, the thunks of axes, the raspy drone of large hand planes, the soft voices. Waves of sweet perfume from the new roof thatch descended from overhead.

Mosabe came up to us, pleased to see Gayle, who was clutching her bare arms in the chill. The house was remarkably cool inside. Due to the roof peak being more than twice the height of the walls, heat in the house rose and seeped out through the thatch. The cool air below was chilled by the porous coral rock walls evaporating moisture they had absorbed from rain. This ingeniously simple system worked like the Bedouin clay vessel wrapped in a wet cord that we had used for cooling drinking water in the Red Sea.

The walls inside the house were plastered smooth and the color of bone. Heavy coconut beams spanned the main room which was just as we first measured it, 20 by 20 feet. The adjoining kitchen was almost 6 by 18 feet, giving us a total of approximately 508 square feet, not including the 5 by 20 front porch under the roof eave. This was much bigger than most island houses, and huge to us after living like peas in a pod aboard Joya.

I set about to assess what still had to be done in the next three days to fulfill Mosabe's promise. I opened the planked kitchen door at the back on the north side where the well would be. The islanders were busily hacking out a huge hole. The west wall of the house was still under construction. Several young boys whitened by coral dust sat upon a pyramid of broken coral dragged up from the reef, chipping it into small flat slabs. The boys carried these hand fashioned little bricks in shoulder slings to a man on a scaffold who mortared them in place. There was a simple kiln in the forest where they melted coral to make the mortar.

The chief of Bodu Fulidu insisted on being solely responsible for the large stack of windows we had shipped from a carpentry shop in Male. He painstakingly planed and chiseled each one to fit in place. I calculated that at his rate of less than one window section per day, it would take him more than a week to finish. Still they insisted they would finish on time.

Possibly Gayle was the clock they were watching, each one of them guessing when the baby would come. Trusting their way was going to be a challenge. Mosabe and the foremen saw me stooping to look out the windows, and sidled up beside me to share my enjoyment of the view. Their heads were only up to my shoulder, and looking straight through the center of the window.

"It'll be a great view from bed," Gayle laughed, stooping with me to see through them. On my way out, my hair caught on splinters overhead in the doorway. The islanders all thought this was very funny. That I was too tall. Not that they made the doorways too short.

When they began pouring the concrete floor, we were very excited by the prospect of moving in soon. Barefoot men with cloth slings full of dripping cement shuffled in and out of the house, pouring their loads over the jumbled stack of antler coral which served as reinforcement.

The men mixed cement in a trough, which looked remarkably similar to a hand-carved canoe. I examined it and Mosabe nodded, pointing to the west. It had drifted from Africa. The islanders must have wondered what such a silly boat could have possibly been used for. There were no rivers, no mangrove swamps, in fact no moving fresh water anywhere in the Maldives. The boat would have been easily swamped by ocean waves and was useless for carrying a large cargo of tuna, but it made a perfect cement mixing trough.

The cost of our little house was about three hundred US dollars, and then a few hundred more for the large stack of wood-framed French windows we had made in Male. We had no electricity, no toilet or shower, no running water, no drains, no septic waste system, no telephone, no mailbox, no bills or taxes, no address, and not even a name for our island on our navigational charts. We were literally off the map.

At first we had no access to neighbors because the channel between our island and Bodu Fulidu was too dangerous for me to cross in a small boat. At this time it often churned with strong monsoon currents and was raked by squalls. Until I mastered my boat, even a short journey could be perilous, especially if I had an equipment failure with natural materials I was unfamiliar with. Beyond these patches of sand lay nothing but thousands of miles of empty windswept ocean.

In the early morning dark of the fourth day, I awoke to the grating sounds of cement being mixed up at the house. The squeals of trowels swiping plaster onto the walls amplified into the sleeping forest. The islanders had been working around the clock as they promised, but had not finished. I looked at the dim light burning up at the house. Gayle's stomach was bulldozing me off the edge of the bed. She had grown so huge she could scarcely turn unless I cranked her tummy over with her knees. I stood up stiffly and pulled on my shorts.

The sand was damp and hard underfoot, every sharp scrap of coconut shell or wood chip was an anti-personnel mine in the darkness. I stopped in the front doorway and watched a man with a soiled white cloth wrapped turban-style around his head, pulling a skimming board across the soupy concrete. A smoky flame flickered from a wick in a dish of coconut oil. He stooped and squinted to level the grade. I thought he must be going blind in that dim light. I walked back to our camp to get our kerosene lantern, and make some tea for the workers.

55
Without Clocks

Our dependence upon the islanders had to be taken quite seriously. In island life people worked together as many appendages of one body; together they formed an inherently intelligent nucleus. We could not be certain exactly why they had decided to watch over us, or for how long they would. If relations were strained, or even if heavy winds or a natural disaster made travel between our islands impossible, we would be left in a very vulnerable state alone on our island.

A dependable source of water was the most important component missing for us to begin our own little village. At the end of the fourth day since our arrival, I stood gazing into the sandy ten foot deep hole that would be our well. The rock sides had only two tiers completed. In the bottom a cream colored crust, resembling the surface of a giant egg shell, had been exposed. Beneath that lay a reservoir of rainwater called a *lens*, which was fresh water that had sunk down through the sand, and was floating over the seawater under the island. On some islands, however, seawater could invade and spoil the ground water *lens*. Only those with good water were inhabited.

We still had no assurance that our water was drinkable. I planned to build a rainwater catch from corrugated aluminum roofing and rain gutter materials I brought with us from Male, as a backup. The islanders had sold us a large cement holding tank, but Shareef could not seem to get anyone to build the rainwater catch. With the skies mercifully clear over our campsite, we were completely reliant upon the islanders to bring us water.

As days passed, the intensity of the work to finish our house faded. Workers seemed to vanish in a camouflage of gusting leaves, leaving jobs unfinished or unstarted. At lunch all the workers assembled around steamy rice pots and fish stew boated over from Bodu Fulidu. I counted twenty-five or twenty-six workers on the site, but no more than five or six working at any one time. Some were eating lunch whom I had never seen working on the house at all.

To make matters more disconcerting, I felt groggy and leaden. Bad water? The climate? Hepatitis from the Male outbreak before we left? I had persistent flu-like symptoms. I yearned for my usual whirlwind of energy to help work on the house. Instead I had to take it easy, take a nap at our campsite in the middle of the day. The islanders must have thought I was feeble or lazy.

After lunch the fifth day with all the workers assembled, I was desperate to organize the men. Shareef translated my idea of creating work groups to complete each project, such as the well, the house wall, or the windows, before moving on to the next. The men listened seeming concerned, then chatted animatedly among themselves. I could only imagine what they said: "Frank does not look so good... Scowling today... Could be those beans he eats... A man has no strength without eating fish... He must be sad with such a worried face... Maybe his relatives will come... Anyone can see his wife is not ready to have the baby."

I returned to camp, where two men stood squarely in front of Gayle, watching her trim her toenails.

"You don't look so good, Frank. How's your head?"

"Pounding!"

Gayle gave me a concerned look, and then leaned back over the aerogramme she was writing to her mom.

"Why are you writing a letter now? You were supposed to help me get the men organized."

"You should take it easy, Frank. You're getting a bit difficult to be around."

"They don't listen to me! But they come to attention when you put your belly out in front of them."

"Walking around right now might not be such a good idea. I'm having a lot of contractions."

"God, what's the date?" I asked.

"August tenth."

"You're ten or eleven days overdue!"

"Four days."

"Can't we at least have one due date? It's safer making decisions from July 31." I sat on the bed, imagining how to cope with having a baby at our campsite.

Gayle glanced up at the attendance of staring heads. "Look at these guys! Some of these people are so thick it's really disturbing. They even sniff around to find out where I took a pee. Between them and the land crabs following me out for a poop every morning, the lack of privacy here is horrendous."

That afternoon I awoke from my nap thrashing and drenched in sweat. A stout-shouldered old lady and a middle-aged frumpy woman, maybe her daughter, both dressed in faded green canvas smocks stood staring at me, with homemade knives in their belts. I sat up and looked around for Gayle. The older lady shouted, pointing her machete toward the lagoon.

Motioning thanks, I stumbled out through the palms.

Gayle's orange and white batik sari laid spread out over the broadleaved plants along the shore. Out in the lagoon her head protruded from an avocado-tinted pool. I walked out a ways towards her and toppled into the sea. I propelled myself down the sandy slope toward the blue opacity beyond. The cool silence soothed my frayed nerves, and the water pressure eased my body aches. The supply of oxygen failing in my lungs erased the dilemma of construction details from my mind. I burst to the surface for air.

"Feel better?" Gayle asked.

I nodded, squinting at the shining halos of afternoon sun flashing from the palm tops.

"Everyone thinks we have a boy," she said. "Wouldn't it be a pleasant surprise if we had a little girl?"

I nodded. "Are you scared?"

"I only worry that the baby will be all right. But I guess that's natural. I've been pleading for him to wait till our house is finished. I've been having a lot of contractions. Only about fifteen minutes apart." She leaned back and let her belly float. "Are you feeling better after your nap?"

"I'm not sure. I'm hanging in there. My joints ache."

"You really have got a nasty cold. Maybe you should wear a mask if you're sick during the birth."

"A mask?"

"Well you don't want to get the baby sick."

"He's going to have your immune system. So I suppose if you are not sick, he won't be."

"Like you always say, señore, why take the chance. Just get some rest, Okay?"

I made my rounds late in the afternoon to check on the day's progress. No one was working at the rainwater catch, only the post holes had been dug; the chief was climbing up and down his ladder for every little thing he needed, his helper nowhere in sight; most frustrating of all, no one was working on the well. I calmed myself by walking away toward the forest and then back, hesitating for a few breaths at the corner of the house. When I walked around, Shareef was sitting outside the kitchen, staring at a fifty gallon drum he was supposed to have buried in a pit full of coral rock to drain our kitchen sink. No one had dug the pit.

"What are you doing, Shareef?"

"I am looking to see how to make another hole in the barrel for the pipe."

"What happened to the men you took with you this morning to dig the pit?"

Shareef stood, tipping his eyes up sheepishly.

"They said it was their time off."

I glared at him. It must be the bends, I thought, the bends from coming up too quickly from the depths of an efficient clock driven culture. I retreated back to our camp without saying anything more, and began pacing the boundary of our supplies. Gayle watched me from the bed as she sat embroidering a vest she had begun for my last birthday.

"No one working on the well?" she asked.

"They're incompetent. I don't want to judge them, but I have never seen any human beings so... I don't know what to say. Superstitious. Any whim or impulse distracts them from what they are doing."

"You are way too tense, Frank."

"What am I supposed to feel? Our baby is due right now, and the only thing I can do about it is strangle Shareef. Which would be very gratifying."

"Come here. Sit down with me for a moment." She held up the vest she was making for me.

It was bolder than anything I would have chosen to wear. A scene of fire-red and dappled-blue waves licking up into a setting sun. "It's kind of hippie-like... but beautiful. Strong. Incredibly beautiful. It's our trip isn't it."

Gayle smiled shyly. "Like this," she said, fingering the tiny teak cloud pendant which I had carved for her out in the Arabian Sea.

"I'm sorry, Gayle."

"For what?"

"I'm sorry I cannot make these guys go any faster."

"Something motivates them."

"But what? Could be which way a bloody crab points its antennae… who the hell knows. I should just try and finish the well myself."

She took my hand in hers. "No, no, you won't. I need you in one piece."

"If we only had a few more days!" I said.

"The house is almost ready, right?"

"Almost, yes. But what that means around here I have no idea. Maybe for the next generation?"

"Honestly Frank, I may burst, or this baby'll pop out with his teeth in, but I'm not giving birth in the woods."

"That's really a frightening image, Gayle!" You shouldn't speak like that."

"Something inside tells me that the islanders won't let anything bad happen to us," Gayle said.

"I try to believe that. In fact I'm sure they would rather be out fishing. They're not just doing this for a meal a day, even a big meal. They are doing this because they have included us in their village."

56
Just Two of Us

That evening all the workers boarded their boats and returned to Bodu Fulidu. It was the first evening since we had arrived that we were left completely alone. With the aqua shadows deepening over the lagoon, I ignited the kerosene wick stove and fried some eggs. It was so silent that the popping olive oil sounded like gunshots. Battalions of crimson-backed land crabs scuttled out from their burrows across the forest floor, clicking their claws on the backside of our cardboard boxes. Here and there a rat torpedoed along the edge of our clearing, and a black and white chicken-like ground bird of some kind ducked out of sight in the shrubs. As it grew darker, the hum of mosquitoes closed in around us. We ate dinner under the mosquito net, holding our plates in our laps.

"It's beautiful out here, but spooky," Gayle said. "Have you noticed we seem to have a lot of rats?"

"This is the first time I've seen them."

"Oh I saw them the first night. At least we're not in the projects. Those suckers jumped out of the bins onto your arms. My brothers always made me empty the trash."

"No."

"Yeah! You didn't have 'em in your swanky neighborhood. The gardeners choppin' 'em all up with their big lawn mowers."

"You act like real life only happened to poor people."

"Well it did, you could say. Certain things. I wonder what else lives here? Not any huge spiders or snakes, I hope."

"It's the crabs that give me the creeps," I said. "They'd crawl up and eat us alive, if they could."

"I'd take crabs over mosquitoes any day," Gayle said. "At least you could eat crabs if you had to survive."

I rinsed the plates in the lagoon and navigated back through the shrubs toward the glow of our campsite. We tucked our pants inside our socks, and put towels over the backs of our necks for protection against the mosquitoes, and brushed our teeth at the base of the banyan tree. Overhead its limbs were interwoven with the shadows as if we were in a giant basket. A glob of white toothpaste foamed conspicuously on a huge root, and I wiped it off feeling the aliveness and vibrancy of everything around us.

I blew out the lantern, and we scrambled under the net drooped over our bed. We lay still, watching the bats chop and cut through the purple zenith. A nocturnal honeysuckle-like fragrance inundated the forest. Stars sparkled in the palms as the moon rose over the lagoon, looking like a lamp emerging from the depths.

Gayle jerked. "Ouch! That hurts… Oh, he moves so low in my pelvis."

Her hand groped for mine and pulled it onto her tummy. "Feel it? There he is."

I kissed her nose. I loved to feel the baby move, to know how alive he was inside her.

"I can't believe this is only the fifth night since we came here," she whispered. "Everything already feels so familiar. A part of me keeps saying this is totally insane, but I am not afraid at all of having my baby here. It feels so right."

Just then a breeze shoved against our mosquito net, rattling the bushes, and bellowing in the tree tops. We clutched each other as ripples chattered over the lagoon. Palm trunks swayed heavily outside our netting, and the sail tied over our bed snapped and strained against its ropes.

"Maybe you should go out and check on the weather," Gayle muttered into my neck.

I groaned, got up and ran naked out onto the beach, prancing on my toes to avoid waves of scurrying crabs. South of us a black squall billowed up into the night, topped with silver-edged clouds, and dragging a black curtain of rain over the glistening sea. It was the first stormy weather we had seen in a week. Further to the south more dark lumps of trouble crossed the horizon.

I sat on the bed, brushed the sand off my feet, and tucked our net closed around the mattress. "How is it out there?" Gayle whispered.

I sat leaning on one arm across Gayle. "A *thumper* is passing to the south. It's okay."

"You haven't called squalls *thumpers* since we were out on Joya."

"It does feel like we're back on Joya. Our island is so small out here. It's like we're not attached to the earth." I looked down at Gayle with her head so softly buried in her pillow, all snuggled up with her hair mussed. She pursed her lips to throw me up a kiss. I looked outside our mosquito net at the dim rainy looking shadows cast over the sand. "I'm afraid there are more *thumpers* out there. The weather is changing."

"They're coming to get us," Gayle sang, in a haunting tone.

I lay back down, and she pulled me to her with her leg over mine, as the errant blasts of wind churned the forest. I listened to her breathing in my ear after she fell asleep in my arms, feeling glad for the alluring and wonderful madness of us together. The edge of the squall passed, and I fell asleep floating on the hollow wash that echoed from the shore.

57
Taking Shelter

    I awoke to the sound of voices rising and falling between surges on the shore. I squinted through the mosquito netting gauze into the early morning blaze. The stooped figure of the old man with a soiled turban walked past. He had leveled our concrete floors, meaning they were going to finish mortaring the well today. I shook my head to check my condition. Just a dull background ache. Not too bad. Gayle still had her head bolstered in pillows. I pulled on a pair of shorts and swallowed a glass of water for breakfast, about all the calories one needed in that heat, and headed for the house.

    The chief had moved our windows inside onto the newly finished floor and was shaving them to fit. We greeted each other as I hurried through the kitchen door to join the old turbaned man at the well. After Mosabe and I stared for a long moment into the hole, I wondered if he too wondered what we were looking at. I turned to outline a concrete path between the well and kitchen, as Gayle had requested.

    I heard Shareef's voice in the kitchen and joined him to test the brass spigot protruding through the wall over a sink inside. A platform constructed outside the wall supported a fifty gallon drum which we would fill with buckets from the well. We were turning it off and on, enjoying the resplendence of water running through it, when there was a loud commotion on the other side of the house. We rushed out to the front porch to see what was going on.

Gayle had an armlock on a corner of our mattress, the heavy back end of it flopping across the sandy clearing like the tail of a stegosaurus as she swung her belly step by step toward the house. Workers danced around her, trying to get a hand on it to help. Shareef was right beside me as we jumped off the porch.

"My God, Gayle! What are you doing?"

"I'm moving in. There was a rat in our cereal bag. I'm not living out here while these guys turn our house into their workshop. The floors are done. There's a roof. There are rats out here. I'm not waiting any longer."

She was sweating and grunting as we staggered along trying to wrestle the bed away from her. "Okay. Okay Gayle, just… let… let it go!" I put my arm around her to try and calm her. "It's okay. We'll just move everything in for you. Let us take the mattress. Okay?"

The chief quickly relocated the remaining stack of windows to the kitchen. The bedroom was finished. The men moved all our furniture and supplies in through the clouds of stone dust being swept out. Then Shareef and Abdullah helped me move furniture back and forth as Gayle directed where she wanted everything. Our bed faced the lagoon with its head against the rear wall, next to an old English oak dresser we had bought in the flea market in Male. Gayle put the baby's cradle against the kitchen wall alongside our bed. For a shelf under the front windows we placed a plank upon two large hunks of coral. The next time I looked Gayle had already organized her shell collection on it.

I climbed a wobbly ladder and tied our mosquito net to the coconut wood rafters over our bed. We placed our dining table between our bed and the kitchen, with the perfect number of chairs: two. In the kitchen I put our kerosene stove on a table and stacked our food supplies around the walls. With the forest rustling outside the empty window frames, another milestone had been reached. We were moved in.

It was now eleven days after Gayle's originally calculated due date of July 31st. To celebrate our first night in the house, we made an East Indian lentil dhal over rice, with crispy papadams on the side. The fumes from the kerosene stove and lamp mixed intoxicatingly with the aromas of curry, garlic, ginger, and steaming rice. The glossy black inside of the windowpanes were empty of any other light, not even the distant glimmer of a passing ship; we were hundreds of miles from any shipping lanes. No matter what sound we made - drawers opening and closing, the rattling of pans, talking, even the hiss of our lantern, it was swallowed by the hush around us.

The vastness of no sound cannot be described as silence really. This kind of soundlessness can actually be heard in the sounds of other things. A leaf tapping another in an errant breeze, a soft stroke of the lagoon on the sand, the dying echo of a wave slap, or the gurgle of a bubble curled into the tail of a fish, and the sound of listening itself but hearing nothing.

We ate as little gnats dropped from the hissing white light of our lantern into dishes of sour mango chutney and homemade yogurt. It would have been nice having a little beer or wine to celebrate, but alcohol was forbidden in the Maldives, according to Muslim law.

"Except Maldivian guys working on the tourist islands put vodka in their cokes," Gayle said.

She suddenly pressed her spoon on the table, and looked down at her belly. She gasped a breath and smiled. "He's doing his soft shoe. Ooooh! There he goes again." Taking a deep breath, she said quite seriously, "I sure hope he has your nice square jaw, and your eyes."

"I sure hope he gets your behind," I said.

"Me, too," she laughed. "What was it your friend in England said, your ass is like two melting pancakes sliding down the backs of your legs?"

"Yeah, that was Michael's mind sliding down the backs of my legs. But he also said your upper lip looked like a deflated tire."

Gayle's face reddened.

"Maybe deflated is the wrong word… sneering, skeptical, sexy…"

"I hope our baby will be beautiful," she said. "And smart. We have plenty of smart people in our families." She looked at me tenderly. "How can anything go wrong?"

"Everything has worked out so far, Gayle. That's a good omen." I rubbed the flats of my feet back and forth on the cement floor, pressing in the coolness to assure every part of myself that it was true.

"I'm afraid there's no more room inside me." Gayle lifted her arm over the back corner of the chair to stretch.

"All I have to do is boil the scissors and shoelace," I said. "All the medical stuff is organized in the dresser drawers."

"Maybe he will come tonight."

The shadow of Gayle's head with her hair mussed on one side loomed up on the mosquito netting. Mine rose up the wall, distending grotesquely into the roof thatch. It was a bit frightening for some reason, but we laughed at our dinner companions.

58
Far from Alone

The night passed without our baby being born. I woke to the sound of crows cawing, their feet clicking on the hard surface of the palm fronds arching over our house. The room clung to the cool night air, but we could feel the heat of the day working its way in. A blade of light slid over the edge of the window onto the floor. With a little luck, I thought, the rainwater catch would be finished today. That would be a step forward. I turned toward Gayle and stroked her forehead.

She opened her eyes, and her body went unmistakably stiff.

"What?" I asked, suspecting the baby had moved.

She squealed, and ducked her head back under the sheet like a panicked shellfish.

"What's wrong with you?" I said, trying to pull the sheet back.

"Frankie, dear, we're not alone," she whispered icily under the sheet.

I turned to look over my shoulder.

Where there should have been a view into the forest, a crowd of brown faces pressed against the wall of windows, heads stacked like coconuts with their noses flattened against the glass.

"Oh, my God." I slid down and joined Gayle under the sheet. Hiding was all I could think to do.

Gayle looked me squarely in the eyes. "Frank. Make them go away. Please. Right now!"

"Okay. Okay," I said. "But I'm naked. Oh, what the hell." I peeked out again, ready to dash for my shorts while clutching a pillow as a shield, but there was no one there, just windowpanes of palms and blue sky.

Our plan to be alone had backfired! Islanders began arriving by the boat load. They had to see us to believe that a pregnant white woman and her husband were living island style and about to have a baby. They anchored on the east side of our island and crept towards us through the forest, often startling us out of our wits as they peered through the windows. I'd be concentrated on working and suddenly realize that brown legs had surrounded me like palm trunks.

Gayle strung up sheets over the windows and still shadowed heads gathered behind the cloth. The anxiety we once felt for dragging anchor, we now felt for dragging back the curtains.

At first, we were gracious and accommodating, but the word spread. People arrived from more distant atolls. The islanders did not seem to notice how distressed we were by their disregard for our privacy. Mornings we hurried to dress, brush our teeth, and get back from shore duty, pulling up our pants, only to find groups already waiting humbly in the beach grass at the side of our house. Their faces were innocent and awestruck by the sight of us.

"When are you going to stop being Mr. Hospitality?" Gayle grumbled.

"They'll get tired of us after awhile. What are we supposed to do, throw them off the island?"

Gayle looked at me with her eyebrows raised, as if I had struck upon a great idea.

The irony was that we had chosen their open-hearted, open-door (usually no-door) community to be alone. How could I be the one to introduce Western concepts of privacy, the keep-out values of our walled and gated culture? I looked out the window at the children sitting on their mother's laps, fathers standing alongside looking slightly uncomfortable. Maybe the women wanted to be near Gayle, to offer their support?

The milk tea began boiling over, while Gayle lurked about like a grumpy mother bear.

"Instead of scowling, why don't you tell them to leave, yourself?" I said, and reached past her to turn down the stove.

"At this rate we'll be out of milk and sugar real quick," Gayle shot back.

How could I not be gracious about their fascination with us? I was just as fascinated by them - the imperturbable sparkle in their eyes, their ease and harmony in such beautiful surroundings. I knew that they envisioned Western life to be fantastically rich and superior to theirs. But tourism was picking up. Even Club Med had negotiated an island we heard. Politics and paper money would cripple the windblown autonomy and the once sustainable lifestyle of each island village. Whatever the West brought to them, their unique life and culture would go on the block. Gayle and I felt the precarious nature of our influence, as well as the remarkable spirit of its people seeping into us.

Heedless of Gayle's warnings to distance ourselves from the islanders, I put on a good face and walked out with the tray full of tea cups knocking together and spilling milk tea over the top of our large aluminum pot. I joined them to extol the virtues of a sandy path. I acted out the strain of traffic jams, of mechanized life, phones ringing, horns honking. I mimed and wagged my head with my hands over my ears. I coughed and choked on pollution, on phoniness, on materialism and arrogance.

"Why are you sputtering around in the trees like a car?" Gayle demanded when I returned. "God knows what the islanders think."

I just couldn't bear them thinking that technology is without a terrible price, or that anyone is richer by sacrificing nature. I couldn't bear to think that they would trade one hand-forged knife, or the mentoring of their children by elders, or the grace and beauty of their coconut wood boats, or their pride as sailors or hook and line fishermen, or any part of their lives for the values of industrialized culture. I lifted my hands to the sky framing the beautiful day, and their blessings. I held my hand over my heart to express what I felt for their way of life.

My impassioned enactments made them laugh, or they looked respectfully perplexed, trying to understand. Any of them would have given a right arm for a boat engine, electricity on the island, and medicine for the staph and bacterial infections that afflicted their children. How would they ever survive the slipstream of ills following Westernization?

Occasionally an islander, usually a man, would rise to his feet and stand nose to nose with me, shouting out some sentiment he had to share. The subject matter never mattered. So we all shouted back and forth under the towering palm heads. And when we parted, we felt we had understood each other somehow.

Gayle shook her head, unable to hold back a smile from the porch.

Without an English/Dhivehi dictionary, I had begun jotting down phonetic notations for their language. I thanked the islanders for their gifts of *cocolo bis*, eggs; or *dumb fallow*, papaya; *kashi*, coconut; or *donkio*, banana.

"I can't just slam the door in their faces," I told Gayle. "How could I explain why we want to be alone? What would I say? I'm not even sure I can explain it myself!"

"Then leave the door wide open," Gayle chided.

"What am I to do? Build catapults on the beach? Fire flaming coconuts at them?"

"You may as well build grandstands around our house. The word is spreading from atoll to atoll."

"Damn it, Gayle. I already explained to Mosabe we wanted privacy. He had no idea of what I was talking about. What can I do?"

59
Appropriating Privacy

By August 14 after nine days on the island, the men ceremoniously hammered a hole in the eggshell-like membrane at the well bottom. We all cheered as clear water rose up inside. The islanders quickly cupped their hands to taste the quality, and then spit the water back out to the side. Sure enough, it was brackish, and only good enough for cooking, bathing, and laundry. But the men pointed encouragingly over at the gleaming aluminum panels of our newly completed rainwater catch, nodding and humming "hmm…" in affirmation. As soon as the dry spell ended, our concrete tank would be filled with sweet drinking water.

Mosabe arrived, his boat cleaving onto the beach. Bilge water sluiced forward along blackened planks carrying white bits of coconut meat and hairy hunks of husk, chunks of wood, and fleshy pink pieces of fish. Mosabe clutched up his faded sarong and stepped ashore. Although there were more than fifty years between us in age, and who knows how many thousands of years of cultural differences, we felt very close to each other. I would never offend him intentionally, but Gayle and I had reached our saturation point over islander visits. She had made me promise to confront him this morning.

"Salaam," he said.

"Salaam," I repeated.

He barked directions to his rowing boys to carry up two jugs of fresh water he had brought for us. We trekked up to our front porch where Mosabe thrust out his white canvas hat with some small chicken eggs buried in a handful of sand. He also pulled a lovely green papaya from the folds of his sarong. I listed these items with a pencil on a scrap of wood I kept pushed up into the roof thatch of our porch. Mosabe was content getting paid after the amount reached a few rupiah.

Once our business was concluded, he grunted his approval and shouted out, *"Sa,"* short for *Kire du sa*, meaning tea, and stomped off into the woods with his boys carrying machetes to cut coconuts for us, the island counterpart of fresh-baked muffins or bread. We made milk tea for his return.

Mosabe whacked off the top of our coconuts with his island-made machete, blacksmithed with a thick and curved ridge over the top of the blade for extra weight. The method was to expose the white meat through the lime green husk, but not break through into the coconut. It was the island pop-top system like on a soda can. When we were ready we just poked a finger through to drink.

The dark musky cavity of a newly opened *karamba* smelled like roots exposed in damp earth. The milk was fresh and sweet. I wiped my chin. Mosabe sliced off a green sliver of a spoon from the outer husk, and split the nut into a couple of bowls containing small portions of the creamy young fruit for us to eat. This was our morning ritual.

While Mosabe and I drank our *karamba* on the front porch, Gayle lingered inside today, making the bed so I could confront Mosabe about the visits.

He peeked his head into the doorway to see what was taking her so long. I wondered how even if Mosabe understood our privacy issues, how he could keep the other islanders away. People here moved together like schools of fish. There didn't seem to be any leaders. To explain I began by taking Mosabe by the hand over to the wall of windows outside our bedroom where I pressed my face up to the glass to stare through. I knelt and pointed to all the foot prints below the window.

Mosabe held his hand up, curling his fingers for me come back to the porch and sit down, indicating with an uncharacteristic grimace that he was also fed up. He waved his arm at the horizon as if he would shoo them all away. He looked me in the eyes either to convince me, or see if I were convinced. Then he continued sipping his tea as if the matter were closed.

Gayle appeared standing in the doorway like an exclamation mark.

By August 18, our worries were compounding with the baby being overdue and islanders arriving in even larger boats from more distant islands to gawk at us. Mosabe was now clearly distressed himself, but obviously unable to intercede. Boats called a *batheli*, with a long bowsprit carrying a billowing white jib and a weathered thatched hut amidships followed each other across the silvered horizon directly to the front of our house. Maldivian families crowded along the gunnels to come ashore.

My mood had grown sour over these visits, and I was feeling desperate to shake my recurring flu-like symptoms. One day about noon, I carried my sleeping bag out onto the beach and crawled in, to try and bake my illness to death. The burgundy lining of my kiln was glowing and my head pounding when I heard someone shout. I slithered out of my bag in a delirium as two large *batheli* sailed into our lagoon. I waved them away, shouting. Then I grabbed handfuls of shells and threw them out into the lagoon.

The islanders stared at me in disbelief, glistening in sweat as my shrapnel splashed across their bows, and for the first time they turned and poled their boats away.

Surprised and saddened by my own behavior, I worried over how very ill I might be. There was no ache in my back from the kidney stone. Had we overshot our mark somehow, becoming isolated beyond what we'd come to find? I could not escape the fact that our problems were mounting.

"Nonsense," Gayle said. "Any pregnant female would snap at her husband or anyone else crowding her. A mother has a right to her privacy. You can bet the islanders understand that. And my baby and I are fine, so don't worry. But I am concerned about you."

"Whatever is wrong with me isn't going to kill me. It's not what's most important right now."

60
Mosabe's Prediction

I believed Gayle, that she was fine, but according to our books her pregnancy risk was now *high,* because of her bout with preeclampsia and the fact that she was over forty-two weeks. Had we opted for a hospital birth back in Los Angeles at this time, she most surely would have been induced. From the research I had done at the time, she would have been pushed in a wheelchair to be shaved, examined, given an enema, and an intravenous drip containing Pitocin to start labor and provide fluids. Drinking anything would be forbidden in preparation for an emergency C-section which after looking at hospital statistics, seemed probable. The procedures would have compounded from there: a fetal monitor belt, constant exams, drugs, ultrasound, nurses recording data, noise, and strangers. Had she resisted a Caesarean section, Gayle would have been subjected to unyielding pressure from the hospital to concede. And I wondered if the hospital could exercise a legal right to take charge, had they determined her decisions endangered the baby? In any case, risks due to human error including the misuse of data as well as the data-collecting itself would only increase. Not to mention the dangers of pathogens in a hospital setting.

Sitting in the palm shade rereading all this made me sad and angry, to think of the disruption to any woman's biorhythms and self-confidence, the corruption of her time-proven capacity to give birth. Why hasn't the medical establishment instilled fear in women for sailing around the world, or riding a bicycle, or playing soccer, or just going for a walk? Of course it's obvious, I thought, most women are vulnerable to hysteria whipped up over the safety of their children, and intervention must be huge business. And it establishes male hegemony.

I put my book over my knee and gazed out over the sea. Less obvious is something far more ominous and obscene, I thought. What has happened to the integrity of complex gene-driven relationships between a baby and mother that must be crucial to a child's development, as well as to the empowerment and affirmation of her mother? That's the wedge driven in. Both baby and a mother are separated from experiences which are fundamental to being human. Something lacking instills dependency and allows for social control.

But it is not my position to argue our choices in the face of maternal and fetal death rates in the world. Our choices were for our lifestyle, choosing empowerment over fear or inadequacy. And pregnant Maldivian women who came to visit helped us relax. They compared bellies with Gayle and laughed. They knew what a healthy pregnancy looked like, that we all grow and develop at different rates. They took forty-two or forty-three weeks in stride.

Mosabe arrived one day with the Bodu Fulidu midwife, without ever asking us beforehand. She had a white rag tied around her head, and energetically reached for Gayle's belly, as she would any pregnant belly in her village.

Gayle fended her off. "Ooooh, no! Keep her back, Frank. I don't need any help. Thank you."

"Why not let her touch you, Gayle? She might have some good advice."

The woman advanced again.

"No. That woman is not putting her hands on my belly. She doesn't look you in the eyes. She's weird."

"I wouldn't insult her. She did come all the way over here to help."

"I am fine, thank you."

I shrugged my shoulders at Mosabe. He bowed and walked back with the midwife through the forest to his boat.

By August 19, the baby was nearly three weeks overdue, and we walked hand and hand around the west side of our Kuda Fulidu to see the sunset. Both of us were trying not to be anxious over the challenge before us. We had reached the *wait-no-longer* point, which we had agreed upon before we came to the island.

Crows squawked and sailed overhead. The westerly breeze rustled the broadleaved shrubs where the beach narrowed to a ledge of white sand. I held out my hand to help Gayle along.

"I know I'm not the prettiest sight right now, but it worries me when you call me your *elephump*. I don't like the bad thoughts I'm having."

"Like what?"

"If the baby is all right? If he's gotten too big to come out... or if I am going to die?"

I was undone to hear her ask such a question. She was so full of life, so young, yet I knew I should seriously consider what she said. I stopped and stared at her bare feet in the sand. Her drawstring shorts somehow stayed up under her tanned and bulbous belly. Taking a breath, I looked up into her eyes, bright with the water born light of leafy green shrubs along the shore. Bright with her incredible courage, and humility. I foundered again at the thought of her dying. An unbearable vision flashed across my mind of sitting alone in the house beside her body. I gasped, kicked up a fan of sand to dispel the errant thoughts of what could happen. The breeze chilled the tears in my eyes. I pulled her hand to continue walking, clutching her hand behind my back, trying to find my voice, my own courage.

"You're not going to die," I said turning, feeling the incalculable sway of our unknown fate. "But you are three weeks overdue."

"Has it already been three weeks?"

"The day after tomorrow. We promised each other to leave the island by then."

"I'm just worried, Frank. It's completely normal. Any woman would be scared right before birth. As long as the baby is active, and I'm healthy, which I am, then it's okay."

"Are you saying we should forget the limits we agreed on?"

"I just don't feel right leaving. What if I go into labor on the boat? Wouldn't that be our karma for not trusting our intuitions to have our baby here!"

Back at our house Gayle wanted to linger on the beach alone. I walked back into our house to get things ready for dinner, while there was still some light. I looked around at our things, or should I say I felt our things were looking at me. My binoculars sat there on the book shelf as if glaring at me for having considered packing them in a crate. I must have lost my mind to be anthropomorphizing our household stuff, I thought. Next I'll be having a discourse with a sponge, if we had one. Then my chess set caught my attention, and I could not shake the feeling I had cheated. I looked around to confirm what I suspected, at our cradle made up with tiny blankets and sheets with the ponies on the padded enclosure, and to our boxes of food. It was true; I was a traitor. "Okay, Okay, Okay," I announced out loud to the room "Enough! We are going to do this altogether." Later when I told Gayle what happened, she told me I should get a job writing Disney movies.

On August 21, the morning we had agreed to return to Male, the main island, if our baby had not been born yet, we began another day. It was a very quiet day, calm with no wind, but not too hot. Neither of us wanted to speak much, or waste our energy trying to sound free from worry. We had now engaged ourselves just as surely as our baby's head, to be born into a new experience of ourselves. There were no longer any alternatives to sap energy from us. It was as if a mirror had unfogged and our commitment to our plan was directly reflected in everything we did.

I stepped out of the kitchen to help Gayle pull water from the well. Steam rose from the wet cement. I took the well dipper from her, a long banyan root pole with a coffee can lashed to the end by coconut twine. I lowered it until I heard the hollow gushing sound and felt the weight of it filling with water. Then I hauled it back up, stiff armed, to avoid scraping the sides of the well.

"Over here." Gayle motioned me to empty the dipper into a green plastic bucket holding a mound of soapy underwear.

"How are you feeling?"

"Fine," she said curtly. "I'm cramping. I'm nauseated. And I don't like how the baby is so quiet. Usually when I get up in the morning he's quite active. And I feel like I'm getting my period."

"But you're not bleeding or anything?"

"No." Gayle tapped the bucket with the side of her foot. "Will you scrub these for me?"

I kneaded the soapy underwear into the bottom of the bucket.

"Save the suds. I got more stuff."

Gayle suddenly straightened and pulled her blouse up over her belly. Some baby part visibly rolled the surface and turned back inside. She breathed a sigh of relief.

"It's good when he lets me know he's okay."

The next afternoon Mosabe visited. I pulled my *dhoni* to the shore next to him as he lashed up a split oar. He glanced up at me from time to time, as I battened down my boat in case I were house bound with our new baby. It occurred to me I had better ask if one of the islander's big *dhoni* could be available if we had an emergency.

The main halyard snagged, and I whipped it free from the mast head. Mosabe was cinching coconut twine in tight winds around the split in his oar, tying off the end of each wind at the middle. I knew a better way of doing this and showed him on my tiller, pulling the ends tight into a bight under the twine, rather than knotted on top.

He examined my sample and laughed admiringly, then proceeded to do it his way on a lower section of his oar. After a moment he stopped and looked me deeply in the eye. "Gayle," he shouted, turning his hand over in the air and patting his stomach. "Maadhamaa! Maadhamaa!"

"Birth tomorrow... maadhamaa?" I repeated.

He nodded once, "Maadhamaa." He held my gaze to be certain I understood that he was not guessing, that he was an elder who had witnessed a village grow. I waved goodbye as Mosabe launched his boat into the chop of the evening breeze. He sailed out from the shadow cast over our shore and into the softly setting light of the sea beyond. His thin figure bent to the tiller home, and I walked up the beach to our house, not even realizing I had forgotten to ask for a standby boat.

PART VI
FROM THIS MATRIX

61
A Baby

The night air was hot and damp with the weight of storms in the West. The island felt hunkered down for a blow. We lay in bed and I told Gayle of Mosabe's prediction that morning.

"And the emergency boat you wanted to ask for?"

"No I didn't. I can't believe it, but I didn't."

"That's not like you," Gayle said.

We went to bed spooned together, listening to thunder in the distance. We had slept for almost 6 hours when I felt Gayle jerking my arm in the dark. It seemed I had just closed my eyes.

"Frank! Frank! The show is on! I just lost my mucus plug." Gayle was sitting holding a flashlight beamed on the sheet between her legs.

"You sure?"

"Positive. I have contractions, blood-tinged mucus. The cervical plug has come out. It's happening."

"How do you feel?"

"Excited. I feel really excited. It's finally happening."

I focused on the luminescent blur of numbers on the face of my watch, which I had put it on last night for the first time since we arrived. It was just after four in the morning. How had Mosabe known?

"I'm not feeling too well, Gayle. Maybe it's better I get some more sleep. For the strength I need to help with the birth."

"It's okay. Right now, I'm just cramping like crazy."

I knew Gayle would understand me going back to sleep. There's a functional detachment we learned at sea, to conserve energy in storms rather than getting too wrapped up in the excitement of the moment. I fumbled the watch off my wrist and gave it to her. "Wake me when the contractions get closer together." Then I flopped face down on my pillow, holding her hand in mine.

"This is the last time there will only be the two of us," Gayle said as I fell back into deep sleep.

I never forgot those words. She told me later that while I slept, snoring heavily, the sun rose as if over the edge of a blue porcelain cup. She said it was the most beautiful sunrise she had ever seen, and that she would paint it someday, the fiery ripples advancing over the lagoon that were hot as her contractions.

Gayle did not wake me until about 8 a.m. "Frank, my contractions are five minutes apart."

"Five minutes apart!" I shouted, leaping up. "Five minutes! Why didn't you wake me?"

"You were so tired."

I noticed immediately that Gayle did not look well. Her forehead was furrowed, cold and clammy. Her skin color was purplish, as if she lacked oxygen. I began massaging her neck and shoulder muscles which had knotted into a hump. The next contraction vibrated under my hands, humming like an electric motor trying to make a revolution. Her whole body seized, and hardened into a rocklike mass.

"Breathe," I said, feeling panicked, and taking the advice myself. "Take - a - deep - breath."

"It really hurts," she sputtered. "You have no idea."

"Okay, but breee – athe."

Adrenalin surged through my own system and must have erased my memory. Try as I might I could not recall what I was supposed to remember. It was like staring at a page that had been erased. Try as I might, I could not focus on my notes either.

I turned back to massaging her lower back.

"Oh.... I've been waiting hours for this," she moaned.

"It feels like I'm massaging a marble statue your muscles are so tense."

"Don't stop."

Sweat dripped off my nose as tropical heat oozed inside our little house. My arms ached to a stop. I grabbed a towel to blot Gayle's forehead and then mine.

"That's enough." She swiped my hand away. "I'm okay now." She kicked the sheet down and scooted back on her elbows. "Give me some pillows against my back."

Her legs stuck out like stretcher handles and I grabbed another pillow. "Breathe...." That's all I could think to say. "Take a deep, deep one!"

There was no bleeding. Nothing obviously wrong. She tipped her head back with each contraction, sinking deeper and deeper into her pillows. Her eyes were out of focus, kind of fleshy and disconnected looking like fruit on the ground under a tree. I was completely unnerved, but somehow steady too.

She struggled to breathe, casting surprised looks at me, wrinkling her brow to strain on another contraction.

"You're doing great," I said, amazed by the strength in my voice. "Slow down. Bring your breath in slowly with the contraction."

Gayle gave a few quick nods.

I pried my watch out of her fist, and collected myself to write in my notebook: *August 23: 8am. Contractions 5 minutes apart. Things seem to be progressing quickly. I don't have a clue what to do other than....* I stared at the page. Why was I recording what I thought? My mind is side tracking me. *Get a grip*, I told myself. *Just record times and signs to refer back to!*

Suddenly Gayle swung her legs over the edge of the bed. "I gotta wash up before this gets any more intense."

"What? You can walk?" She leaned on my hand and stood. "Do you need me to hold you? What if a contraction comes?"

She took a step, then another. Then stooping like Mahatma Gandhi on a stick she headed determinedly out to the well. I followed closely behind and pulled water as fast as I could to fill a bucket. I warmed it with hot water from a pot simmering on the stove. I tried to help Gayle take off her shirt. She pushed me back, suddenly leaning over and bracing herself on her knees. "I need to rest a minute."

I took the moment to dash back into the kitchen and refill the pot, adjusting the flame in the thick blue smoke - no tea or meal to make, just water for scissors and laces. When I looked out the doorway, Gayle had seated herself on the rim of the well. Horrified, I dashed out and snatched her wrist.

"Let me go. Let me go, Frank"

"Oh my God, that's so dangerous, Gayle.

"I just need to sit," she pleaded. "I'm having a contraction."

"What if you fell down the well!" I said, positioning myself to hold her.

"My God it could have just happened." My imagination developed the scene like a photo, the horror of Gayle tipping in with her feet sticking up. The well wasn't more than fifteen feet deep, but I didn't have a ladder. She might have delivered the baby down there before I could rig a hoist, a seat, and figure a way to get her up over the edge. What if I dropped her back down? A woman in labor falling down a well was not a chapter in our birth books. And no 911 to call. Or anyone to help. Just one or two seconds more... I struggled not to think.

I grabbed an upside-down bucket for Gayle to sit on, and began soaping up her back and arms. She was too sensitive to be touched anywhere else. I dried her off as she teetered back along the cement path through the kitchen door. I eased her back onto the bed.

Mercifully the villagers had not shown up yet. Gayle asked for a couple of bananas. I was hungry too, but dared not take the time to even peel it, to better prepare and watch after Gayle. I hurried around cleaning and straightening up the house. I caught myself doing things twice, sweeping the same part of the floor again, like reaching around in the dark for a handhold. I filled the oil lamps for a night delivery, organized all my notes and birth books. Then I cooked some rice in case Gayle wanted soothing food at some point. I laid out her tea cup and spoon.

Most of our birthing supplies in the dresser were for emergency use. I pulled out the package of sheets from the bottom drawer, which we had sterilized by baking them in the oven in our bungalow in Male. The birthing book stated they would no longer be sterile after a week. "By the time I get done with them, there won't be a thing sterile about them anyway," Gayle had said.

I remade the bed while she stood with her hands on the dresser top, clutching each side of it as if she might heave it into midair. I got her back to bed, and pulled more fresh water from the well, filling the fifty gallon drum on the platform outside the kitchen sink spigot. I put another pot of water on the stove just in case, and stirred the already boiling scissors, shoelace, and ear syringe.

Then I brought a laundry bucket inside, and reminded Gayle. "You've got to pee. To avoid rupturing your bladder during birth."

She held my forearm to climb out of bed, but another contraction stopped her midway. I took her into my arms, her stomach quivering against mine as her grip tightened on my forearm. "Oooooooh."

There was nowhere to go, nowhere to turn. I pressed my face to the side of her face. We rocked slightly together. I tried to lead her breathing with mine as her contraction eased. She squatted on the bucket for a pee, and then short-stepped her way back to the bed. I was tucking her in, pushing the mosquito net under the mattress, when I heard the *thunk* of an oar against a boat out in the lagoon!

The sound came from the east side of the island. Then again, another oar *thunk*. Mortified, I looked at Gayle, but she hadn't heard it.

"I gotta go for a minute," I whispered. "Will you be okay?"

"Don't leave me," she rasped.

"I have to. Mosabe and his men are here. I've got to intercept them." Gayle pulled at the tangled sheet to cover herself. I hauled it up for her with both pairs of our hands gripping the edge.

She turned her head as I went out the door. "Tell Mosabe that we'll have a nice fresh coconut for him tomorrow," she rasped.

"I'll tell him. Just keep breathing, okay? I'll be right back."

I bolted out the door. The whacks of machetes already echoed in the forest. I hurtled barefoot over trunk-sized roots snaking out from the banyan tree, holding my elbows up to shove the smaller dangling roots aside. I sprinted along the southeastern shore over sharp blades of beach grass, and bounded off the elephantine root balls of palms leaning out over the beach. Glittering reflections of the sea seemed to spray from shrubs as I passed. Up ahead I glimpsed Mosabe's white head through the palms. I tried to appear calm as I came to a breathless, heel thumping walk.

Mosabe took one look at me. "Gayle?"

I nodded. He turned his head, and shouted out to his men in the forest. One by one they gathered behind him with their stout brown legs cocked out in the sand, their shoulders and hair sprinkled with wood chips. He took a cluster of young *karamba* coconuts hanging from one man's fist, and directed his men back to the boat. "Gayle," he said, extending the coconuts to me, and patting his stomach to demonstrate the goodness the milk would be for her.

As I turned to leave, he suddenly grasped my arm. He led me a ways further up the path, glancing over his shoulder to be sure his men weren't following. He stopped, and looked into my eyes. Patting his own chest, he whispered, "Mosabe, Ufan." He pointed at the ground, meaning our island. "Mosabe," he repeated.

I realized he was offering to stay and help me. I thought for a second of the friendship he was extending me. We'd be the oddest couple of midwives the Maldives would ever have on record! I pointed at him and then myself. He nodded his head firmly.

I took his hand. "Shukuriyya, Mosabe." I bowed my head, and pointed him back to Bodu Fulidu. "Shukuriyya."

He paused for a second longer, to be sure I meant it. "Salaam," he said, and his square thin frame marched off in his ragged shirt through the palms.

By noon, Gayle looked exhausted. She could not focus on anything. And anything I said sounded trite, such as: *Don't worry. This is just part of having a baby; I love you; how do you feel; you're doing great.* But it was all I could say because I had to be on the alert for anything going wrong. As I did not know for sure, a good heart full of optimism was best.

I switched from arm to arm as my muscles cramped working on her back. What good advice it would have been, I thought, for one of these birthing books to have suggested a father getting his arms in great shape for massaging his wife during birth.

Some of Gayle's contractions lasted two minutes, with one minute in between. Others were four minutes long, with a fifteen-second interval. Trying not to appear desperate even to myself, I flipped through my books, bristling with torn paper markers notated with: First Stage, Transition, Second Stage, Placenta Delivery, Bleeding, Tears, Suturing, Cord Cut, Delivery. Head, Suctioning,

Baby Breath Rate, Heart Rate, Resuscitation, Breech, Cord Prolapse....

What had happened to the *regular intervals* the books referred to? With contractions whipping around like the loose end of a high-voltage wire, they all seemed to be one continuous contraction.

Gayle glanced over at me flipping through books, my eyes unable to focus on the print. "It really hurts, Frank."

I shoved the clutter of books and notes aside and began massaging her again. "I can't figure this," I said. "Your contractions are erratic, but nothing seems to be wrong."

"It hurts more than I ever thought...."

The clarity in the tone of her voice caught my attention, reminding me of something I had read. She had been breathless for an hour or so. Murmuring incomprehensibly and gasping. Now her sudden composure could be a sign of the next stage of delivery.

"You can do this, Gayle. Trust your body."

"I feel like I might barf," she whispered.

I grabbed a bucket, but she suddenly arched her back as if she were drawing a bow. Then she tilted her head forward, compressing downward on the next contraction, gasping for air.

"Ride it out. Breathe!" I shouted. "You are stretching your cervix open. It's all working."

Her neck became terribly rigid, her muscles articulated as if they were being exaggerated in an anatomical drawing. I stood vigorously massaging her shoulders so that her blood would be able to circulate.

"Ooooooh, yes. Touching helps me feel where I'm tense."

A contraction began dragging her down by the heels. I added more pillows behind her back, but she flattened them like pennies on a railroad track. When I ran out of pillows, I shoved stacks of rolled up towels behind her, then bundles of clothes.

The sun rose high over the house. Waves of midday heat seeped in. The curtains lifted as if they would burst into flame. Gayle's moans were the only sounds in the silence.

I put a glass of water up to her lips and blotted her brow.

"What time... is it?" she asked scarcely able to enunciate her words.

"About 1:30."

"How many hours?" Her hand grasped mine. It was clammy, strangely strong.

"That makes it about... uh... nine or ten. That's since four this morning, when you first woke me."

"This is harder than anything I've ever done." She opened her mouth as if she were going to scream. But no sound came out.

"That's it, Gayle," I said. What I meant by *it*, I had not a clue.

Regaining herself, Gayle said, "I don't mean to be rude, Frank, but I don't think I'm going to have another baby. I'm not such a toughie as I thought. Once is enough."

"It won't be much longer now." But I thought, *what if I am wrong?* What if her labor took two or three days, like some accounts I had read about?

"I can't stand much more of this," she shouted suddenly, throwing her head back. "It hurts. Nothing helps!"

"You're running a marathon, Gayle. That's why your body hurts. You're okay."

"Then why's it taking so long?"

"It's not," I said unconvincingly, dreading this downturn. "You're having a baby in the time it takes. It's coming."

"But how much longer?" she cried, looking fixedly into my eyes, tears welling up and trickling down her cheeks. "Nothing seems to be happening. I don't think I'm dilating."

"You're dilating. That's what this is all about – the pain is the opening. Try not to worry. Concentrate. Breathe through it."

I stroked her head, and Gayle looked into my eyes, her reality-check-look, the most piercing she had in her arsenal for invoking my honesty. "Am I all right, Frank?"

I swallowed hard on that one. *Am I all right* with that look in her eyes meant *Am I and my baby going to live?* That was the question she entrusted to me, knowing I could never answer it.

In Sufi texts I had read that *the outer world is only language for the inner one.* For how many thousands of years have women enjoined their husbands in birthing? Had I never read a single account of the transition phase of birth, I think I would have known to stand firm now. The higher pitch in Gayle's voice, the concentration and resonance of her energy could have been nothing less than something breaking through.

"You're probably in transition, Gayle. Just that little bit of cervix left, and then it changes. Remember, you get the pushing feeling, the baby moving. All that is about to happen. Just hang on."

By 2:30 the sun had begun its descent over the back side of our house, and shafts of light now angled through the windows behind the bed. The front curtains blued from the afternoon shadow reaching across the lagoon. Gayle's breathing had begun to sound like asthma. Her voice had become more raspy, her breath short. I grabbed one of our books closed upon its bevy of torn paper bookmarks.

"Here it is, Gayle. *Short-winded and hoarse.* They're the symptoms of transition," I said. "You're in second stage! You're pushing the baby out!"

I had also read a midwife account of a *resting phase* that hospitals often interpret as a *failure to progress.* A *resting phase* may be experienced after the baby's head has passed through the cervix. Labor contractions may suddenly vanish as the uterus contracts upon the emptied uterine space. Some mothers relax or even sleep before contractions resume.

But Gayle did not rest. Instead the strangest symphony of grunts, hiccups, hisses, and whines began rising and falling on her breath. Then her breathing deepened dramatically. "I feel it moving," she said with new exuberance. Her face relaxed between pushes, then flushed pink from a sudden abundance of oxygen. The muscle tone of her thighs became smooth and soft. The change in her behavior and appearance was so abrupt it was disconcerting. She seemed suddenly to be having the ride of her life.

Gayle climbed into a squat to deliver, to help open the cervix, but she had become so limber and low-slung that I could see that the baby would have been born folded up like an accordion. "That doesn't look like it's going to work," I said.

"I'll lean back. Stack the pillows up behind me."

I noticed a bulge between her legs the moment she leaned back in an angled squatting position. It was 4:25 p.m. Could the two hours of *second stage* have already gone by? I had forgotten to record when transition had begun. In fact, I had recorded nothing since the beginning of labor.

The bulge continued growing bigger as I leaned down to stare at it. Suddenly the absolutely worst thought crossed my mind: Had she shoved her internal organs downward with such force that they were coming out? I looked more closely and to my astonishment the internal organ I feared coming out had hair!

"Hair!" I shouted. "It's a head! The baby's coming out. Stop pushing! Pant!"

"Are you sure?" Gayle gasped, trying unsuccessfully to tip her head up to see, reaching down to feel with her fingers.

I grabbed the hand mirror, and she angled it at the sliver of wet hair. The bulge grew with the next contraction. Her upper tummy was already deflating. Gayle dropped her head back down on the pillow and began to go tense.

"Don't push. Don't push! Pant! Wait until the baby's head has crowned. It's not ready."

We had sutures, anesthetic, and diagrams for fixing minor tears, but second or third-degree tears deep in the perineum and muscle, or especially the cervix were surgical problems we had to avoid. It was crucial that Gayle allow the perineum to slowly stretch over the baby's head.

The skin pulled back over the bulge, thinning to a pearly translucence. It became so taut I was afraid to try and massage it over the rest of the head, as I had read could be done.

"That's it! Pant! Wait till I tell you it's over the head."

Gayle began to quiver and shake, holding her breath. Then a muted cry spilled from her lips. She sounded like a distant siren, her cry suddenly deepening to a bear-like groan. I watched her whole body shove reflexively downward in one huge push.

The round of her birthing skin split in slow motion, tearing across like a wet sheet of paper. Not in the perineum as we expected, but the upper part of the labia minora. The opalescent womb-wet head thrust forward, with a slow irrepressible force, landing directly into my open hands.

In the next seconds nothing happened. Gayle lay cracked open like an egg, and I cupped the round of a baby's cheek and the back of his head in my palms. A sleeping chrysalis.

The cord was wound once around his neck but slipped off easily with my finger. I forgot to suction his mouth. He was already pink anyway. His presence, the amniotic aura of his face, drew my face close to his. Then, as if commanded to speak, his lips suddenly twitched, uttering a gurgling little cry. Not a complaint, but a wobbly declaration of life. Then he cried again, more forcefully with a clear intonation that I would recognize for the rest of my life as his voice.

I glanced up at Gayle tipping up her face to look between her knees. "He's pink," I said. "He's not breathing cause he's still getting oxygen from the umbilicus."

I remembered the ear syringe and sucked out his nose and mouth, but his passages were clear. Then Gayle's contractions fired back up, and with two big ones a little person shot forward, slippery as a fish into my hands. A boy! He lay across my palms with his fists clenched and knees up as if he had slid off a tiny throne.

Gayle broke into an awe inspired smile. "Oh, he's so beautiful."

I laid him up on her stomach with the cord reaching up between her legs. Her arm curled around him in a primordial movement, a mother's first embrace. After what seemed like only a minute or two, she nudged his cheek with her nipple, and in it went. He lay with his head attached to her breast, his stomach attached by the umbilicus to her uterus in a complete circuit of human genesis.

62
Violet Waters

The shadow of the blood river pulsed within the translucent white rope of the umbilicus which enabled our little boy to breathe easily, or miss a breath entirely, but his healthy pink color assured us he was getting enough oxygen. When the cord blanched, I would need to cut it. I noted that the tear in her labia had ceased bleeding. Everything felt and looked all right. It seemed pointless to count his breaths, take his pulse or make a record. We disregarded calculating an Apgar score done by some midwives and all hospitals to determine the baby's condition: scoring for heart rate, respiratory effort, muscle tone, reflex irritability, color, etc. etc.

The *what if* question had little impact on our decisions, especially since we had arrived on the island. In fact it would have been difficult to find a reason he was not healthy. We could see perfectly well that he had all his fingers, ears, and toes, and that his fontanel seemed nice and flat, which meant there was no swelling from pressure or depressions from dehydration. His little backbone was straight. His testicles were beautifully formed. He moved easily.

Gayle too, seemed fine. She decided not to have me stitch her labia, although the tear was almost an inch long. The drawers full of our emergency supplies would never be needed: not for resuscitation, cardiac massage, breech presentation, a prolapsed umbilical cord, fetal distress, hemorrhage, or delivery of twins, and so on ad infinitum.

As I write this I realize there's no way to explain or justify the magnitude of trust we had for our abilities to have a baby ourselves. Our circumstances illicited that response. Without an attachment to any other option, we slid over a threshold in our understanding of ourselves, to a place we still shared with parents thousands of years back, sitting with their newborns under the same stars with the complete nature of their experience and design known to them. And that was what the island had drawn out of us. I could say the island found itself in us, and drew our ship to it.

After about fifteen minutes, the cord blanched slightly and stopped pulsing, which indicated that the supply of oxygen had stopped. I tied a boiled shoelace around the cord about two inches from the baby's stomach, using half hitches, then secured that with a sailor's reef knot across the top for good measure. My scissors were not the sharpest, and the umbilicus was tough as an old piece of rigging rope. It took several digs to cut through. The baby's end oozed slightly. I tied it again with another lace as a precaution. The mother cannot bleed from the placental side of a cut cord, since it is not directly connected to her vascular system, so our decision was not to tie it and let it drain naturally onto a piece of sterilized gauze.

Nursing stimulates the uterus with the hormone oxytocin, causing the placenta to lose its grip upon the shrinking uterine wall. Not tying the placental side of the cut cord might be another unknown cue. Not thinking too much might be a good thing, because the human species has certainly got it figured out. So we waited patiently for the placenta.

I glanced out of our bedroom windows for what seemed to be the first time that day. A lime-green forest resplendent with budding stems and glowing leaves pressed in around us. The sun crinkled in silken ripples across the lagoon. A boisterous crow cawed. An evening breeze swayed the palm fronds beneath the thatched roof line. "Look, Frank," Gayle whispered. "He's listening to the wind. He nurses. Then he listens."

I straightened up the bed and sat down to dab our little one with a bit of cotton dipped in sterilized olive oil, even though he was very clean - squeegeed clean.

"Don't clean the creases, remember?" Gayle said.

I left the snowy vernix under his arms, knees, around his neck, and so on. I had read it was nature's protective coating produced by the sebaceous glands and skin cells.

"I think one ear is smaller than the other. Look. See," she said, tipping her body with him lying like a pollywog on her breast.

"I don't know. It's hard to see a difference."

"He must have got one of your father's big floppy ears," she said with a laugh that was good for me to hear.

The fifteen minutes passed that the books said would take to deliver the placenta. I listened to Gayle's cooing to her baby, as I glanced at my watch. Then twenty, thirty minutes passed with no contractions. How long could we wait without worrying? The answer to that question was another which had been conspicuously avoided in our texts. Traction or pulling on the umbilicus is dangerous if the placenta has not yet detached from the uterine wall. One test used by midwives is to push the uterus up, and if the cord follows up the birth canal, then the placenta must still be attached. But without this kind of experience, we decided again upon patience.

"Here it comes," Gayle said after forty-five minutes. "I'm having contractions." The placenta plopped out, along with a large glob of slippery skin which was the amniotic sack, and also the outer fetal membrane called the chorion, which first forms with the placenta. All appeared to be intact so there was no obvious reason to worry about anything being left inside Gayle's uterus.

"Oh my…." Gayle said.

Photographs of the placenta had not prepared us for its actual size. The umbilicus stood over the newspaper like a glistening tree trunk rooted in a thick mat of large blue veins radiating outward from the base. It was surprisingly solid and meaty to touch. I flipped it over to study its underside to look for missing pieces that might have been retained by the uterus, and could cause bleeding.

The bottom part resembled the velvety foot of a huge mollusk. Unaccustomed to the sight of internal organs, I ran my finger over the reddish-brown lobes of villi that had absorbed nutrients from Gayle's blood for the last nine months. Then I carried it out to the kitchen and plunked it into a pot. Gayle heard the pot lid clink down.

"You put it in the pot," she whispered.

"I didn't have any other place to put it"

"I'm not eating any of that thing. Period."

We had read of mothers eating the placenta in some cultures. It was rich in vitamin K, a natural blood coagulant. It had also been shown to increase lactation, and was thought to cure a number of ailments. There were actually recipes for eating it raw. Placenta sushi!

"I just don't see how anyone could eat it," Gayle had said. "It's worse than cannibalism. It's eating yourself!"

At sunset Gayle and our baby were about to fall asleep, and Gayle motioned me close to her face. "I think we should plant something over the placenta outside."

"Okay if you want, but what about the sea? Our son was conceived at sea."

"That's fine. I just want to rest now. Make sure it doesn't float back up on the beach."

I carried the pot with the placenta out to the lagoon, walking out over the bone white sand that was peach tinged in the low evening sun and dappled with palm shadows. The lagoon had turned to violet. At the water's edge I bowed my head for a moment, more grateful and excited than I needed to contemplate. Then I cast it out far as I could. There was hardly a splash.

As the ripples radiated outward, I prayed for the sea to bless and protect our son, for him to know himself and to love what he knows. I prayed for the joy and wisdom that had blessed us with his birth to guide him always. I stood there feeling my gratitude, and my relief as the last ring of ripples disappeared over the edge of the reef. It was then that I felt the pang, the thrill of being a new father, and hurried back up to the house.

63
Soft Knocking

The morning after the birth I awakened to a cooing duet only a nursing mother and infant could compose, followed by a volley of slurping noises that sounded like a bilge pump losing suction. I nudged my head up to Gayle's forearm and noticed something unusual about her skin. I sat up. "Good God, Gayle! Have you seen your skin? It's orange. Look at your arm. Your face. Christ, and your eyes are bright yellow!"

We had expected the baby might jaundice, due to a newborn's slow liver function at birth, which elevates bilirubin levels. None of my books could explain why at the time. But we had not expected Gayle to jaundice. She lifted her forearm for a look. Our son protested the disturbance.

"You've got hepatitis! Just like people in Male before we left. Your yellow eyes mean for sure you've got it."

"Don't panic. I feel fine. We're both fine. Look, his skin is pink."

I looked at our little guy closely, and smoothed his white skin under my fingers. . "He seems okay."

"And no one in Male seemed to get that sick."

"No, but the locals might have developed an immunity that we haven't. Don't forget the Korean tourists who died in Sri Lanka."

"We're fine Frank. Read up on it to be sure. So that if I do have Hep, what that means for our baby."

After doing some research, I plopped down on the bed next to my golden maiden to consider our options. "It basically says that young babies are rarely affected by hepatitis A. Because their livers are so *regenerative*."

Gayle rubbed her nose against the baby's. "I told you."

"You can't eat oil or hard to digest food or anything that puts a load on your liver. And you'll have to take plenty of Vitamin C and B."

"Okay, Dad."

"You have to rest to get over this, Gayle. That could be weeks. I'll do all the work."

Little did I know what that would entail. Gayle looked down at our baby and then glanced back at me. "I think he looks like your dad. He's got your dad's cheeks and nose."

I went out on the porch and sat down on the edge of the landing. The caw of a crow folded into the waves slapping the shore. I gazed at the tanned tops of my feet pressed into the sand. They were wide as my dad's, but not so heavy-boned. I remember my dad's white monstrous feet in the bathroom as he stepped out of the shower when I was a toddler. Feet that size can only be a dad's feet. How much I would have loved for him to sit beside me now, feet to feet in the sand. I wondered how big his feet would be compared to mine. I suddenly yearned to experience myself grown with him. His brooding shadow would have vanished in the light here. And his Zeus-like size would have settled into human proportions. And I would have taken him in my boat, to celebrate with him what I have discovered in my blood.

No islanders showed up until the second morning after the birth. I heard someone softly knocking and there were Mosabe and

Abdullah crowded shoulder to shoulder in the doorway. Abdullah pointed at the cradle for permission to come in and see the baby. Gayle emerged from the kitchen cinching up her sarong, and invited them in. They hurried over to the crib. Abdullah bowed deeply with his hands clasped in prayer. Mosabe crowded up impatiently behind him. I couldn't help but notice that Mosabe did not bow, stood straight as an arrow as if to assert his authority. I supposed he was the undisputed village head, of both islands. It had never occurred to me till later that the first new born baby to a land, his placental blood seeped into the sand, would have some indisputable sovereignty that Mosabe must have felt at the time.

They both stared into the crib. Mosabe looked up, shuffling in place, averting his eyes from mine. Abdullah lifted his head with an uncomfortable smile, and began bowing as if he'd been wound up with a key. "*Reethi, Reethi*" he said, but beautiful was not what he was thinking. I glanced at Gayle. Her cheeks had dimpled and flushed, as they do when she is amused by embarrassing situations.

"Let's face it," she said to me over their heads. "Their babies are gorgeous, they've got cinnamon skin and perfect features. These guys have never seen a little white baby before."

Compared to island newborns, our boy must have appeared pale as a sick crab. Not only that but his features were puffy, and his head molded to the shape of a papaya rather than beautifully round like theirs.

I stepped up and put my arms affectionately around Mosabe's and Abdullah's shoulders. They nearly jumped out of their skins. The commotion woke the baby who began to cry.

I picked him up and held him to my chest. "Say hello to Mosabe and Abdullah." I turned him around to face them.

They nodded approvingly to each other, greatly relieved to see me embrace such an odd looking baby.

"*Naan?*" Abdulla asked swaying his open palm.

No I told them. No name yet.

Abdullah bowed again, and Mosabe pointed his machete toward the forest, to indicate he was going for coconuts.

"They'll get over the shock eventually," Gayle laughed. "Why don't you take him for a walk so I can get some rest?"

A firm breeze polished the sea a shiny indigo. I pulled up a flap of the sarong he was wrapped in, to protect his face from flying sand. I walked off down the beach buffeted by warm gusts with our little one snuggled up into my neck. We had rooted like pioneers on this scrap of land. A new village had begun and this was now our son's homeland. I peeked at the tiny little face, the thin little lips already flexing around so many things to say.

64
Honoring Family

Three weeks after our son's birth, Gayle changed back from yolk yellow to her normal flour white and freckled complexion. My health also improved on her liver-easing diet. I still had not seriously considered I had some stage of hepatitis, even after Gayle's outbreak. Just as Gayle had adjusted her due date to get to the island, I had too many responsibilities to be sick at that time.

Abdullah appeared by himself at our house a couple of days after the birth. I had never seen him on our island without Mosabe. They were inseparable sidekicks, although he must have been thirty or more years Mosabe's junior. He was a handsome man, darker and shorter than Mosabe, no more than four and a half feet tall. His head could not have been more than twice the size of my fist, but his feet were much wider than my double E. He often held his thumb under his chin which had a pious shadow of a beard. His appearance always introduced a contemplative moment. His muscular physique did not seem to fit his gentle demeanor until one day I came across him deep in the forest, leaping back and forth as gracefully as a leopard over a palm tree he had felled. He swung his axe to shape a plank in the shadow-dark of the canopy, breathing through his mouth and feasting on the aroma of pungent wood.

This particular morning Abdullah stood in our doorway with a scrap of white cloth draped over his head. He was barefoot and barechested in a maroon sarong holding a tiny cloth bundle on his palm, very delicately as if not to wake it. With the fingers of his free hand he unfolded the cloth to reveal a curved sliver of nautilus shell. There was a hole in one corner, with a piece of string through it. He motioned to give it to our baby, went over and placed the shell on his bed, bowed, and left.

Mosabe hurried up from the shore to see what had been going on. Then he told us, patting his chest, that he would bring us a much better shell tomorrow. True to his word, he rushed shamelessly into our house with a larger piece of shell, embellished with a serrated trim around the edges.

Abdullah leaned forward and curiously eyed the fancier gift from Mosabe, but did not appear in the least offended. On the contrary, he offered to bring us yet another, and even better shell the next morning. To stop the competition, I asked Abdullah to tie his first shell gift around our baby's neck. Seeing this, Mosabe marched off into the forest as if the issue were closed.

While Gayle recovered from hepatitis, I had no time for anything but cooking, cleaning, and washing from morning till night. A regular job back home would have been a vacation. By the time I scrubbed my first load of laundry, another pile had grown outside the kitchen door: king-sized sheets, bath towels, and buckets overflowing with soiled diapers. Everything had to be done by hand, scrubbing on an old fashioned steel corrugated washboard. Every liter of water to rinse soap from the piles of cloth had to be hauled from the well with the well stick.

Sodden bombs full of meconium flew out the kitchen door as I worked. The slightest soap residue in such a humid heat was caustic to our skin, and especially to the baby's. All had to be endlessly twisted and wrung out, rinsed again and again until cottony white clouds of diapers floated in clear water without a soap bubble. Then I laid them out to dry over every shrub and branch in the clearing around our house. It looked like diapers had been air dropped over our island.

Island women who had come over to gather fallen palm fronds for their fires, emerged from the trees as I did laundry at the well. The last two weeks after the birth had been a welcome hiatus from visitors. The ladies squeezed around me working out on my washboard, elbowing each other in amusement with their machetes extended from their fists. I'm sure a man doing laundry was stranger than anything they ever imagined, especially one who didn't eat fish. But they told me I was good for delivering my own baby, and I felt genuinely appreciated.

Evenings I staggered into the house and collapsed across the dining room table, my forearms swollen and hard as green pineapples. The kitchen still had to be cleaned up from the day's meals. Our lanterns had to be filled and lit. The house swept. Dinner made.

"How's it going, Dad?" Gayle whispered, nursing inside the mosquito net.

"We forgot the washing machine," I groaned.

"Told ya!" she cooed laughing. "But no, you didn't want modern conveniences."

"I say, forget the diapers. Let's do it island style. Only use diapers at night."

Gayle looked down and whispered to our sleeping boy. "Poor Daddy is going to expire out there. We're going to have to try something new."

I began dashing baby into the woods whenever he started grunting. Or held him out the window, often leaving a pooh trail across the floor. I washed his bottom out in the lagoon. Somehow islanders knew exactly when to walk out with their babies. I practiced studying his face and his squirter for any telltale twitch or warning. I could not get it right at first, missing the almost imperceptible relaxation around his nostrils, when his geysers hit me in the eye with uncanny precision. We saved on diapers, but added pee soaked sheets and towels to my washing load.

Then our baby developed a nasty rash and gas pains. His response was to cry all night. I paced him back and forth bundled up to my shoulder, till my back ached so badly it forced me to take the risk of laying him down. I handled him like a land mine as my exhaustion felt like a matter of life and death. Invariably, he started bawling again the instant his body touched the sheet. I was desperate for some childcare advice.

I asked Gayle if she thought we should take him to Male to get him checked out.

"We'll figure this out," she said, blowing on his blisters to dry them. So we kept him aired and changed in fresh gowns. Gayle sunned his bottom, and comforted him every waking moment. Somehow after stocking the island with absolutely every imaginable thing, we had overlooked Talcum powder. But Mosabe insisted on sprinkling a handful of white flour on the rash, which definitely helped.

Gayle stopped eating lentils and other foods she suspected of causing colic, and I found that by pressing my fingers into his stomach, I could scoot his gas bubbles along, in a sort of intestinal soccer game. A fart was a score.

We also had an East Indian book on baby yoga with pictures of babies folded up like pretzels. A bit unsettling at first folding your baby, but the *gas release pose*, with one foot across to the opposite shoulder produced plenty of relieving toots. And so it went with many little ceremonies making our home work, but without ever having a discussion about when we would leave.

In a letter to her mother Gayle wrote: *I have felt freedom here like never before. I watch sunsets that are unimaginable. I am amazed by it all. The palm trees are so free. They curve in every direction and are almost sensual. They gently sway in the fresh fresh breeze. Our shoreline is emerald green under emerald blue. I pick up beautiful polished shells on the beach. They are just waiting to be found like jewels. I don't think we'll ever see beauty like this again.*

65
Storm Riding

Gayle and I watched the squalls of the South West Monsoon grow larger and more powerful. They scraped the sky, dragging their black curtains along, inking out islands one by one across the horizon. When one veered our way, its mantle of darkness crackled and exploded overhead, furiously raking the palm heads. If we were caught away from the house, we dashed back through blasts of wind so laden with falling water that waves seemed to be bursting over the island.

Our routine was to wash in the torrential showers cascading off the thatched roof. We scrubbed ourselves naked and shampooed our hair, hurrying as the clouds parted. Then as suddenly as the squall hit, it sailed away, leaving us often shivering and rinsing our hair in the last rivulets off the thatch. When the sun beamed into the forest again, every plant steamed as if on fire, and our holding tank spilled fresh water over the top.

I had another engagement with the squalls in my boat out at sea that I kept secret from Gayle. When I saw one coming, I ran for my spars and rigged my *dhoni*. I bounded out over the waves, as the storm bit down on the last sliver of daylight. I held my position upwind as the wind stiffened and bawled. The surface of the sea turned to black velvet, and then to a crazy vista of foam tumbling like white feathers. With every ship's line humming, fairleads to rudder pintles stressed to the brittle edge, every stitch and seam pulling, only then would I helm my boat away from the wind, her bow sluggishly plowing the backs of waves and throwing plumes of spray as I pointed homeward. In the full force of wind, that dank and water laden blast, I let the sail fly into a loop as it was designed to spill wind. The white canvas curled up into the grey smoke, wagging violently in the storm's teeth. I flung the tiller this way and that to counter the force turning me back on the face of the rollers. Waves and spray hissed over the deck, and sluiced aft into the bilges. At the peak of the squall's force I was close to the safety of our lagoon, and with the deck boards drumming it began to pour, the torrential rain smoking up the sea.

I spotted Gayle running out to the south point, her sarong whipped around behind her, with our son clutched to her breast. I waved victoriously, careening past her into the safety of our lagoon. She stood on the shore as I trudged in with my sail wrapped on its spar, and balanced over my shoulder.

"Are you crazy! Are you out…" The wind stole the rest. She hurried alongside me. "You've got a family to think of now! You want to leave your son fatherless? What're we going to do if you don't come back?"

"I didn't come here to wash diapers every minute of the day." I shouted into the wind and walked past her.

She caught up with me. "What about the friggin islanders who got blown to Africa?"

"That was the Northeast Monsoon. This one's headed for Australia."

Gayle was referring to an account of some islanders blown across the sea in their boat, unable to fight their way back against monsoon winds and currents. They had helmed their way over unfathomable depths for thousands of miles in an open boat with a patched lateen sail. They had uplifted their palms to the rain, coaxed fish to a hook, and had sailed on with nothing but the baking sun and shivering stars for a compass. One can only imagine how thin the skin of their small open boat, and how deep their will to survive. But after weeks turning around in the stars they sighted the blue anvil-headed clouds over land. In my heart I knew those men. How they trudged ashore with their stories that nobody could understand. I knew the sea-eye that would steady generations of mariners born to them, as O'Riordan's had steadied mine.

My trips out into the weather aroused a belligerence and helplessness, even in a sailor like Gayle. She would not be consoled, bracing her shoulders, her eyes hard and angry. At sea she had relied upon me unflinchingly, but to face trusting my permanence as a father tormented her.

66
Kokko's Name

The weather eased and the seasonal storms diminished. Fishermen sailed home afternoons, routing through our lagoon. They grinned as their boat slid by a few yards from me flailing diapers, with schools of sliver-sized fish nipping at my fingertips in clouds of baby poop bits. They lined up along the gunnels and held up their prize fish for the day. I held up a clean diaper. They laughed, calling out questions I could not understand, and *Salaams* to Gayle and Kokko.

That's what they called our baby, Kokko, pronounced coco. So we called him that too. No other name seemed right. Not my father's name, Homer, or Alexander, Arthur, or Ludovick, or any other of my family names. All of them sounded leaden and gray in this sunny tropical expanse. Gayle never offered any of her family names. She insisted our son would let us know what his name was. I searched the Maldivian language for something that sounded right.

"You can't call a boy *Fousse*," Gayle said. "Or *Mudu*. Whatever that means?"

"It means 'waves' and *Fousse* means 'clouds'."

"Whatever – 'cause when he goes to school, the kids will tease him."

It seemed a bit late to worry about what people would think, but I skipped mentioning *Doe Monico* and *Tou Tou*, Maldivian names which might have survived from times before Islam was introduced to the Maldives in 1153. They were Buddhist before then, settled by people from southern Asia. The name Maldives was believed to have originated from the Sanskrit *maladivpa*, meaning "garland of Islands."

I decided to sail over to Bodu Fulidu and ask Mosabe about a name for our son. I tugged my boat through the shallows toward our lagoon entrance, gripping the snub of bent wood protruding from her bow. It was a gloriously warm and blustery morning. Avocado-green wavelets lapped against my thighs, and the scent of warm salt water was thick in the wind. I held the whipping mainsheet in one hand and leapt aboard, thrilling to the charge across the ruffled blue channel through our reef. In my whole life I would never forget being barefoot on warm wooden planks, and accelerating over those waves. I tightened up the mainsheet bent around a crook of hardwood on the gunnels. From there it led aft to a post where I stood on the helmsman's platform. *Dhoni*s are designed to be sailed this way, standing and steering with one foot to give the helmsman a better view of reefs and fish ahead.

Gayle waved from the porch at the side of our house as I surged back across our beach outside the lagoon on the wave crests toward the green mound of Bodu Fulidu. I turned to let my shoulder blades soak up the morning sun.

Mosabe was not at his forge, where I anchored on the north end of the island. A teenage boy squatted at the hearth, vigorously squeezing a bellows into the firebox. Several machete blades made from car spring steel and various smaller knives without their handles lay pushed to one side. Mosabe's wooden mallet lay next to a pair of unfinished rudder pintle brackets.

I waited around for awhile, and then walked to Abdullah's house in the center of the village. Children with big brown eyes watched me pass from their shady verandas. A handful of them found their voices and rushed excitedly ahead, shouting the news of my arrival.

Abdullah emerged from his thatched hut, holding his infant daughter, and patted a bench for me to sit in the shade of his pitched roof. He shooed away the kids hanging on my knees, and we sat in silence. Crows cawed noisily, sailing overhead like charred pieces of sky, and thudded onto palm fronds to protest my visit. The sun blazed on the tops of my feet. I pulled them back into the shadow, and rubbed the burning skin. A group of barefoot girls crossed the clearing chatting with each other, arms full of coconut husks for kitchen fires. Down on the shore, another group of girls laid fillets of tuna upon racks to dry in the sun, pushing tall sharpened slivers of a palm frond into each piece to discourage marauding crows and seabirds. The absence of most of the men and boys meant the tuna were running.

Abdullah's wife stepped out from the doorway and handed me a glass of mango juice. She was in her thirties, beautiful, with fine Indian features, sinewy muscular arms, and shiny black hair. She wore it knotted to one side and tied at the end with a broad piece of white cloth. I felt suddenly shy in her presence.

None of us spoke. That was their way. I could have left without uttering a word, and that would have constituted an agreeable visit, but today I was on a mission. I asked Abdullah about a name for our son, turning my palm up, and sifting it back and forth island fashion to request an answer.

"DonKokko," he replied without hesitation, wagging his head with a smile.

The *Don* part was new to me.

A man walked by, and Abdullah called him over. He introduced him as his brother and then stood beside him, lowering himself at the knees and patting his chest.

"Kokko," he said.

"Ah! So Kokko means little brother."

"Ahhhh," Abdullah said, nodding his head as if he understood English.

"Don," Abdullah said, pinching the skin on my arm. It wasn't till later that I discovered Don meant fair, not white as I first thought. Our son's name was DonKokko, "Fair Little Brother."

It was early afternoon when I trudged back up our baking hot beach. Gayle was swinging in the shade in the *joli* the islanders had given us. A *joli* is a net seat within a wood frame, usually suspended from the curve of a palm. Her sarong flapped back and forth across her legs as Kokko slept in her lap. I plopped down on the edge of the landing, a pool of seawater dripping off my shorts.

"Kokko means 'little brother,'" I whispered.

Gayle swung the joli by kicking her legs straight with her toes poked in the sand.

"Like you said," I added. "Kids will always find something to torment each other about."

"It was mainly one black girl," Gayle whispered, "named Glenna. She had a clubfoot. She used to wait for me walking home from school. She beat me up and tore the arms off my doll. And some other stuff I'd rather not talk about."

Gayle had never before told me what happened with this person before. Mosquitoes hummed around my legs. I buffed the air to shoo them away.

"The complete name is DonKokko. That's what they call him over at the village. Don means something like white."

Gayle smiled and looked down at our son, dragging her foot to stop the swing. "So you are DonKokko." She lowered her head to his. "Congratulations, you have a name."

67
The Chess Crisis

Mosabe turned up several times a week for morning tea, but his visits became uncharacteristically curt and businesslike. After handing us whatever fresh fruit or eggs the islanders could spare, he stomped off into the woods.

"He's just getting old and cranky," Gayle said.

But I suspected that our morning chess games were the source of his chagrin. The islanders called the game *razzuvaa* and played it in the shade of breadfruit or banyan trees. I first noticed the game being played in Male, but did not identify the nondescript carved disks as chess. Then our friend Abdullah Kamaldeen explained, to my astonishment, that his great-grandmother was French, and that she had washed up in the Maldives from a shipwreck. "So why not chess?" he asked.

Mosabe always insisted on having the dark wood pieces. Some things never change. He played the game as if it were simple as opening a *karamba* coconut, but then after getting himself checkmated, he stomped off into the woods. From the day we started playing he returned almost every morning with only one thing on his mind, revenge. His behavior so annoyed me that I grew less inclined to delay beating him.

I delivered the coup de grace one morning in retaliation for Mosabe confiscating a treasure I had found on our beach. I was making my usual daily patrol to see if anything on our island had changed, always alert to anything that might have washed up on the beaches. For me it was like checking the mail every day or the newspaper to find out what was going on in the world.

I scanned the empty spit on the north end, and then the sweeps of undisturbed sand along the coves on the western side. I walked up to the dished skid marks of a giant sea turtle. Fans of damp sand had been sprayed out by her flippers as she dragged herself up to the forest edge. I walked up to a fleecy mound of its nest sand, and dug down, happy to feel the spongy ping-pong ball-sized eggs in my fingers.

I rested there for awhile, thinking of the turtle I once saved in Male. I had found it in the marketplace, bound and gasping on its back with sand in its eyes. When I purchased it at least fifty people followed me down the road, begging me to give it to them. They were exhilarated knowing I was going to release it, something of so much value for humanitarian reasons. I held the turtle high over my head so no one could leap up and grab it. At the end of the breakwater, over a sea of delighted eyes and brown faces dancing around me, I heaved it out. Everyone gasped. With scarcely a splash, the turtle vanished in a surprisingly quick turn, buttoning itself back up inside its emerald camouflage.

On this morning I stood up from the nest and looked out over our lagoon, as the dorsal of a baby black tip shark knifed the surface, dashing after its prey. Fat white globs of cloud sat on the horizon like reflections of the tensions I felt developing in my chess games with Mosabe. Just surface tension, I thought. Maybe something about Gayle and me, our presence that could not be assimilated? Our unavoidable cultural differences from the islanders did seem to hold us on the surface like pontoons, at times.

There was never any sign of the outside world on the beach. No scrap of trash ever floated up. No crate with lettering, no bottle, no piece of crumbling Styrofoam. No shredded pieces of poly rope, or splintered 2 x 4's with rusty bent over nails. Not even a piece of driftwood washed up. Yet some part of me yearned for these little mercies, something to remind us of where we had come from. Even shouting out at the top of my lungs to get a sense of my physical presence was like sinking into silence underwater. Some days even the sight of my own footprints gave me a shock.

I had given up hoping to find something washed up on the shore. When I spotted a greenish glint down the beach, I rushed excitedly up to the dome of a large glass float used on fishing nets. It had sunken into the sand, and I tugged it out with a scrap of rope still attached. I washed it off at the water's edge, turning the fiery green orb around and around in the sunlight. This was an exciting prize indeed! I hung it ceremoniously under the curve of a palm when I got home.

"Ah ha, are we decorating today?" Gayle said, standing with her arms akimbo. "What I would give to walk into a real store."

Just then Mosabe emerged from the woods and sauntered up, his attention fixed upon the fishing float. He ungraciously demanded I hand it to him, which I did. Then he thrust it into the hands of his helper, and directed him back to the boat.

"Come on, Mosabe!" I protested. "It came from the sea!"

Mosabe firmly shook his head. Anything that washed up on the island belonged to him. He made it clear by so many words and curt gestures, his voice an octave higher than usual. He held up the flat of his hand to let me know that the subject was closed, and we walked up for tea and chess.

Furious, I opened our morning chess game exactly by the book, the chess book I had dug out from Joya's library. I had been studying it like a military manual, and nailed him in ten moves. Mosabe stared at the board, then snapped his head up with a shell-shocked expression.

I turned up both my palms, just as he had done when he took away my glass globe.

He grunted, and marched abruptly off. A short ways up the path he stopped and turned. I hesitated, but he was obviously waiting for me, so I followed. His white head bobbed along the sun-burnished cuttings strewn along the wind path cut across the island's center. Wafts of stale urine drifted back to me from his faded persimmon and white checked sarong, the same he always wore. The black blade of his machete hung from his fist, looking as if one arm were longer than the other. Halfway across the island, he ducked off the path.

He stopped in a forest and gazed quietly around. Then he waved his arm across the trees, and explained that this was his new *dhoni*. At first I didn't understand, but he walked me from tree to tree silhouetted against the sunny blue channel, showing me limbs in the breadfruit tree that would become his stem and stern post, the knees and crooks that would become ribs, banyan roots that would become spars, and the palm trunks that would become the curved planks turning up to his bow. He literally had boats and houses growing in the forest.

No cutting would take place until the shape of the boat had been dug and smoothed into the sand. Then the trees would be cut and fitted into the hole, measured with slivers of palm frond snapped to length. First the hull planking would be laid in, and then the frames and knees and so on. It was as if a chair were being built around someone in a sitting position. This was completely opposite in technique to how we construct boats in the west, inside out with frames first and then milling the hull planks to fit.

By bringing me to this place, Mosabe was showing me how his island life was the shape of nature herself. That our invitation to live on the island meant fitting in. We were part of this design, and we had no place there beating him at chess. Ridiculous as this may sound in a freely competitive society, and comical as Mosabe's indignation was, breaking with his tradition was a deeper and more grievous taboo than a foreigner might suspect.

68
Reclaiming

Crows sailed over Gayle and me on our evening walk with Kokko, ratcheting their heads to ogle us as we wended along the scallops of the shoreline. They landed noisily behind us, squabbling and squawking on the sand spit where we came to watch sunsets, on the northwestern end of the island. Then groaning irritably as if commanded to silence, they stood with their glossy black feathers ruffled in the breeze, their eyes shining like crimson coals.

Squalls approaching flashed with lightening as spokes of gold light wheeled over the skyline, shafting down through the towering grey and stormy processions from the southeast. Gayle looked down at Kokko sucking noisily at her breast, and pressed her fingertips near her nipple to angle it into his mouth. Then she looked up and stared out.

"Is something wrong?" I asked.

"It's just that whenever I imagine our island, it's as if we're already in some other place. And I get sad."

"I'm not sure I understand."

"It's just 'cause we won't be here together, not like we are now. I doubt if we could ever know ourselves the same somewhere else."

I pulled her close with my arm around her, and we sat in the sunset in silence. The skin on our naked feet drawn up to each other in the sand turned to a peach pastel. The sky brightened to an intense turquoise and the sand darkened. I kept an eye on battalions of land crabs closing in from behind. They tested the already too small a distance separating us. Walking back I thought how the island and its creatures had slowly made a place for us. Like every other living thing that had washed ashore, our roots were growing deeper.

Gayle suddenly dashed across the wet glimmering sand toward a budding shape. I followed with Kokko bundled up asleep in my arms. She stooped over the water's edge to rinse her find. "What is it?" I whispered.

Gayle held a shiny bronze cowry shell up into the afterglow of the sunset. It glistened with gilded ridges corkscrewing around it. It was the kind of shell that had once been used as money in ancient Asia.

"I am saving this for Kokko. For his naming memory."

Gayle and I had never considered what the ramifications of Kokko being born on the island were for the islanders, especially Mosabe. But we came to realize that no islander's existence could be separate from his island. People were from a place. Place names were like family names. Kokko was from Kuda Fulidu. Mosabe was not. My guess was that Mosabe had been surprised by the ramifications of our son being born there. New islands have not been settled for a very long time.

After Mosabe's and my estrangement, due to the last chess match, I became more aware of subtle changes and tensions. Mosabe had always guarded secrets about the island, but as our teacher, he had always welcomed our discoveries. But now when I asked where he found large bunches of juicy leafed dandelions, he just laughed. The only ones we could find were small and stringy, and we needed the nutrition. Nor would he show me where he picked his sweetest karamba, even with my original promise never to pick them.

In search of Mosabe's secret patch of dandelions, I parted ways with Gayle and Kokko to hunt "the lions," as we called them on the way home from sunset walks. They grew deep in the forest domain of the fierce *madhiri*, Dhivehi for mosquitoes. At the perimeter of a small hidden meadow, I pulled my hunting outfit from my sack, carefully swaddling every exposed part of my body. Then with my face poked through the neck of a t-shirt like a nun's, my forehead bound by the arms of a sweatshirt draped over the back of my neck, and the backs of my hands cinched with socks, I charged into the meadow. The biggest lions grew under the dripline of shrubs. With the humming black devils swarming all over me, I picked furiously. Welts burned on my bare knuckles, my eyelids, and every sliver of bare skin exposed as I bent to my work.

Gayle shook her head at the sight of me clutching hard won bunches of dandelions in our doorway.

"Don't say no yet," I said. "I'm going to stir fry 'em with garlic, dried onions, and shiitake mushrooms. That should take the bitterness out of them."

"Not to discourage you, but I'm having sprouts and rice."

"Come on, Gayle. You need the nutrients. It's our only fresh vegetable."

"Why don't we plant our seeds?"

That was the first time Gayle had mentioned our seeds. I had forgotten about them crumpled up in newspaper in a rusting tin can on the top kitchen shelf. Kokko woke in his cradle in the bedroom and started crying.

Gayle went and sat down on our bed to nurse. Once he had latched on she looked up at me. "Why did we go to all the trouble to find those seeds if we weren't going to plant them?"

"Just like I told you, so we wouldn't starve if there were some kind of world disaster."

"So why can't we be independent without a disaster? And eat some real vegetables?"

"Because I never envisioned settling down on the island long enough to grow a garden."

What had that old Chinese wizard in Singapore instigated? Stuck in his boots like a big frog with that light in his eyes, sowing our voyage with these seeds. He must have sensed we were not planting a backyard garden. That his seeds would be carried far. That they would grow our future.

It stormed hard that evening. The dandelions tasted bitter and unappetizing. I picked out the mushrooms and chucked the rest in a bucket. The weight of the storm thudded on the thatched roof and beat on forest leaves like trap drums. Cascades of water plunged past our windows. We cleared up the dishes, and as I brushed my teeth at the kitchen sink, I noticed water creeping under the backdoor. I stared as it grew into a large black puddle.

The whole island was only a few feet above sea level, far beneath the jaw of a freak wave or a tsunami. Some islands even sink back into the sea as the coral dies beneath them. I wedged some soiled diapers into the crack, and as I did so heard the faint sound of music coming from our shortwave receiver in the bedroom. It was a gentle, fluttering organ part that I loved from a Saint Saens symphony.

I walked into the dim lantern glow of the bedroom, the wick ember smoking for lack of fuel. Gayle stood in the center of the room, swaying with her arms folded across her breast. Kokko slept in a small bundle on our bed.

"What are you doing?" I asked, walking up to her.

"Just standing here."

She reached for my hand, and folded herself into my chest. We began to dance slowly. How did we ever find each other and this place? I held her tight, melting together, carrying each other's weight. We turned slowly around and around the end of the bed, as flying storm debris scraped the windows, the glass panes pressing the lantern glow inward. The rock walls of our home stood around us, the only solid thing between us and the motility of our world.

69
Feridu Medicine Man

Late in October the Northeast Monsoon pushed forward against the Southwest Monsoon. In the standoff the wind came to a standstill. The tension could be felt in the heat and weight of the humidity. Everything went limp and upturned leaves sagged with the weight of rainwater crowded with mosquito larvae.

The time of the *madhiri* had arrived. They arose in swarms, females frantic for the blood they needed to produce their eggs. We were the only naked and featherless meat on the island! Mosquitoes bounced weightlessly around our net in the morning, and hummed after me as I dashed out to light the smoky green coils used all over Asia to ward them off.

After I had smoked out the *madhiri*, I laid my straw mat down to do my Surya Namaskar, or sunrise yoga. Pink cumulus clouds smoldered on the eastern horizon kindled by the rising sun. Sweat poured off my body and splattered on my mat as I stood and bent back down into prone positions. Outside our window even the cold blooded lizard that warmed up every morning on a palm trunk, crawled around to the shady side to escape the flame.

After yoga, I went out for my morning shore business. Every village had a beach designated as a latrine, which we had discovered on a stroll along the southeast side of Bodu Fulidu. I headed the opposite direction from Gayle's tracks in the sand. She was obsessively private about her toilet, and had a place near some bushes overhanging the amber shallows. Squatting in my spot, I listened to the fish getting excited and breaking surface behind me. I laughed reflexively to think of Gayle's horror the day a fishing boat full of men glided silently around the bend and surprised her.

That morning, the chief's boat cruised into our lagoon and Mosabe stepped ashore with some unusually tall black men, who had long disheveled hair and broad African noses. They were from Feridu Island on the southern horizon. When fishing was heavy during the monsoon change, Bodu Fulidu boats sometimes went there looking for extra crew. We stood in a clearing at the side of our house as a self-important man stepped forward, and looked Gayle up and down as if she were a textile he might purchase.

Gayle looked at me. "Tell him I'm married, if he hasn't figured it out yet."

Mosabe explained to Gayle that this was the Feridu medicine man, and that he had come over to help her reduce the size of her tummy. Mosabe had seen Gayle covering up and doing sit ups.

Only the day before I had found Gayle measuring her hips with a cloth measuring tape. "Are you mailing yourself somewhere?" I asked.

Contemptuously she twisted a chunk of her abdomen. "It's been two months; I should be back to 110 with a 24-inch waist."

"You look great, more mature, in my opinion. Like a woman."

"Woman my ass. I'm fat. I took apart my favorite jeans for a pattern to make new ones. I had to search all over Singapore for the denim. Now I'm gonna fit into 'em no matter what."

The Feridu medicine man began dancing around Gayle to help her lose weight to the delight of the other men. He bent over at the waist, scratching the ground with his feet like a chicken.

Gayle braced and scowled at him, her head cocked to one side in her tough stance.

ISLAND BORN

Undaunted, he continued chanting and gesturing up and down her body.

"Uh huh," Gayle said.

He picked up a handful of sandy soil around the base of a palm, offering to make a tummy pack for her.

Gayle squinted at him. "Thanks. But no thanks."

He squinted back, the pair of them unflinching eye to unflinching eye. The medicine man began leaping back and forth towards her like a scarecrow knocked about in gusts of wind.

The rest of the men were now beside themselves with laughter. The chief and his brothers hung onto each other's shoulders. Mosabe spun around like a leaf dangling on a bit of web.

Gayle marched toward the chief. He saw her coming and stiffened. She glared him right in the eye. "What's wrong with you male idiots? There ain't nothin' wrong with this belly!" She smacked it with her hand. And then again, with a solid thud to prove its firmness. "Go ahead. Hit it! Go ahead!"

The chief looked mortified. His brothers slunk away behind him.

"You guys don't even know what a hard belly is. Come on. Let me feel your mangoey paunches." She reached out, but they dodged her, quickly retreating down the beach, laughing themselves silly all the way to their boats.

Gayle turned to me. "What's wrong with those guys?"

I shrugged my shoulders. I knew her feelings were hurt. Her tough act never fooled me for a second. After they left, she sat brooding on the porch with Kokko clutched to her breast.

"Do you want to talk?" I asked.

"I don't know.... If I lived here for any length of time, I think my friends would be you and Kokko, and that would be it."

"You gotta admit, that Feridu guy was pretty funny."

"Yeah, if you're a guy." She gave me a glowering look I knew well, one drained of warmth. This especially happened when she drank. Another person took her place, one estranged even from her loved ones. Then she could do things she had done in Djibouti, bringing craziness into any moment.

"I need to take a walk," she said.

She handed Kokko to me, and trudged off down the beach. Her sarong twisted around the back of her calves in the breeze, and sand feathered off her heels. Maybe she would turn and I would hold up my hand, as if to touch hers in the air, to let her know how much I loved her. How I would be a safe harbor for her. But she did not look back.

70
Poison

Mosabe wanted revenge for his chess losses and insisted playing every morning he arrived. Annoyed by his persistence and bored with the game, I just ended it quickly most mornings. Still he arrived and strutted around our front porch as if he were constipated, itching circles around his neck, rudely demanding tea. I had put the chess set out of sight in the hopes he would forget about it, but his eyes darted about furtively in search of it.

Gayle thought I should have let him win, but I didn't. Then a week passed without a visit. The sands on the shore were unsettlingly smooth, no groove from his bow plowed up on the beach. Another week passed, and I began to worry I might have lost my bearings in an unfamiliar culture. We were all playing by very different rules, but the severity of Mosabe's indignation caught me unawares.

Mosabe broke his conspicuous absence by showing up one morning, very suspiciously lighthearted and friendly. After handing me a few eggs and some pitiful specimens of fruit, he motioned for me to come for a walk with him. Clearly he had something planned. I followed him over the short grasses under the palms to the east shore where he cut into the deep woods. Pushing the foliage aside like a swimmer, he pointed out plants for different remedies.

Then he stopped at a tall, spindly-looking weed, and stated dramatically that the root was a very bad poison. He flicked his head back to show that anyone who consumed it would ascend to Allah, just to be sure I got the point. I felt instantly very white, and alone. The seamless connection between his insults over his chess loses and now showing me a poison plant seemed all too obvious.

The only violent crime involving Maldivians that we had heard of had happened twenty-five years before, when an islander stabbed his adulterous wife. Even on the capital island of Male, there were no locks on doors, no back streets with bad reputations. Gayle walked anywhere, anytime, day or night. Without land animals to hunt, the islanders kept no weapons designed to kill anything. No spears, bows and arrows, blow guns or firearms. Even the island method of fishing by hand and throw-net seemed gentle.

Yet Mosabe's behavior worried me, and I wondered if there was a more sinister side to the islanders. I remembered hearing of a crocodile that had floated all the way from Africa to the Maldives. It was a miracle it survived but unsettling to hear that they had clubbed it to death. Our pets from Joya had not fared much better. Monkey, who had gone to live with Postmaster Rashid in Male, had settled in a tree in Rashid's front courtyard, and spent his days eating fruit and candy from dishes wedged into the branches. The heavy weather gear Gayle made for him had been replaced with a white lace pajama. He had it made, we thought, until we got the bad news. "Probably poisoned," Rashid confessed. "Someone must have been jealous."

Then following Monkey's death, we had sad news of our cat, Circe. We had trusted Abdullah more than anyone to care for her. He had bowed, saying that it must have been like parting with one of our children. Indeed, Abdullah's wife had fed Circe her own breast milk. The news that Circe had fallen down a well was a shock.

I began to wonder what Mosabe's medicinal services to the Sultan might have been, in the old days. Could they have included concocting poisons to get rid of opponents? But I reprimanded myself for such thoughts. No matter how Mosabe had earned this island, he had accepted us into his village, and had always watched over us. If I had mentioned to Gayle that Mosabe might be plotting to poison me, she would have burst out laughing.

71
Assimilation

We tried to ignore the rats at first. They scurried through the early morning hours, attacking land crabs outside our windows as they zigzagged in a windmill of legs to escape. The rats charged with their heads down scooping the crabs onto their backs to devour them belly up. Their carnivorous ferocity did not harmonize well with our yogurt and papaya breakfasts.

The chief and his three brothers visited one morning, and I pointed out a rat chasing a crab. Before I had lowered my finger the men leapt like gazelles into the bushes, hissing directions to each other as they beat about with sticks.

"I knew those guys had it in 'em," Gayle said, carrying Kokko back to his cradle. "That's how to deal with rats!"

I had no intention of chasing rats around with sticks every day, and the rats must have known it. Before long rats were poking their noses through our front doorway to see if we had gone to bed yet.

"They're coming to get us," Gayle sang over her dinner plate.

Sure enough they began coming in late at night, testing our food containers, gnawing, and crashing things to the floor. I dashed into the kitchen as dark shapes torpedoed under my feet and scaled the walls to escape. Soon as I returned to bed, they were back at it, and we resorted to clutching pillows over our heads to try and sleep. Mornings we swept up the broken glass mixed with our ruined supplies.

To protect our food from being spoiled, I transferred the grains and dried foods into burlap bags and suspended them with ropes from the ceiling beams. Above each bag I fitted a tin lid with a hole punched through the center for the rope. This type of rat guard is typically seen on ship's shore lines in port. For added protection I pushed straight pins through the ropes above the rat guards, chuckling vengefully over my ingenuity.

"Very impressive," Gayle said. "The pins are a nice touch for a pacifist."

"I wouldn't call myself a pacifist, but I am a good negotiator."

Still the rat guards failed. The rats dropped like paratroopers from the kitchen rafters onto the burlap sacks and chewed their way in through the sides.

Gayle smirked. "Honey, remember the ad on the pest control trucks? You know that guy with the hammer behind his back talking nice to a rat. Bait'em and smack'em. That's how you do it."

"And turn this place into a slaughter house? Bloody splotches all over the bedroom floor? No thanks. I didn't come to this island to spend every day clubbing rats. You could never kill 'em all anyway. There just has to be a better way."

"You want to negotiate with a rat?"

"Yeah. That's the way nature works."

"Here we go again. If I remember correctly, you gas bombed the cockroaches on Joya in Djibouti."

"Okay I'm a hypocrite. But I'm not going to start killing rats."

"Islanders do."

"I didn't come here to be a Maldivian. Don't worry; I'll take care of it."

The next day I dragged an empty fifty gallon steel drum into the kitchen and put our most vulnerable food supplies inside, layering what I figured we would need for each day. What I could not fit into the drum, Gayle packed in our oak dresser. We relocated our clothes into boxes.

All that night the rats gnawed the back of the dresser, rousing me to shake and kick the dresser to scare them off. We were exhausted and the stakes were getting higher. The nightly Rat Festival, as we called it, caused my illness to flare up.

We were at a loss for what to do until one evening I stood in the kitchen doorway sweeping and chatting with Gayle and a rat whizzed by. I reflexively whacked it with the broom. To our astonishment, the rat flew through the air and smacked the kitchen window. It was one of those unexplainable connections that changed everything.

That night we crept out of bed while the rats were at it. Gayle stationed herself outside the kitchen window. On my signal she flung it open and bellowed with such a bloodthirsty shout, that a dozen rats scrambled past my feet through the bedroom doorway to escape. I whacked several and one flew right out the open window. Gayle let out a victory yell.

We called our campaign "rat golf." Over the next few nights we took turns teeing off with the broom. We even kept score. A rat out the window was a rat-out in one. We even developed technique, letting the rat run close to our legs to put more lift into the swing. Stunned rats toppled out onto the night sand like stuffed animals.

Amazingly, the rats grew scarce. Unlike city rats that probably would have come in anyway, these shyer country rats showed some respect for territory. They poked their noses in the front door, but scurried away when they saw us.

If nature were testing us, then Lua as we called her, was our final exam. She was a huge tarantula type spider that marched down the wall over the stove while Gayle was cooking dinner. I heard her gasp. I lifted my head and listened from the bedroom. The only sound was the pot top clinking over boiling water.

"Gayle, you okay?"

She appeared in the doorway, hurrying toward our bed. She lifted the mosquito net and leapt in. She wagged her index finger toward the kitchen trying to speak. "Go in there, Frank."

"What?"

"Please! Just go in!"

I poked my head in the lighted doorway, seeing just the pot boiling on the stove. I stepped cautiously in, and there on the wall over the stove was the biggest hairy black spider I had ever seen, bigger than the palm of my hand.

"You see it!" Gayle called from the other room.

I backed cautiously out of range, so it could not jump on me, and bellowed. "AAAAAAH!" But the spider did not budge. I heard Gayle whimper in the other room.

Now that this bloodless bundle of pipe cleaners had proved to me that I was the one who was going to die, it shot up the wall and disappeared into our roof thatch.

This new resident in our house continued to appear on the walls during heavy rains. Abdullah told us that little red bumps would grow on our arms if Lua bit us. He ran his fingers around on his forearms to simulate baby spiders hatching out of our flesh. Mosabe cackled like an old witch to see our horror.

The night Lua descended over the baby's crib was the last straw. I blocked it with a long handled oar-like paddle I had made specifically for giant spider combat. I slapped the wall until it slithered back into the roof. Then I dashed outside. There it was on the moonlit wall outside. I slapped the top of the wall above the behemoth to block its escape back into our thatch, and it sprinted with terrifying agility across shadows on the wall face. I thrust my paddle to angle it toward the ground. Forced to plop down onto the sand, it went limp as a shamed dog. I had to scoot it across our clearing with the flat of the oar against its butt. At the forest edge it crawled away stiffly as if it had osteoarthritis. That was the last we ever saw of Lua.

The saga with island critters continued when we found unexplainable itchy welts on our bodies in the mornings. Our ignorance of tropical island life may have amused the islanders. I imagined their discussions on woven platforms in the sandy clearing shade at the center of their village. *Did you see? Now they've got bed bugs. Frank has got bites all along his ribs. It's because of the bedding they use... And he talks to that old crow.*

Abdullah peeled up our mattress and showed us a bed bug, which we had never in our lives seen before. He helped us carry out our wooden bed frame and sink it in the lagoon, its posts sticking out of the water like grave markers. We baked the mattress in the midday sun on the beach. The bug baking and drowning scheme worked and that was the last we saw of those critters.

To my horror the crow I thought I had befriended hopped down one day, and began pecking at our baby's face in his swing seat. Island crows don't know they're supposed to eat garbage. Baby eyes would obviously be just fine. I set about making a wicked bean shooter, which I then kept on the front porch.

72
Seeking Allies

On Mosabe's next visit after pointing out the poison plant to me, he demanded to know when we were leaving the island. I was stunned. We had never mentioned leaving. I had gotten word that my dad was ill, and had told Mosabe so he would be sure to deliver our mail from their monthly supply boat to Male. He lingered by the front door. I didn't know what to say. Then he announced that a German tourist had rented an island in another atoll for a hundred dollars a month.

From my point of view this added another motive for Mosabe wanting to poison me, if not to kill me, at least to make me sick enough to leave the island. For the money! The German tourist was paying about nine times more than we were. Mosabe had once happily promised twelve dollars a month for our island for my entire lifetime. The German's rent would have made an islander instantly rich. We had built a substantial house by their standards and had gone through many trials to settle into island life, including having a baby there. We did not appear to be going anywhere soon, and Mosabe was getting old.

Gathering up our towels that had been drying on the line strung between the front porch posts Gayle asked, "If we don't pay him more, what will he do? Do you think the islanders would turn against us?"

"He's just being a brat," I said. "We could pay him more, but that would start an unhealthy relationship with him and other islanders. We already made a deal he was happy with."

"He's been acting very strange lately. I told you to let him win at chess."

"I'm thinking I should sail over to Matiwari Island. Introduce myself. Talk to the guy over there who's got an engine *dhoni*. Make some new connections."

"That's a good idea," Gayle said. "I've got a feeling you should do that soon."

Matiwari was the only other inhabited island within reach of my small boat. The sail there was a relatively safe since we were embraced by the same reef system. Gayle packed a lunch for me and carried Kokko down to see me off.

I kissed her forehead and then Kokko's. "These worries about Mosabe are probably absurd."

"Please come home safe." She handed me a bottle of water and a plastic bag containing my cotton pants rolled up with my vest, to put on if I got sunburnt or cold sailing home late.

I set sail against a fresh headwind. When I cleared the northern tip of our island, a frothing seascape charged past me. My boat seemed to be standing still. Over at Bodu Fulidu I spotted a large sail bursting open. Within half an hour, the larger boat had overtaken me. The stout brown figure of Abdullah waved from under the foot of his sail. I waved back and followed him through a shortcut passage in the Matiwari reef.

We anchored along a sandy spit and walked together toward the village, greeting several islanders along the way. They did not smile like villagers on other islands, and I cringed to think they were the ones I had thrown shells at in the lagoon, that day I was sick on the beach before Kokko's birth.

Abdullah introduced me to an overweight man with self important airs. We sipped *karamba* sitting on a woven platform under palms fluttering high overhead. Turned out he was the owner of the only other motor *dhoni* in the area, a welcome connection in the event we were stranded due to poor relations with our closest neighbor. As Abdullah chatted with his friend, I gazed out over the reef curving like a wedge of honeydew melon out in front of us. Island ladies stooped in the clearing, sweeping the sand with their bundles of sticks. I noticed them casting unusually somber glances my way. I thought maybe it was the recent murder, a German tourist, not the one who had rented an island in an atoll to the north of us, but another who had stabbed his girl friend in Male, just before we left for our island. The authorities had put her body on display. The whole island had lined up to see it. Not even our Maldivian friends in Male looked us directly in the eye after that.

Then not only were we white and by association capable of horrors in the islanders eyes, there was the fact that we were living on an uninhabited island away from our home and relatives. This alone might have suggested a criminal past to the villagers. Banishment from one's island, family, and friends was the worst punishment in the Maldives at the time, that we had heard of. Even the German boy who murdered his girlfriend was not repatriated to stand trial, as German authorities had insisted. Instead the Maldivian court gave him a life sentence of banishment to a small village on one of the Maldive Islands. Banishment to a tropical island! Sometime later we heard that the young man had built a house, married a Maldivian girl from the local village and had a baby. In fact, his circumstances were similar to ours, except our exile was self imposed, which might have incriminated us further, because we had chosen complete isolation. There may have been no other comprehensible explanation from the islander's point of view.

Given our problems with Mosabe, these thoughts settled into me. I excused myself from Abdullah and the motor *dhoni* owner to walk down the shore. Some men were heaving on the gunnels of a fishing *dhoni*, sliding it up the beach on log rollers. I threw my shoulder against the hull to help. The trick to this teamwork is to be in sync with the Maldivian work chant; otherwise you miscue busting a gut pushing while the islanders take a breath, or suddenly get dragged along. I kept my eye on their knobby dark feet cranking the sand, as the boat lurched up the crest of the beach. As I walked away, I turned to look back, squinting against the sun. The dark silhouettes of the men lifted their arms and waved. I waved back, feeling the relief of being so simply woven back into their community.

Sailing homeward around Matiwari Island's windward side, the foot of my sail dipped the lime-green sea, and swooshed closely past some men and women wading out on the reefs with their eel gaffs. I tacked and headed past hunks of dead coral that emerged like broken teeth from the swells. Along the shore a gnarled thicket clawed up to the water's edge with its roots dangling out, as if calling the sand that would be uplifted someday. Uplifted like the sense of home we had hung our roots out for in this community.

As Matiwari fell into the distance, the hum in my tiller directed my hand. The warmth and pull of my sails swept me away from my worries over Mosabe's intentions. I lay back on deck, squinting at the tip of my white canvas sail as it rocked firmly across the blue.

A sudden urge to sleep overwhelmed me at the helm. To wake up I tied off the mainsheet and slipped into the water over the stern. I hung onto the transom with one hand, and steered the trailing edge of the rudder with the other. Stretching back into the effervescence streaming off the hull, I gazed down through the bubbles at the vermilion and emerald fluorescence of brain corals sliding under me. I cleaved through reef fish, over loopy tentacles and waving antennae, the tightening coils, and sandy spurts. Surprised reef sharks pumped their black-tipped tails away in flight.

Then hauling myself back on deck, I sat in a hot puddle, as my skin began to pinch with drying salt. I licked the salt crystals on the warm skin of my shoulder. I thought about what Gayle had said, *if we could ever know ourselves the same somewhere else?* Her raw temperament and wild disposition found no better footing than a fan palm rooted in a freeway crack back in L.A. Now that she had flourished in the open sea and these islands, I wondered if she would be able to cope with a paved over life, or if she would be better off in our life style of self-imposed banishment?

The sandy white rim of our island rose on the horizon, and I spotted the small figure of Gayle standing out on the northern spit. When I got close enough she waved back, and turned to stroll homeward with Kokko bundled in her arms. I intercepted them and leapt out into the shallows. I clung to my boat in a commotion of sloshing water and whipping canvas and urged Gayle aboard.

"It would be Kokko's first sail," I begged.

She smiled and swung her foot over the gunnel. I jumped in over a poisonous lionfish, just avoiding a painful sting from spines concealed in its lovely bronze-feathered plumage waving in the bright water under the hull.

The sail barked taut against the sheet hook, pulling us over a marbled wake, with the lion fish's feathers churning above the surface behind us like the ribs of a fan. The splash of our bow wave echoed back from the blue-china shade over the beach. Moments later Gayle tipped Kokko's head up to show me that he had fallen fast asleep.

73
Mosabe's Checkmate

The day Mosabe sailed over to inform me that he was going to make me medicine, I was repairing our rainwater gutter torn off its supports by a strong squall.

"Your old buddy is here," Gayle shouted out from the back of the house.

We met on the front porch. We had not shared another word about the German on an island somewhere north paying more rent. Mosabe jutted out his hand ceremoniously with three small *cocolo bis*, and three finger-sized *donkio*, which was very much appreciated, since we'd had no eggs or bananas for some time. He also pulled out a jar of *hokuro*, a thick golden coconut honey that we loved for sweetening our tea, and melting over whole wheat pancakes with yogurt.

"Sa?" I asked, stuffing our accounts board back up into the roof thatch. He declined my tea, and pointed at my stomach, like a kid who'd captured some crawly thing in a jar. He shouted that he would bring medicine tomorrow. "Maadhamaa. Madhammaa," he repeated.

I slapped my stomach and told him I was perfectly healthy, that I did not need medicine.

He disagreed, holding up the flat of his palm, and marched off to gather ingredients for my potion. I watched to see which direction he went, and sure enough it was where he had shown me the poison plant. I considered spying on him, but the thought only made my suspicions more chilling. I walked into the kitchen to be with Gayle.

"Why are you standing around behind me. You're making me nervous. The tea is not ready yet. Relax. Go sit down."

My hand shook when she handed me my tea. I had to put it down to keep from spilling.

"What's happened to you?" Gayle asked, looking at me curiously.

"Mosabe is planning to poison me." I tried not to appear as nervous as I was. "But I don't know for sure. He's gone to get…"

Gayle smiled. "He sure did seem to be in a bouncy mood today."

"It's no joke. He showed me a poison plant in the forest. Now he wants to make me medicine."

"It was probably something for me, to help me lose weight, since he's so obsessed about it."

"No it was poison. He made that very clear. I looked it up in our plant book. I think it is called *black nightshade*. It's a Eurasian plant with hairy poisonous foliage. I'll show you," I said looking around for the book.

"The book is on the nut bins."

I went and opened to the page I had marked. "See it's got white star-shaped flowers just like this. I'm telling you, something doesn't feel right. Maybe it's about how much that German is paying for rent. The chess games… I don't know."

"You do get overly competitive, Frank."

"I should have just refused to play."

"Don't you think Mosabe is a bit old to be a murderer?"

"Maybe he feels more youthful if thinks he's going to get rich. Who the hell knows what he did for the last Sultan."

"He's got you bad." Gayle laughed again.

"Look what happened to Monkey and our cat!"

Sobered to hear of the demise of our pets, she glanced out the window and turned back to the stove. "Keep it down, here he comes."

Two helpers accompanied Mosabe. Witnesses! I thought, feeling slightly relieved. That lessens the chance he's planning to do me in.

Mosabe cast me a professional look as he passed, holding up his bunches of pharmaceuticals for me to see. I took a much harder look at the plants than I wanted him to notice. But I could not find the tall spindly poisonous ones in his load. He could have concealed them in the center of the bunch, I thought.

Gayle thrust Kokko into my arms. "He may need to pee." She motioned me toward the door. I walked a few steps, and stood staring numbly out the front window as Kokko pressed his nose with both fists, chewed his thumbs, and peed on the floor. I reached under the crib, retrieved a used diaper still lying there from last night, and wiped up the puddle.

After I carried Kokko out to the well to wash him off, I strolled down the beach. It was overcast and very humid, a storm brewing. The dull metallic undulations over the lagoon radiated an uncomfortable heat.

The next day the sea built into a maelstrom. Creamy froth tore from the dark-lipped swells. Three Bodu Fulidu boats raced for the safety of our lagoon with their canvas billowed out in front of them, spars bent to the point of snapping. I hurried out and sat on a sandy rise in front of our house to paint the scene with my Chinese ink and brush set. The first raindrops plunked down into the ink and forced me to finish it in a few strokes. Then I went back to the house with damp sand clumping to the underside of my toes like warm dough, keeping watch over my shoulder on several fishing *dhoni* ploughing into our lagoon to anchor in the sheltered water inside of our reef.

Shivering men from Bodu Fulidu always rushed up to our porch while they waited out the squalls. We gave them hot tea, joked, and smoked cigarettes. But today these men, whoever they were, did not come up to our house. I watched them from between the palms as they crawled under their sails, the wet canvas molding to their huddled shapes. Maybe they were from a distant island, I thought.

"Maybe… maybe the word is out about us," I said to Gayle standing beside me looking over the lagoon.

"And what could they be saying?" Gayle said. "They are probably sick of Mosabe thinking he is hot shit, beating them at chess all the time."

We settled at the dining room table to wait out the thunderous drumming on our roof. I pushed our dictionary toward Gayle, opened to the botanical drawing. "See there it is. *Black Nightshade*."

"You showed me already, Frank. I really don't think that old fart Mosabe has got it in him to poison anyone."

"Even if I refuse to drink it, he would probably figure out another way to do it."

Gayle looked at my storm painting, propped up on the library shelf, the ink-dark fury with the three white sails, moth-like in the grip of the storm. "Not bad," she said. "It's got the feeling."

We were suddenly startled to hear the sound of laughter carried in the wind, and went to the window. Two men were hurrying up the beach from a small *dhoni* pulled up on the shore. "Where did they come from?" I said.

The waves were splashing over the transom of their boat, and their sarongs were soaked and clinging to their thighs as they carried a huge bloated black coconut between them. It looked like a bearded head. They clutched it by the shaggy weed, grown from floating so long in the water. Clumps of white goose barnacles tangled in its beard like broken teeth. The men began sharpening a stake where they clearly intended to cleave it open. Neither our staring nor waving elicited any response.

A spontaneous conviction in my gut compelled me to stop them from splitting open this dead thing next to our house. I leapt off the porch and ran out, but by the time I arrived the deed was done. The men were running back to their boat laughing like hyenas.

Gayle and I both knew of an ancient Maldivian custom of burying an evil wish under the floor of another's house. I searched on my hands and knees through the vines, for every shattered cranium-like piece, and smelly decomposed glob. I threw them all back into the sea. Then back at the house I scrubbed my hands with soap and rainwater spilling off the roof, before going back in the house.

"That was pretty weird," Gayle said, as rain tinkled in its ghostly way on a pile of empty jars out back.

I sat down beside her nursing Kokko, and felt the curve of our son's head in my palm. "I'll switch teas on Mosabe tomorrow. Just in case. I'll just give him back his own medicine."

Gayle looked down at Kokko. "Shhh, he's asleep." She motioned my ear down to her so she could whisper. "Even if it isn't poison, whatever that old fart makes will give you the shits."

I stood to leave, but Gayle waved a pair of Kokko's plastic briefs with another split in them at me. They had several black patches already. There was no explanation for why I had brought a bicycle repair kit to our island. It was just one of those things. There was still a couple of hundred feet of Joya's heavy Dacron rope laying in a corner, which I also could not resist bringing.

Mosabe's boat arrived first thing the next morning. I had just washed my face at the well, and water dripped from my whiskers as I watched Mosabe tramp up the beach.

"He's here," Gayle called out through the back door.

"I see him," I said hurrying into the kitchen.

A coppery-colored pot of Assam milk tea wafted a buttery perfume into the low beams of morning sunlight through the kitchen windows. As Mosabe's figure approached, I waved hello through the window.

"I can't switch teas on him," I whispered. "What if he drops dead on the front porch? I could be accused of murdering him."

"Maybe you guys should dig at least one grave before you settle this. Digging would be hard on my back."

"Christ! If this all turns out to be a big joke, fine!"

I carried the pot and two glasses out to where Mosabe had suspiciously chosen to wait in front of our house, instead of coming up to the porch as usual. Tea slurped out the spout and messed the tray. Mosabe opened his palm revealing a folded piece of newspaper, and announced that this was the medicine he had brought for me.

I poured our tea ignoring his enthusiasm. He took a glass of tea and ticked his packet over it with his index finger, spilling in some of the tan powdery granules.

Powder! I thought. How the hell did he get dried powder from those leaves overnight? Maybe it's not the same stuff, I thought. There was no escape, only my refusal to drink.

Mosabe held the glass out to me.

"I can't," I said, holding up my hands.

He hesitated, slightly surprised. He stared at me as I grimaced to express the bellyache I would get, my knees sinking and my toes curling in the sand. Then I straightened and blurted out, to my own amazement. "I will die if I drink it." I passed my finger over my throat like a knife and tipped back my eyes.

Mosabe clipped off a little grunt that could have been a laugh. Stretching out his arm, he insisted again, pushing the glass almost under my chin. I took it, noticing his dreadfully youthful glare.

In desperation I glanced back toward the kitchen. Gayle waved frantically through the window, shaking her head for me not to drink it.

I pushed the glass back toward Mosabe. "You drink it first," I told him.

He looked at me fixedly, with a charmed expression as if he would never forget the moment. Then with a loud laugh, he grabbed the glass of *sa* from my hand. Gayle had made the tea drinkably hot, the way we both preferred it. He tipped it up to his mouth, his eyes fixed on me over the rim, and drained the whole thing.

I stared at the empty glass in disbelief.

Clearing his throat, he shook the glass upside down over the ground to empty out the last drip, a typical island wash job. Then he dumped a measure of powder into my glass of tea, and gestured for me to drink it down.

Well whatever trickery he might have been up to, I could bear it no longer. If this was my fate, then I had brought it upon myself. Time to be done with it. So I just drank it all, right then and there.

When I looked up at that old toothless man, he laughed heartily. My first thought was that he couldn't have poisoned me and be looking so sweetly at me. He took my hand in his, and my nightmare dissipated in its embrace, its warmth. I suddenly understood; true friends know each other through tenderness, the tenderness they find in their hearts for each other's limits. Mosabe shouted out to Gayle, "Karamba?"

74
Baking

After three months on the island, we reached deeper into our barrels of supplies. There was still plenty of flour, and it surprised me when Gayle announced one morning that she wanted an oven. "I can make coconut cakes. Wouldn't that be great?" She beamed. "Just think. Home baked goods out here."

Island ovens were permanent coral rock structures with hearths and chimneys, requiring the efforts of several men for at least a week to break coral into bricks and mortar it all together. At this point I would have thought an oven stood outside our time frame for living on the island, but then we had no timeframe, just an assumption that we would agree on leaving at some point after the birth, probably after we had used up our supplies.

Our baby had now aroused a longing in me for home; just the thought of bringing Kokko to my parents gave me a thrill. It was the biggest contribution I had ever made to our family, returning home as a father with my own son. On the other hand, Gayle, who had so agonized at first over having a baby away from her mother, had not mentioned going home at all. There seemed to be much more than a cake baking in her mind.

Yet Gayle's insistence on an oven also gave rise to a new and disarming stability she felt for us as a family. I couldn't have hoped for more after all the trials of Djibouti and so many precarious steps along the way. I had realized by now that Gayle had a habit of creating affirmations out of conflict, and now she had done so again, taking this huge and unexpected step toward homesteading our island.

That night after Kokko fell asleep, Gayle and I washed out by the well, dishing heated water over each other's backs. Two lanky crane-like birds grumbled hoarsely from their nest high overhead in the banyan tree. Their long white necks stretched out to keep an eye on us.

"They're like nosy neighbors," Gayle said, rinsing soap from the reappearing curves of her body.

She looked beautiful glistening nude in the moonlight. "I've been thinking there might be a simpler way of making an oven," I said.

"Forget about it."

"But you've seen those things, Gayle. They're built to last for generations."

"Mosabe said he would build it for me, so why not let him?"

"I thought we had an unspoken agreement. That we came here to have Kokko. We stocked the island for about six months."

"I said forget about it." She leaned over to gather up her toiletries.

"But why? Why would you put the islanders through all that effort? Letting them think we're going to stay?"

Gayle spun around. "You had the islanders build you a boat. How would you feel without it? Not being able to sail out into the reefs every day? Baking is just as important for me. And Mosabe knows it."

Gayle wrapped herself up in a towel, pinching it to her body with her elbows and began scrubbing her teeth with a fibrous stick splayed out on the end, the same type of toothbrush the islanders use.

I reached through the kitchen door and got mine off the shelf. "Mosabe knows it. Why don't I know it?"

Gayle took her tooth-stick out of her mouth. "We've been traveling for years, Frank."

"But how much longer do you want to stay? What's on your mind? That's all I'm asking."

"I don't know how long. Long as it takes to bake bread."

Gayle leaned on the well rim to rinse off her feet. She was composed and fragrant as a gardenia. I followed the flap of her sandals on the cement path, and closed the planked kitchen door behind us. Lightning whitened the windows as Gayle walked into the bedroom. Thunder shook the house, and it began to pour.

"Oh, I could have rinsed my hair under the roof, if that had come a few minutes earlier," she lamented.

Our shadows stooped and stretched around the walls of the room as we readied for bed. We crawled in on either side of Kokko, who was fast asleep, and lay there listening to the rain subside, softly tapping the thatch. I could feel her thinking in the dark, but before I could speak there was another lightning flash. Gayle's eyes were looking straight into mine, a ghostly porcelain white with black irises. She slid quickly over and put her arms tightly around me under the sheet. She held me without letting go. And I held her. We both somehow knew that time was running out.

"Gayle."

"What?"

"I'll make you a temporary oven tomorrow, okay? Until Mosabe can finish his."

"Ok. And if we stayed a little longer, you could write about our island," she whispered.

"You think so? I'm afraid I would offend people. That what we're doing out here is irrelevant to most people's lives?"

"I would be interested to read about us."

"I just know I love you, Gayle."

"Frank, hold me."

We held onto each other until her fingers slackened their grip in sleep, letting go one by one as she drifted off.

In the morning I rummaged through our books for the copy of Robinson Crusoe, and found the part I remembered, where he had baked with a fire built over an earthenware pot turned upside down. Of course, the real Crusoe was Alexander Selkirk, who survived on his deserted island by chasing down goats, and killing them with his bare hands, eating them raw, but I decided to give Defoe's fantasy a try.

Moldy branches were all I could scavenge from our island for fuel. I built a fire over one of our clay yogurt pots with Gayle's cake inside. I staggered back and forth from smoldering clouds of smoke, clawing at my eyes, and gasping for air to tend the fire. After the embers died down, Gayle and I scraped away the soot and squatted to peek under the charred edge of the pot. There was a perfect looking wheat-germ cake.

We ate the whole thing on the spot like kids, burning our fingers and lips, laughing and running down to wash our faces in the sea. In the following days she baked a coconut cake, and pineapple upside-down cakes with canned fruit. Mosabe suggested altering the kiln which the islanders had used to construct our house, for Gayle's oven. It was a short ways off in the forest.

I was tending the pot-oven fire when Mosabe arrived one day. He stood on the beach, looking stunned as I danced in and out of the flames covered in soot. His own eyes grew watery at the sight, and he turned to conceal a few spasmodic gasps of laughter. When he got a grip on himself, he motioned for me to follow him into the forest. He stopped at a low palm tree, and stabbed his finger at some large empty pods that were tipped out from its head. I jumped up and ripped them down. These burned hot over the pot oven with only thin wisps of white smoke. Mosabe promised again to build her oven soon.

75
Fitting In

A few days later Abdullah and Mosabe marched officially up to our door. Abdullah advised me, wagging his finger, that Kokko should not be wearing baby gowns or going around naked. He should have a shirt and a pair of pants, like all baby boys on their island. After the toddler phase, they graduate to a sarong. Mosabe nodded in agreement, his toothless lips turned inward like a seam.

As Mosabe and Abdullah discussed Kokko's first island clothes with Gayle, I tried to envision our boy as a young man dressed in a sarong. Such a deceptively simple piece of clothing, perfectly designed for island life. It was nothing more than a rectangle of material wound around the waist and folded in against the stomach to hold it. It could be rolled up or down like a blind to adjust the length, long to keep mosquitoes off the legs at night, or rolled up short in the heat. To wade out to a *dhoni*, islanders hiked it up into the shape of tight-fitting shorts, by pulling the back edge up between their legs. If it was stormy and cold, a sarong could be unrolled completely and pulled up over the head, so that islanders looked like a group of walking tents.

By the time our son graduated to a sarong, his hair would be sun bleached and his shoulders deeply tanned. He would run along the beach twice as tall as his island friends. They would sail off, hanging their weight together upon a halyard to raise a sail. I often leaned on my rake to watch very young island boys charge out into the waves, chatting and holding each other's arms as they ducked the flying crests. I would teach my son, as their fathers had taught them, how to love and know the sea. We would homeschool him when the time came. There was no hurry. Joy in this glorious nature would be his teacher, with so many skills and challenges for a child's development. Joy would be his way of understanding his life from the beginning, hitting him in the face like sea spray.

Our island was no mirage. Gayle recognized it from the beginning; we could grow strong here as a family. There was nothing crazy about baking with a coral rock oven, tending gardens, and mastering maritime skills. And when our son rejoined a western world, the whispers and splitting thunder in monsoon winds, the ever shifting patterns of virgin sand and blown shreds of weed, the calligraphic sea of swaying light, the visitations of ancient turtles, and intimacy with every fiber grown from the forest, all and much more would hone his focus upon intelligent life.

Gayle looked knowingly over at me, as Abdullah explained the measurements he was taking, breaking wood slivers to the length of our baby's limbs. I looked back into her gaze for an eternal moment, lost in her brown curls entwining the blue sea in the window, in the chattering voices and snapping sticks, and I suddenly understood; we had grown almost small enough to fit in.

Our food was running out. We discussed switching from being vegetarians to catching and eating fish like the islanders. Our medical supplies drawer was almost empty. Gayle had used all our antibacterial ointment on an islander child with a horrible bacterial infection on her head. After that, grown men sailed over to get a Band-Aid for the tiniest scratch and soon our Band-Aids, antifungal cream, Tylenol, gauzes, disinfectant, and eye-drops were all gone. As the rest of our island supplies dwindled, fewer letters arrived. The thinning of our connections to the outside world was in its own way the birth of us on our island.

76
Swallowed Up

I stood on our porch watching a moth-like procession of sails stream across the crinkling glitter of the horizon in a thin overcast. I felt unsettled over what could have caused such an exodus. But then it felt wonderfully strange and even familiar to think of being the only ones left in our galaxy of isles and reefs.

Gayle sat beside me on the porch stoop.

"The islanders are on their way somewhere. Look at that, not just from Bodu Fulidu," I said pointing to a procession of dots on the horizon. "They're coming here, somewhere close to the north of us. It's odd to see so many on the move. What if all the islanders left?"

"What do you mean, left?"

"Just disappeared for some reason? And we were the only ones out here?"

"We would survive," she replied. "We've got coconuts, a breadfruit tree, and all the fish we can eat. And it's all free."

"But how does that feel to you? Being stranded out here with no one, indefinitely?"

"We've got each other."

"I mean there are a million reasons anyone could think of not to live out here. No emergency medical, no family, no variety of food, no friends or at least Caucasian ones, no society to interact with."

"It's peaceful living the way we do. There's always a lot to think about."

"And...?"

"It's beautiful and clean, and very healthy. Our time is our own. A complicated life doesn't make you feel you have everything you need."

By midmorning Mosabe's *dhoni* careened past our house under full sail. He stood pointing his finger behind our island to the north, shouting "*Hasfathaalu boatu.*" The hospital boat had come.

Gayle and I had never heard of a hospital boat making rounds in the islands. Since Kokko had never had a medical examination, I thought it was an opportunity for us. We didn't even know his birth weight. I had rigged up a counterbalance with one-pound cans of powdered milk suspended in a box off one end, but Gayle refused to suspend him off it, and I forgot about it after he was born.

"Maybe we should go. Just get him his first check up," I suggested.

"There's nothing wrong with Kokko, so why rush out to a hospital boat?"

"Because it's there. Maybe someone speaks English."

"If you're lonely, go out there yourself."

"Just sail out with me to keep me company then. The breeze is on the beam, both ways perfect and safe."

Gayle agreed, but by the time we had sailed north to the lagoon between us and Matiwari Island, a logjam of *dhoni* jostling at the ship's side were already casting off. Women handed children back down to their husbands, and sails billowed up toward home. As we sailed up to the huge white stern of the ship, smoke belched from its stacks, and it rumbled away leaving us behind in its wake.

"I still don't know why you got so worked up about coming out here in the first place," Gayle said, ducking the mainsail as I threw over the helm toward home.

"Maybe I am missing home, our own culture," I replied carefully.

"Like missing? Or wanting to go?"

"Like feeling that I left something undone."

"Going back is not going to fix that, Frank."

"I missed something growing up. And always go more native, more extreme to compensate. I told you how I awoke mornings as a kid, hearing the drone of rush hour traffic in the distance. I always hated that sound. I was afraid of it. Like my future would be the death of me. Now I have to learn how to trust it."

The breeze swept away the veil of overcast, revealing a cap of dense white clouds over a sparkling ocean. We sailed alongside the top of the reef. It was bronzed and crispy-looking, as if the sun had fried it in the shallow pools at low tide. I gazed under the foot of our sail into the glassy swoosh of our bow wave, and O'Riordan's words came to me once more: *You can never come back completely.* I saw him sitting in his easy chair by the fireplace, hands draped over the hook of his cane, wheezing with laughter.

Gayle dragged her fingers through the water, and I pulled my legs up out of the burning sun, and leaned on the helm around the reef toward our lagoon entrance.

77
Seeds

News of the world outside seemed increasingly dangerous and foreign to us. We stopped listening to the BBC and Voice of America on the shortwave, to the anxious voices crackling through showers of magnetic energy, granulated to sand in the airwaves.

One day we heard a prop plane that sounded like the twitter of a small bird lost at sea. I ran out on the beach, searching the miasma of clouds, hoping I would not see it. Hoping not to see it! And on days when the breeze carried the faint *putt putt* of the Matiwari engine *dhoni*, I felt a twinge of dread. The same dread I felt in my childhood.

Then the letter arrived from my mother, telling me dad was ill, *a heart problem*, she wrote. I knew that even if he had passed away, she might not have told me at first, said something like he had gone fishing with one of his friends. I also knew she wouldn't have said anything at all, if it wasn't serious.

In the lacy afternoon shadows I stood surveying the crumbling cement path to our well. No antler coral had been used to strengthen it, and I would have to remake it. The windows in the house were sticking, and some would not close completely to keep out the driving rains. My boat needed a coat of shark liver oil to preserve it. Everywhere I looked, I saw things that needed mending. We had begun sifting weevils from the last of our flour, and floating the bugs out of our rice.

The Northeast "fair weather" Monsoon bulged on the horizon. It was already the end of November, uncomfortably hot and humid. Gayle was suspiciously quiet. She sewed new curtains for the kitchen, reorganized our front window shelves, and unpacked the canning jars along with the last of our things from Joya. Recently she had placed a photograph of her mother and some shots of her cousins on the dresser. She was still moving in.

The stick and shell mobile I had made for Kokko hung motionless over his crib. It was so hot we decided to go for a walk to cool off on the west side of the island which was exposed to wind this time of year. On our way home the breeze stiffened, buffeting the forest edge, knocking us off balance along a crumbling sand ledge. Gayle suddenly stopped. Shielding Kokko from the wind, she turned to look back at me.

"What?" I asked, my voice lost in the gusting rattle of leaves from some hearty shore shrubs.

Her hair swept back against the pastel haze of the shore. Her eyes were penetrating. She smiled, and I thought I heard a laugh sucked away in the wind.

"What?" I asked again.

She leaned forward. "I was just thinking," she shouted with an enthusiastic tone, "that before our stores get much lower we should plant our seeds. Get them in now."

I hesitated for a stunned instant. She turned and walked on. I followed, nodding.

Gayle stopped again and turned to face me. "We could also get a goat. For milk and cheese."

She looked at me with such an open heartedness, such a transparency that my imagination gave in and bloomed with our future together there. Visions that I hadn't allowed myself rushed in and held their ground. Visions of more children in the doorway of our thatched house, barefoot little ones climbing palms, home schooled, romping on the beaches. The hair of our girls would be sun bleached and oiled with coconut oil like island women. They would learn to grate, crush and expel the oil themselves on a breadfruit plank. They would dive for treasures, and race their *dhoni* against their brothers. I was full of wonder for the childhood they would have… And one day we would take them back with their gifts.

Gayle turned, and walked on. I followed slightly behind, as if still wading toward a dream. I remembered the small sparrow-like bird that had rested aboard Joya, like many migrating birds had in the Mediterranean. It was weak, and I put it in my sea toque. After a few days it tried to fly off against a very strong wind. But realizing its mistake, it fluttered back to within a few feet of our calls, and our outstretched hands. But it couldn't make it the last few yards, and dropped into the waves.

This little creature's attempt to get back had moved us so deeply that we jibed the ship, sprang into emergency man-overboard procedures. It was a miracle that through plumes of blustery spray we spotted such a tiny thing, being flung in and out of sight on the crests. And a miracle again that in all the upheaval of the sea, I managed to hang over the rail and scoop it up as we surged past. I cradled it in my sea toque again, its feathers fluffed up around its little black seeds for eyes. But after a few hours it died, and we laid it back into the plunging waves.

I stopped Gayle at the front porch with my hand on her shoulder.

Her eyes searched mine.

"We might not ever get back here, if we leave," I said. "I think we should give it a try."

"What about your dad's health?"

"If I hear anything more from mom, if there is an emergency, then we can go and come back again."

We sat on the edge of the porch. The last beams of sun stretched out through the palm shadows onto the beach. The lagoon was violet, violet as when I threw Kokko's placenta out.

"Remember your mom told you that Homer had written you a letter after Kokko's birth?" Gayle said.

"Yeah, of course. But I don't think it's ever going to arrive; it's been more than two months. I know he sent it because Mom would never make that up. Dad never sent me a letter in my life."

"Well it'll come."

"You think so?"

Gayle pushed her toes through the sand. "It will come because I know what your Dad wrote in that letter."

"How could you know?"

"Homer talked to me. I may have been the only one he talked to."

"About what? You just used to sit around together kinda silent."

"He didn't talk much, but he talked about you."

I waited, while she relaxed and looked out over the water.

"You know his handwriting, right? How he scribbled so it looked kinda jerky like twigs crumbled on a page."

"Yes."

"Well, he wrote that he knew you had it in you, Frank. He saw how energetic you always were. How insistent. His bet all along, he said, was that you would do something different. He worried at first how unsettled and anxious you were as a kid, but he expected you would come around. He wasn't as disappointed as you might have thought when you didn't go into business with him. Follow in his footsteps. He said, he was relieved. That was his actual word. 'Relieved.' He said that was how he felt when you set sail, and he realized you had grown into a man. With his own dream. And he wouldn't have to try and prove anything to you anymore, because he couldn't anyway. He never wanted to be hard on you like his father was on him. He wrote that you will be the kind of father that a son loves."

That's what you think he wrote?

"I know it is. 'Cause we feel the same about you."

In that moment I would have done anything for Gayle, and I think she finally knew it; we would always be together in this place. She kissed me on the cheek, and put her face next to mine. "Frank, I have decided something," she said. "I'm the only daughter my mom has. She'll love to have another grandchild to dote over. And Kokko deserves to have the rest of his family, too. It might be pretty weird being back. But I think we can handle it."

78
Sowing

Mosabe rowed over and invited us to a festival on Bodu Fulidu. The old man burst with such youthful exuberance, I didn't have the heart to tell him we had decided to leave the island.

On the morning of the festival, we heard drumming across the channel. Sails slid over the sea toward Bodu Fulidu like filings pulled by a magnet.

"Well, I'm not going. For Kokko's sake," Gayle said. "All the ladies'll want to hold him. They have a way of pulling him out of my arms."

"But you've only been to their island once since we first arrived."

"They have practically lived on our island with us. We all know each other. Anyway I don't want our little fella exposed to diseases right before we travel."

At sunset I set out alone across the molten petals swaying over the darkening waters of the channel. I saw the figure of Mosabe emerge from the edge of the forest where he had been watching over my passage. After anchoring my boat, I wadded in and followed him along the dark twisting path, over serpentine banyan roots. Not a soul was in their homes. Everyone had gone to the center of the village.

We came upon a surprisingly large, open-sided tent of *dhoni* sails, which the islanders had erected. The canvass was all aglow with oil lamps. Every man's boat must have been stripped of sail to make it. Inside the lanterns shone upon the crowd of honey-skinned faces. The islanders turned to watch me weaving into the audience. People grasped my arms, pulled my shirt, and held onto my fingers. Their eyes were full of excitement as they pointed me to an empty chair beside the chief.

On stage two kneeling rows of young women dressed in white gave a drumming performance on the mouths of urn-shaped cooking pots, which they held suggestively between their thighs. Abdullah gave me a scandalous wink as they began whirling their long black hair over the pots. After that, there was a slapstick skit by some young men who worked the crowd up into gales of laughter.

Just before it was over, some of the chief's male relatives led me away by the hand, to one of their homes for dinner. The rice was not the musky millet set out on long tables for everyone else, but a high grade white rice they had prepared especially for me. I felt intensely lonely for Gayle. They must have sensed it because directly after dinner, they motioned for me to follow them back through the forest to the shore. The shapes of several men waited at their oar positions in one of the island's biggest *dhoni*. My *dhoni* had already been tied to the stern.

We set across the channel and the muscles in their arms flexed in the half-moon light. The ridges between colliding currents flashed as we crossed the water. The men sang *mmmmm, mmmmm*, as the boat surged with the pulse of their stroke, and the paddles whispered back across the surface.

I walked up our beach toward the dark windows of our house, and stood unmoving in the front doorway, waiting for my eyes to adjust. The gauze of the mosquito net was luminescent with moonlight. Gayle lay with Kokko at her breast. She lifted her head. "Did you have a wild party?" she whispered.

"Oh, I thought you were asleep."

"I was worried."

She held out her hand for me to come and sit on the edge of the bed. I told her all about the festival, how excited the boys got over the drumming girls and how they dropped money into their pots, the dinner, the islander's hospitality.

"Did you tell Mosabe we are leaving?"

"No… The time just didn't seem right."

Suddenly I remembered the papaya I brought, and handed it to her. "On my way back to the boat, a child reached out and gave this to me."

Gayle sat up and asked me to get her a knife and spoon.

"Now?"

"Yes, I didn't make dinner with you gone. I'm starving."

The yellowish-orange fruit looked pale in the moonlight as she ate. I held out my hand for the seeds. When she had finished, I threw the seeds off the front porch, out into the moon-green shrubs under the palms. No sooner had they left my hand, than I envisioned papaya trees already grown there.

"What about your *dhoni*?" she asked, soon as I walked back inside.

"What do you mean?"

"The islanders made it for you. Aren't you going to bring it home?"

"What would I do with such a heavy coconut-wood boat? It would be a useless artifact back in the States. A dead thing."

"But you love your boat."

I shook my head. "She belongs here. Mosabe will make good use of her. He'll let kids sail her over here to collect coconuts. They'll take special care of her because she was mine."

79
O'Riordan's Laugh

Mosabe's gaze quavered with the news. So did mine as I told him. In his ninety or so years, tossed in the waves of island lives, leaving an island was simply unheard of.

"*Dhanee?*" he said, waving his hand toward the horizon.

I nodded.

Mosabe turned to Gayle for confirmation. "Gayle, Kokko, *dhanee?*" he asked again.

"The next time you see this little fella he won't be so small," Gayle said standing before him.

Mosabe stared at Gayle, setting his jaw upon what he could not say. He looked very thin and old in his faded shirt and threadbare sarong. It was as if the sun were absorbing him and the breeze lifting him very gently away, thread by thread. I told him we wanted to give the house and everything in it to him, my boat too.

He nodded just once, just as he had that day he agreed we could live on the island. He rose and said he would get some *karamba* for us to drink. Then turning to Kokko in Gayle's arms, he leaned forward and spoke directly to him, man to man. I only caught a few words, but his meaning could not be mistaken. It was what one chief would say to another, with the exclamatory energy and confidence that was affirmed by his birthright. "DonKokko, you are chief of this island. And the island will always be the source of your wisdom and strength. You must honor it in your heart, just as all the island chiefs have done before you." Mosabe swept his hand from one side of the horizon to the other. "Do not forget your birthplace. Do not forget your people."

Then Mosabe stepped off the porch into the glare of the sun, waved his machete over his head, and vanished up the trail, as if absorbed by the light.

What had I done? O'Riordan must have asked it, too, clinging to the wreckage of his ship in the hurricane. Wherever such fierce beauty gathers up the soul, some human vulnerability will betray it. O'Riordan never stopped reaching. I would hear that old man laughing for the rest of my life.

80
Casting Off

There was a hell of storm the night before the motor *dhoni* from Matiwari came to pick us up. The shadow of the forest bent to the ground. Kokko awoke crying. A racket of wind screamed through the palms above us. Flying debris thudded onto the roof. I sat up in bed worrying if a cyclone had dipped south. At first there was no rain, and it sounded as if the hide were being ripped off our low-lying isle.

I stared up at our roof, as I had stared at the underside of Joya's deck so many times before, listening for the tone of the wind in the rigging, the whitewater plunging past. I recognized the iron-like groan in the racket overhead, the same fierceness as the storm in Male on the eve of selling Joya. It was the groan of an old foe. Then I thought my eyes must be playing tricks on me. I caught a glimpse of stars over the edge of the white rock wall. I stared up into the dark of the rafters. Again, the glimmering smudges of stars skidding through the clouds. It was like a transparency on the underside of the thatch. I went numb, realizing I could not have possibly seen stars inside the house.

Then I leapt up. "Gayle, the roof is blowing off the house!"

"What? What's happening?" Gayle cried out, cradling Kokko.

"The roof is blowing off! It's tipping up off the wall!"

Saying the words brought me to my senses. Gayle cradled Kokko to her chest, as I leapt from bed. Thunder boomed and the roof thatch drummed with the downpour as Gayle dashed about shoving belongings into a corner with her free hand, clutching Kokko in the other. I dragged a tarp over it all, leaving a space big enough that we could all crawl under. We might be able to hold the tarp down with weights and clutch it over us. But heavy palm fronds now thudding on the roof would also land on us inside our roofless walls. We might have to flee to the beach, away from the forest and out into the weather just as we had done aboard Joya.

I grabbed coils of Joya's rope and rushed outside with them looped over my shoulder. I climbed up the slats nailed to a palm and clawed my way up the slippery roof thatch through sheets of cascading water. Palm fronds tore loose sailing through the air, and smashed into other palms overhead. Large dark shapes skidded down the roof past me. Once I had straddled the peak I threw the end of the line down to Gayle. She rove it through the windows and heaved the coil back up. I cranked my hips along the peak, literally lacing the roof onto the walls.

The next morning the sun rose over a serene, hyacinthine slab stretching from horizon to horizon. The air was crystalline, fresh and cool in the aftermath of the storm. We had packed very little: our shells, books, and clothes, and the *joli* I had made for Kokko. I could not remember any time so mercilessly still.

Gayle kicked the still unopened box of pickled bean curd which I had insisted on shipping from Singapore. The ceramic jugs clinked together inside.

"I told you," she laughed.

By midmorning Mosabe, Abdullah, the chief and his brothers, and several men from Bodu Fulidu arrived and carried our things in a duffle, a sail bag, and three or four boxes. The northeast wind began to blow, the first breath of the new monsoon launched with last night's storm. It was crisp as a slap.

We turned away from our house, and walked through the palms to the Matiwari motor *dhoni* waiting on the leeward side of our island.

The shaded water was perfectly transparent, magnifying the bone-white fragments of shells strewn over a bed of fine sand. Further out the wind kicked up ripples, and hushed them away from our island. We hesitated on the shore to say goodbye, but no words came.

Mosabe spoke first. The energetic punch had vanished from his voice, as if the island and even the sky overhead had shrunken around us, leaving just enough room for our feet facing each other from shore to shore. He spoke of presents.

First, he handed me a child's-size knife to give to Kokko when he had grown. He had made it at his beach forge and turned the handle on his hand lathe. He pointed out how special the handle was, made of white plastic instead of wood.

Then he thrust out two husked *kashi* coconuts, just the same as the ones you get in supermarkets at home, which were presents for our families from him. He handed over these treasures, one to Gayle and one to me.

"Take care of yourself, you old fart," Gayle said.

Mosabe bowed to Gayle, "*Salaam.*" He touched his heart with his right hand.

Then to me, "*Salaam.*"

We climbed aboard the *dhoni*. The propeller began thumping hard under our seats, and the boat slid from the glassy shade over the shore. The gap widened quickly, the water deepening beyond any reasonable impulse to jump out. We stretched away, our arms raising to wave again and again.

Once the southerly point of the island had eclipsed our view of the islanders, Gayle bundled Kokko up against the wind. I stood to wave one last time over the frothing-white distance, but could not see anyone to wave to.

The *dhoni* captain chose to motor close across the south end of the island rather than head out any further. The shady white rock walls of our house came into view, and the last glimpses of our island life slid by: our sandy front yard under the palms; the porch with its thatched overhanging roof; a tall bedpost through the front window draped with our pale blue mosquito net; then the front door open upon our planked dining table, the glass-bodied lantern on top filled with amber kerosene for the evening meal. Against the back wall in shadow I made out the old oak dresser we bought in the Male flea market. It was still full of unused birth supplies and clothes we had left behind.

"Look, there's Kokko's cradle," Gayle exclaimed, pointing as if we were just arriving, rather than leaving.

We slid past the corrugated aluminum panels of our rainwater catch. They flashed through the palm trunks out back. We craned our necks until the forest had completely cut off our view, and the house had disappeared in the forest.

When we passed my *dhoni* in the lagoon, I stared back at the naked stick of my mast rocking violently in the wake of our departure. I stood on my seat to see if I had anchored her too near shore at low tide. The wake passed, and she settled back down, floating gracefully upon the fullness of her bilges. Asmar of Turadu Island had especially designed her for my weight and height. From a distance I could see how she was the shape of me in the islands.

For an instant I almost saw Gayle rush out, cradling Kokko in her arms, waving to me from the beach as she always had when I sailed home. I would have hurried up from the lagoon, excitedly recounting my seaward adventures, thrusting my sail-wrapped spar up onto the porch rafters.

Out from the lee of our island, the captain pressed the engine kill-switch. The engine wheezed into the sound of rushing water. The sail billowed out into the windswept blue, snapping taut with a loud retort, and we felt our boat surge out over the swells toward Male.

Suddenly I remembered the Tupperware container on the top shelf in the kitchen, the one that contained the seeds from the old

Chinese man in Singapore. I had wanted to plant them back in the States.

"Our seeds!" I exclaimed. "We left them."

"It's okay." Gayle touched my leg. "I already planted them."

All that could be done had been done. Gayle's garden would grow. I settled back down with her on the warm planks amidships. She cradled Kokko in her lap, shielding his face from the sun nipping around the trailing edge of the sail. She wore her green batik scarf, woven around her head as she sometimes did on windy days. From time to time we glanced back over our shoulders at the verdant mound of our island growing smaller in the distance, dissolving into the blue opacity. Finally it dipped under the wave crests yawing up into the mottled cloud, and did not rise up again.

Gayle reached across Kokko asleep in her lap and took my hand. She squeezed it in the seesaw glare of the swells, and gazed at me with the shimmering light of the waves in her eyes. We both understood that we would always be each other's link to what had happened, and to whom we had become. The island we had searched for had been inside of us from the beginning. I mouthed, *I love you.* And from her lips, *I love you too.* Our hands did not let go, as the steady sway of the sea found its way into our backs.

About the Author

Frank Burnaby is a poet, traveler, sailor, and storyteller. He worked as a gifted and successful lighting designer in Los Angeles for many years. Then moving to an island in Pacific Northwest, he devoted his time to raising his sons, writing, and to the creation of a wilderness school focused on the developmental needs of 7-13 year old children to experience nature.

As a youth, he survived his parent's good intentions of enrolling him in military school for seventh through ninth grades. There he learned to disassemble and reassemble his rifle with his eyes closed, and to pull weeds for not having a mirror shine on his shoes. For high school they sent him away to a boarding school in New Jersey.

In 1969 after a stint at San Francisco State University film school, Frank boarded a freighter bound for North Africa. Hitchhiking across Turkey, Iran, Afghanistan, Pakistan, he made his way through India and South East Asia 0to remote islands in Indonesia by native boat, and finally on to Hong Kong where he taught English.

Landing back in New York City he drove a taxi nights, and studied acting at Herbert Berghof Studios. He worked quickly as an actor including an offer to be a principal in a travel adventure feature film, but instead of pursuing an acting career, he started a thriving vegetarian taco stand on the edge of the meat packing district.

Drawn to the sea and his own dream of sailing to a tropical wilderness, he took a job as an apprentice shipwright in a Los Angeles marina. Soon after, he set off with his soon-to-be wife, Gayle, to purchase a small vintage sailboat in England. He was 27, and she was 17. The ensuing five year voyage, eastward across the Indian Ocean, and their amazing story living on an uninhabited island changed his life forever. This is the story, *Island Born*.

• • • • •

www.ingramcontent.com/pod-product-compliance
Lightning Source LLC
Chambersburg PA
CBHW071233160426
43196CB00009B/1047